BREAD FOR THE DAY

DAILY BIBLE READINGS AND PRAYERS

2025

 AUGSBURG FORTRESS

Minneapolis

BREAD FOR THE DAY 2025
Daily Bible Readings and Prayers

Editor: Rebecca Ajer Frantz
Cover design: Laurie Ingram
Cover and interior art: Mary Button

Contributors to the weekday prayers: Kurt Lammi, Dayton, Ohio (January); Matthew Folkemer-Leonard, York, Pennsylvania (February); Stacey Nalean-Carlson, Decorah, Iowa (March); Kent Narum, Saint Peter, Minnesota (April); Reed Fowler, Saint Paul, Minnesota (May); Mytch Pierre-Noel Dorvilier, Dakar, Senegal (June); Edward G. Horstmann, Greenwich, Connecticut (July); Wilbert "Wilk" Miller, Essex, Connecticut (August); Phil Potaczek, Ottawa, Illinois (September); Fanya Burford-Berry, Chicago, Illinois (October); Phil Ruge-Jones, Eau Claire, Wisconsin (November); Matta Ghaly, Portland, Oregon (December). Table Prayers for Time after Epiphany, The Three Days, Pentecost, Autumn, and Thanksgiving by Meta Herrick Carlson, and for Lent, Easter, Summer, November, and Christmas by Phil Ruge-Jones.

ACKNOWLEDGMENTS
Scripture quotations are from the New Revised Standard Version Bible © 1989 Division of Christian Education of the National Council of the Churches of Christ in the United States of America. Used by permission.

Hymn suggestions and prayers of the day for Sundays and festivals are from *Evangelical Lutheran Worship,* © 2006 Evangelical Lutheran Church in America; *This Far by Faith,* © 1999 Augsburg Fortress; *Pastoral Care,* © 2008 Evangelical Lutheran Church in America; and *All Creation Sings,* © 2020 Augsburg Fortress.

Materials prepared by the Consultation on Common Texts (CCT), published in *Revised Common Lectionary* © 1992 and *Revised Common Lectionary* Daily Readings © 2005. Used by permission.

"A prayer to begin the work day," "A prayer to begin the school day," "Morning blessing," and "Evening blessing" from *Reformation 500 Sourcebook: Anniversary Resources for Congregations,* © 2016 Augsburg Fortress.

Materials prepared by the English Language Liturgical Consultation (ELLC), published in *Praying Together,* © 1988: "Blessed are you, Lord" and "My soul proclaims the greatness of the Lord." Used by permission.

pISBN: 9781506487908
eISBN: 9798889832645

Manufactured in the USA

Contents

September

October

November

December

Additional Resources

Prayers to Accompany Your Reading

Morning Devotions

Worship with me, O Lord. Come open my heart and let me sing harmony to your tune. Let your voice vibrate a new string and your words awaken a lost language. Worship with me, O Lord. Stir me from my slumbers. When I awake, I am still with you. Worship with me, O Lord. Amen.

Scripture

Author of all creation, we give you thanks for inspiring the writers of the Bible, your holy Word, to share your word. Help us to turn to it through all the many days of our lives so that we may find guidance for our living. Amen.

Community

Loving God, as we read your word, help us to discern its meaning for the life of our community. May it empower us to witness to your love in the world in many new ways. Amen.

Discipleship

O God, may we be like Samuel who, when you called him, said, "Here I am!" Empower us to listen to your word and to hear your call to us so that we might more fully live out our vocation as your disciples in the world. Amen.

Devotions

O God, you are our loving parent who gave everything for us so that we might come to know the depth of your love for us. As we read your word and meditate on it, use it to deepen our relationship with you so that we might truly grow in faith. Amen.

Introduction

Daily prayer is an essential practice for those who seek to hear God's voice and cultivate an inner life. Whether you pray alone or with others, with brevity or in sustained meditation, the rhythm of daily prayer reveals the life-sustaining communion to which God invites all human beings. Such prayer is a serene power silently at work, drawing us into the ancient yet vital sources of faith, hope, and love.

The guiding principle of the selection of daily readings in *Bread for the Day* is their relationship to the Sunday readings as presented in the Revised Common Lectionary (a system of readings in widespread use across denominations). The readings are chosen so that the days leading up to Sunday (Thursday through Saturday) prepare for the Sunday readings. The days flowing out from Sunday (Monday through Wednesday) reflect on the Sunday readings.

How this book is organized

- Each day's page is dated and named in relationship to the church's year. Lesser festivals are listed along with the date as part of the day heading. Commemorations are listed just below in smaller type. Notes on those commemorated can be found on pages 407–415.
- Several verses of one of the appointed scripture texts are printed. The full text citation is provided for those who would like to reflect on the entire text. In addition, two or three additional reading citations with short descriptions are provided.
- Two psalms are appointed for each week: one psalm for Monday through Wednesday and a second psalm for Thursday through Saturday. In this way the days leading up to Sunday or flowing

out from Sunday have a distinct relationship with one another in addition to their relationship with the Sunday readings.

- Following the scripture text is a hymn suggestion from *Evangelical Lutheran Worship* (ELW), *All Creation Sings* (ACS), or *This Far by Faith* (TFF) and a prayer that incorporates a theme present in one or more readings.
- Household prayers and blessings appropriate to the changing seasons are placed throughout the book. Simplified forms of morning and evening prayer, morning and evening blessings, and prayers with children can be found on pages 423–430.

How to use this book

- Use the weekday readings to prepare for and reflect on the Sunday readings.
- Use the questions printed on page 431 to guide your reflection.
- Use the resources for household prayer placed throughout the book. See the Contents on pages 3–4 for a complete list.
- Record prayer requests on the first page for each month.
- In addition to being used to guide individual prayer, this book may be used to guide family prayer, prayer in congregational or other settings during the week, prayer with those who are sick or homebound, or prayer with other groups.

Even though Christians gather on the Lord's day, Sunday, for public worship, much of our time is spent in the home. We first learn the words, gestures, and songs of faith in the home. We discover our essential identity as a community of faith and mark significant transitions of life in the home. To surround and infuse the daily rhythm of sleeping and waking, working, resting, and eating with the words and gestures of Christian prayer is to discover the ancient truth of the gospel: the ordinary and the human can reveal the mystery of God and divine grace. Like planets around the sun, our daily prayer draws us to the Sunday assembly where we gather for the word and the breaking of the bread in the changing seasons of the year. From the Sunday assembly, our daily prayer flows into the week.

Prayer List for January

_____

_____

_____

_____

_____

_____

_____

_____

_____

_____

Wednesday, January 1, 2025
Name of Jesus

Luke 2:15-21
The child is named Jesus

When the angels had left them and gone into heaven, the shepherds said to one another, "Let us go now to Bethlehem and see this thing that has taken place, which the Lord has made known to us." So they went with haste and found Mary and Joseph, and the child lying in the manger. When they saw this, they made known what had been told them about this child; and all who heard it were amazed at what the shepherds told them. But Mary treasured all these words and pondered them in her heart. The shepherds returned, glorifying and praising God for all they had heard and seen, as it had been told them.

After eight days had passed, it was time to circumcise the child; and he was called Jesus, the name given by the angel before he was conceived in the womb. (Luke 2:15-21)

Psalm
Psalm 8
How exalted is your name

Additional Readings
Numbers 6:22-27
The Aaronic blessing

Galatians 4:4-7
We are no longer slaves

Hymn: From Heaven Above, ELW 268

Eternal Father, you gave your incarnate Son the holy name of Jesus to be a sign of our salvation. Plant in every heart the love of the Savior of the world, Jesus Christ our Lord, who lives and reigns with you and the Holy Spirit, one God, now and forever.

Thursday, January 2, 2025
Ninth Day of Christmas

Johann Konrad Wilhelm Loehe, renewer of the church, died 1872

Proverbs 1:1-7
Grow in wisdom and knowledge

Let the wise also hear and gain in learning,
    and the discerning acquire skill,
to understand a proverb and a figure,
    the words of the wise and their riddles.

The fear of the LORD is the beginning of knowledge;
    fools despise wisdom and instruction. (Prov. 1:5-7)

Psalm
Psalm 147:12-20
Praising God in Zion

Additional Reading
James 3:13-18
The wisdom from above

Hymn: We Eat the Bread of Teaching, ELW 518

God of all wisdom, you are the source of all truth and our ever-patient teacher. Strengthen us in our learning, uphold us in our growth, and empower us as we live out what you teach us.

Friday, January 3, 2025
Tenth Day of Christmas

Psalm 72
Prayers for the king

Give the king your justice, O God,
  and your righteousness to a king's son.
May he judge your people with righteousness,
  and your poor with justice.

May the kings of Tarshish and of the isles
  render him tribute,
may the kings of Sheba and Seba
  bring gifts.
May all kings fall down before him,
  all nations give him service. (Ps. 72:1-2, 10-11)

Additional Readings
Job 42:10-17   Luke 8:16-21
Job's family   *Jesus' family*

Hymn: O God of Every Nation, ELW 713

God our ruler, you are the one in whom we place our trust and to whom we are devoted. Grant wisdom and insight to all earthly leaders so they might become reflections of your love to the world.

Saturday, January 4, 2025
Eleventh Day of Christmas

Isaiah 6:1-5
The Lord high and lofty

In the year that King Uzziah died, I saw the Lord sitting on a throne, high and lofty; and the hem of his robe filled the temple. Seraphs were in attendance above him; each had six wings: with two they covered their faces, and with two they covered their feet, and with two they flew. And one called to another and said:

"Holy, holy, holy is the LORD of hosts;
the whole earth is full of his glory."

The pivots on the thresholds shook at the voices of those who called, and the house filled with smoke. And I said: "Woe is me! I am lost, for I am a man of unclean lips, and I live among a people of unclean lips; yet my eyes have seen the King, the LORD of hosts!" (Isa. 6:1-5)

Psalm
Psalm 72
Prayers for the king

Additional Reading
Acts 7:44-53
Solomon's temple cannot contain God

Hymn: Holy, Holy, Holy, Lord God Almighty, ELW 413

Eternal and majestic God, all of heaven praises you and sings "Holy, holy, holy" before your throne. Stir up your Spirit within us so that we may join their song. Help us see and celebrate your presence among us.

John 1:[1-9] 10-18

God with us

He was in the world, and the world came into being through him; yet the world did not know him. He came to what was his own, and his own people did not accept him. But to all who received him, who believed in his name, he gave power to become children of God, who were born, not of blood or of the will of the flesh or of the will of man, but of God. And the Word became flesh and lived among us, and we have seen his glory, the glory as of a father's only son, full of grace and truth. (John 1:10-14)

Psalm

Psalm 147:12-20
Praising God in Zion

Additional Readings

Jeremiah 31:7-14
Joy as God's scattered flock gathers

Ephesians 1:3-14
The will of God made known in Christ

Hymn: Praise the One Who Breaks the Darkness, ELW 843

Almighty God, you have filled all the earth with the light of your incarnate Word. By your grace empower us to reflect your light in all that we do, through Jesus Christ, our Savior and Lord, who lives and reigns with you and the Holy Spirit, one God, now and forever.

Blessing for a Home at Epiphany

Matthew writes that when the magi saw the shining star stop overhead, they were filled with joy. "On entering the house, they saw the child with Mary his mother" (Matt. 2:10-11). In the home, Christ is met in family and friends, in visitors and strangers. In the home, faith is shared, nurtured, and put into action.

Twelfth Night (January 5), Epiphany of Our Lord (January 6), or another day during the time after Epiphany offers an occasion for gathering with friends and family members for a blessing for the home. Someone may lead the greeting and blessing, while another person may read the scripture passage. Following an eastern European tradition, a visual blessing may be inscribed with white chalk above the main door; for example, 20 + CMB + 25. The numbers change with each new year. The three letters stand for either the ancient Latin blessing *Christe mansionem benedicat*, which means "Christ, bless this house," or the legendary names of the magi (Caspar, Melchior, and Balthasar).

Greeting

Peace to this house and to all who enter here.
By wisdom a house is built,
and through understanding it is established;
through knowledge its rooms are filled
with rare and beautiful treasures. *(Prov. 24:3-4)*

Reading

As we prepare to ask God's blessing on this household,
let us listen to the words of scripture.
In the beginning was the Word,
and the Word was with God, and the Word was God.

He was in the beginning with God.
All things came into being through him,
and without him not one thing came into being.
What has come into being in him was life,
and the life was the light of all people.
The Word became flesh and lived among us, and we have seen his glory,
the glory as of a father's only son, full of grace and truth.
From his fullness we have all received, grace upon grace.
(John 1:1-4, 14, 16)

Inscription

This inscription may be made with chalk above the entrance:

20 + C M B + 25

Write the appropriate character (left) while speaking the text (right).

The magi of old, known as

C   Caspar,

M   Melchior, and

B   Balthasar

followed the star of God's Son who came to dwell among us

20   two thousand

25   and twenty-five years ago.

+   Christ, bless this house,

+   and remain with us throughout the new year.

Prayer of Blessing

O God,

you revealed your Son to all people by the shining light of a star. We pray that you bless this home and all who live here with your gracious presence. May your love be our inspiration, your wisdom our guide, your truth our light, and your peace our benediction; through Christ our Lord. Amen.

Then everyone may walk from room to room, blessing the house with incense or by sprinkling with water, perhaps using a branch from the Christmas tree.

Monday, January 6, 2025
Epiphany of Our Lord

Matthew 2:1-12
Christ revealed to the nations

In the time of King Herod, after Jesus was born in Bethlehem of Judea, wise men from the East came to Jerusalem, asking, "Where is the child who has been born king of the Jews? For we observed his star at its rising, and have come to pay him homage." When King Herod heard this, he was frightened, and all Jerusalem with him; and calling together all the chief priests and scribes of the people, he inquired of them where the Messiah was to be born. They told him, "In Bethlehem of Judea; for so it has been written by the prophet." (Matt. 2:1-5)

Psalm

Psalm 72:1-7, 10-14
All shall bow down

Additional Readings

Isaiah 60:1-6
Nations come to the light

Ephesians 3:1-12
The gospel's promise for all

Hymn: Christ, Be Our Light, ELW 715

Everlasting God, the radiance of all faithful people, you brought the nations to the brightness of your rising. Fill the world with your glory, and show yourself to all the world through him who is the true light and the bright morning star, your Son, Jesus Christ, our Savior and Lord, who lives and reigns with you and the Holy Spirit, one God, now and forever.

Time after Epiphany

The season of Christmas rejoiced in Emmanuel, God with us. In the time after Epiphany, the story moves from Mary's arms into the world, where Jesus teaches, heals, and feeds those he meets, manifesting the good news of heaven in daily life. On the Epiphany of Our Lord (January 6), hearts and homes join the whole church in recognizing God revealed in Jesus. The time after Epiphany invites us to consider: How might our faith in Christ shine in our lives, shared for the sake of friends and family, neighbors near and far?

Table Prayer for Epiphany and the Time after Epiphany (January 6–March 4)

Generous God,
your delight for creation is revealed in Jesus,
who sets wide tables and feeds multitudes,
who breaks and becomes bread for the whole world.
May this meal strengthen our bodies and illuminate our spirits
so that our whole lives shine with love from heaven.
Grant this through Christ our Lord.
Amen.

Tuesday, January 7, 2025
Time after Epiphany

Ephesians 4:17—5:1
Life lived in Christ

So then, putting away falsehood, let all of us speak the truth to our neighbors, for we are members of one another. Be angry but do not sin; do not let the sun go down on your anger, and do not make room for the devil. Thieves must give up stealing; rather let them labor and work honestly with their own hands, so as to have something to share with the needy. Let no evil talk come out of your mouths, but only what is useful for building up, as there is need, so that your words may give grace to those who hear. And do not grieve the Holy Spirit of God, with which you were marked with a seal for the day of redemption. Put away from you all bitterness and wrath and anger and wrangling and slander, together with all malice, and be kind to one another, tenderhearted, forgiving one another, as God in Christ has forgiven you. (Eph. 4:25-32)

Psalm
Psalm 72
Prayers for the king

Additional Reading
Daniel 2:1-19
The king searches for wisdom

Hymn: Blest Be the Tie That Binds, ELW 656

God of all truth, you bring your people together as one family united in your love. Forgive us when our actions do not reflect that love, and lead us so our words and deeds overflow with your grace.

Wednesday, January 8, 2025
Time after Epiphany

Ephesians 5:15-20
Wise living in evil days

Be careful then how you live, not as unwise people but as wise, making the most of the time, because the days are evil. So do not be foolish, but understand what the will of the Lord is. Do not get drunk with wine, for that is debauchery; but be filled with the Spirit, as you sing psalms and hymns and spiritual songs among yourselves, singing and making melody to the Lord in your hearts, giving thanks to God the Father at all times and for everything in the name of our Lord Jesus Christ. (Eph. 5:15-20)

Psalm
Psalm 72
Prayers for the king

Additional Reading
Daniel 2:24-29
Daniel reveals the dream's meaning

Hymn: Jesus Shall Reign, ELW 434

Loving God, source of all goodness and life, you pour rich blessings upon us every day. Remind us of your provision, lead us away from the temptations of this world, and help us to sing your praises all our days.

Thursday, January 9, 2025
Time After Epiphany

1 Corinthians 1:18-31
The power and wisdom of God

Where is the one who is wise? Where is the scribe? Where is the debater of this age? Has not God made foolish the wisdom of the world? For since, in the wisdom of God, the world did not know God through wisdom, God decided, through the foolishness of our proclamation, to save those who believe. For Jews demand signs and Greeks desire wisdom, but we proclaim Christ crucified, a stumbling block to Jews and foolishness to Gentiles, but to those who are the called, both Jews and Greeks, Christ the power of God and the wisdom of God. For God's foolishness is wiser than human wisdom, and God's weakness is stronger than human strength. (1 Corinthians 1:20-25)

Psalm
Psalm 29
The voice of God upon the waters

Additional Reading
Ecclesiastes 1:1-11
There is nothing new under the sun

Hymn: Be Thou My Vision, ELW 793

God of all, you came to us in the person of Jesus Christ, bringing forgiveness and discernment to our world. Open our eyes to see your wisdom, our mouths to speak your praises, and our hearts to share your love.

Friday, January 10, 2025
Time after Epiphany

Psalm 29
The voice of God upon the waters

Ascribe to the LORD, O heavenly beings,
    ascribe to the LORD glory and strength.
Ascribe to the LORD the glory of his name;
    worship the LORD in holy splendor.

The voice of the LORD is over the waters;
    the God of glory thunders,
    the LORD, over mighty waters.
The voice of the LORD is powerful;
    the voice of the LORD is full of majesty.

The voice of the LORD breaks the cedars;
    the LORD breaks the cedars of Lebanon.
He makes Lebanon skip like a calf,
    and Sirion like a young wild ox. (Ps. 29:1-6)

Additional Readings
Ecclesiastes 2:1-11
Toil for pleasure is ultimately vanity

1 Corinthians 2:1-10
The Spirit reveals the depths of God

Hymn: Open Your Ears, O Faithful People, ELW 519

God of all creation, by your word you create life. We celebrate your majesty, power, and strength. Stir up your Spirit within us that we may be changed by that same word and share it with others.

Saturday, January 11, 2025
Time after Epiphany

Ecclesiastes 3:1-15
All that is, is God's doing

What gain have the workers from their toil? I have seen the business that God has given to everyone to be busy with. He has made everything suitable for its time; moreover he has put a sense of past and future into their minds, yet they cannot find out what God has done from the beginning to the end. I know that there is nothing better for them than to be happy and enjoy themselves as long as they live; moreover, it is God's gift that all should eat and drink and take pleasure in all their toil. I know that whatever God does endures forever; nothing can be added to it, nor anything taken from it; God has done this, so that all should stand in awe before him. That which is, already has been; that which is to be, already is; and God seeks out what has gone by. (Eccles. 3:9-15)

Psalm
Psalm 29
The voice of God upon the waters

Additional Reading
1 Corinthians 2:11-16
God's wisdom is taught by the Spirit

Hymn: We Are Called, ELW 720

God of all, you bless us with strengths and interests. You call us to use those gifts for the sake of others. Guide us in seeing how our gifts can serve our neighbors.

Sunday, January 12, 2025
Baptism of Our Lord

Luke 3:15-17, 21-22
The baptism of Jesus

As the people were filled with expectation, and all were questioning in their hearts concerning John, whether he might be the Messiah, John answered all of them by saying, "I baptize you with water; but one who is more powerful than I is coming; I am not worthy to untie the thong of his sandals. He will baptize you with the Holy Spirit and fire. His winnowing fork is in his hand, to clear his threshing floor and to gather the wheat into his granary; but the chaff he will burn with unquenchable fire."

Now when all the people were baptized, and when Jesus also had been baptized and was praying, the heaven was opened, and the Holy Spirit descended upon him in bodily form like a dove. And a voice came from heaven, "You are my Son, the Beloved; with you I am well pleased." (Luke 3:15-17, 21-22)

Psalm
Psalm 29
The voice of God upon the waters

Additional Readings
Isaiah 43:1-7
Passing through the waters

Acts 8:14-17
Prayer for the Holy Spirit

Hymn: Christ, When for Us You Were Baptized, ELW 304

Almighty God, you anointed Jesus at his baptism with the Holy Spirit and revealed him as your beloved Son. Keep all who are born of water and the Spirit faithful in your service, that we may rejoice to be called children of God, through Jesus Christ, our Savior and Lord, who lives and reigns with you and the Holy Spirit, one God, now and forever.

Monday, January 13, 2025
Time after Epiphany

Psalm 106:1-12
God saves through water

Praise the Lord!
> O give thanks to the Lord, for he is good;
> for his steadfast love endures forever.

Who can utter the mighty doings of the Lord,
> or declare all his praise?

Happy are those who observe justice,
> who do righteousness at all times.

Remember me, O Lord, when you show favor to your people;
> help me when you deliver them;

that I may see the prosperity of your chosen ones,
> that I may rejoice in the gladness of your nation,
> that I may glory in your heritage. (Ps. 106:1-5)

Additional Readings

Judges 4:1-16
Israel's enemies drown

Ephesians 6:10-17
The Christian's spiritual armor

Hymn: All Creatures, Worship God Most High! ELW 835

God of all hope, you are our deliverer. In days of trouble and worry, you remain with us, pouring your steadfast love upon us. Keep us centered on you, and help us sing your praise forever.

Tuesday, January 14, 2025
Time after Epiphany

1 John 5:13-21
The life of those born of God

We know that those who are born of God do not sin, but the one who was born of God protects them, and the evil one does not touch them. We know that we are God's children, and that the whole world lies under the power of the evil one. And we know that the Son of God has come and has given us understanding so that we may know him who is true; and we are in him who is true, in his Son Jesus Christ. He is the true God and eternal life. (1 John 5:18-20)

Psalm
Psalm 106:1-12
God saves through water

Additional Reading
Judges 5:12-21
The song of Deborah

Hymn: Change My Heart, O God, ELW 801

God, you came to us in Jesus Christ, bringing life and forgiveness. When we follow the empty promises of the world, open our minds and hearts to receive your life and forgiveness once again.

Wednesday, January 15, 2025
Time after Epiphany

Martin Luther King Jr., renewer of society, martyr, died 1968

Numbers 27:1-11
Daughters also promised inheritance

And the LORD spoke to Moses, saying: The daughters of Zelophehad are right in what they are saying; you shall indeed let them possess an inheritance among their father's brothers and pass the inheritance of their father on to them. You shall also say to the Israelites, "If a man dies, and has no son, then you shall pass his inheritance on to his daughter. If he has no daughter, then you shall give his inheritance to his brothers. If he has no brothers, then you shall give his inheritance to his father's brothers. And if his father has no brothers, then you shall give his inheritance to the nearest kinsman of his clan, and he shall possess it. It shall be for the Israelites a statute and ordinance, as the LORD commanded Moses." (Num. 27:6-11)

Psalm
Psalm 106:1-12
God saves through water

Additional Reading
Luke 11:33-36
Your body full of light

Hymn: Jesus Loves Me, ELW 595, TFF 249

God of families, your love sustains and supports our deepest relationships. Work in and through us as we navigate found families and those we are born into.

Thursday, January 16, 2025
Time after Epiphany

Psalm 36:5-10
We feast on the abundance of God's house

Your steadfast love, O LORD, extends to the heavens,
> your faithfulness to the clouds.
Your righteousness is like the mighty mountains,
> your judgments are like the great deep;
> you save humans and animals alike, O LORD.

How precious is your steadfast love, O God!
> All people may take refuge in the shadow of your wings.
They feast on the abundance of your house,
> and you give them drink from the river of your delights.
For with you is the fountain of life;
> in your light we see light. (Ps. 36:5-9)

Additional Readings

Jeremiah 3:1-5
Unfaithful Israel

Acts 8:18-24
God's gifts cannot be purchased

Hymn: Great Is Thy Faithfulness, ELW 733, TFF 283

God our rock and our protection, in the midst of a chaotic world you hold us tightly in your compassionate embrace. Your steadfast love fills us with life and sees us through each day. Thank you for holding us forever.

Friday, January 17, 2025
Time after Epiphany

Antony of Egypt, renewer of the church, died around 356
Pachomius, renewer of the church, died 346

1 Corinthians 7:1-7
Guidance for the married

Now concerning the matters about which you wrote: "It is well for a
man not to touch a woman." But because of cases of sexual immorality,
each man should have his own wife and each woman her own husband.
The husband should give to his wife her conjugal rights, and likewise
the wife to her husband. For the wife does not have authority over
her own body, but the husband does; likewise the husband does not
have authority over his own body, but the wife does. Do not deprive
one another except perhaps by agreement for a set time, to devote
yourselves to prayer, and then come together again, so that Satan may
not tempt you because of your lack of self-control. (1 Cor. 7:1-5)

Psalm
Psalm 36:5-10
We feast on the abundance of God's house

Additional Reading
Jeremiah 3:19-25
Israel is a faithless spouse

Hymn: Will You Let Me Be Your Servant, ELW 659

*Holy God, you designed us for relationship. Strengthen all marriages, and
keep spouses faithful to one another. Help them honor and cherish one
another in good days and bad, reflecting your ever-present love for us.*

Saturday, January 18, 2025
Confession of Peter

Week of Prayer for Christian Unity begins

Matthew 16:13-19

Peter confesses: You are the Messiah

[Jesus] said to [his disciples], "But who do you say that I am?" Simon Peter answered, "You are the Messiah, the Son of the living God." And Jesus answered him, "Blessed are you, Simon son of Jonah! For flesh and blood has not revealed this to you, but my Father in heaven. And I tell you, you are Peter, and on this rock I will build my church, and the gates of Hades will not prevail against it. I will give you the keys of the kingdom of heaven, and whatever you bind on earth will be bound in heaven, and whatever you loose on earth will be loosed in heaven." (Matt. 16:15-19)

Psalm

Psalm 18:1-6, 16-19
My God, my rock, worthy of praise

Additional Readings

Acts 4:8-13
Salvation is in no one other than Jesus

1 Corinthians 10:1-5
Drinking from the spiritual rock of Christ

Hymn: My Hope Is Built on Nothing Less, ELW 596/597, TFF 192

Almighty God, you inspired Simon Peter to confess Jesus as the Messiah and Son of the living God. Keep your church firm on the rock of this faith, so that in unity and peace it may proclaim one truth and follow one Lord, your Son, Jesus Christ our Savior, who lives and reigns with you and the Holy Spirit, one God, now and forever.

Sunday, January 19, 2025
Second Sunday after Epiphany

Henry, Bishop of Uppsala, martyr, died 1156

John 2:1-11
The wedding at Cana

When the steward tasted the water that had become wine, and did not know where it came from (though the servants who had drawn the water knew), the steward called the bridegroom and said to him, "Everyone serves the good wine first, and then the inferior wine after the guests have become drunk. But you have kept the good wine until now." Jesus did this, the first of his signs, in Cana of Galilee, and revealed his glory; and his disciples believed in him. (John 2:9-11)

Psalm

Psalm 36:5-10
We feast on the abundance of God's house

Additional Readings

Isaiah 62:1-5
God like the bridegroom and the bride

1 Corinthians 12:1-11
A variety of gifts but one Spirit

Hymn: All Hail the Power of Jesus' Name, ELW 634, TFF 267

Lord God, source of every blessing, you showed forth your glory and led many to faith by the works of your Son, who brought gladness and salvation to his people. Transform us by the Spirit of his love, that we may find our life together in him, Jesus Christ, our Savior and Lord.

Monday, January 20, 2025
Time after Epiphany

Psalm 145
Praise God's faithfulness

I will extol you, my God and King,
>   and bless your name forever and ever.
Every day I will bless you,
>   and praise your name forever and ever.
Great is the LORD, and greatly to be praised;
>   his greatness is unsearchable.

One generation shall laud your works to another,
>   and shall declare your mighty acts.
On the glorious splendor of your majesty,
>   and on your wondrous works, I will meditate. (Ps. 145:1-5)

Additional Readings
Isaiah 54:1-8
God is married to Israel

Romans 12:9-21
Live in harmony with one another

Hymn: Faith of Our Fathers, ELW 812/813

God of the ages, throughout all generations, you work in the lives of your people. As you have inspired us through the faith of those who came before us, use us to be inspiration for the generations that follow.

Tuesday, January 21, 2025
Time after Epiphany

Agnes, martyr, died around 304

1 Corinthians 1:3-17
Appeal for unity

Now I appeal to you, brothers and sisters, by the name of our Lord Jesus Christ, that all of you be in agreement and that there be no divisions among you, but that you be united in the same mind and the same purpose. For it has been reported to me by Chloe's people that there are quarrels among you, my brothers and sisters. What I mean is that each of you says, "I belong to Paul," or "I belong to Apollos," or "I belong to Cephas," or "I belong to Christ." Has Christ been divided? Was Paul crucified for you? Or were you baptized in the name of Paul?

For Christ did not send me to baptize but to proclaim the gospel, and not with eloquent wisdom, so that the cross of Christ might not be emptied of its power. (1 Cor. 1:10-13, 17)

Psalm
Psalm 145
Praise God's faithfulness

Additional Reading
Song of Solomon 4:1-8
The bride's beauty extolled

Hymn: We All Are One in Mission, ELW 576

God of all, in the body of Christ there is diversity. Remind us of our unity in the face of our differences. Forgive us when we think we are better than others. Bring us to a greater understanding of our life together in you.

Wednesday, January 22, 2025
Time after Epiphany

Luke 5:33-39
Christ the bridegroom

Then [the Pharisees and their scribes] said to [Jesus], "John's disciples, like the disciples of the Pharisees, frequently fast and pray, but your disciples eat and drink." Jesus said to them, "You cannot make wedding guests fast while the bridegroom is with them, can you? The days will come when the bridegroom will be taken away from them, and then they will fast in those days." (Luke 5:33-35)

Psalm
Psalm 145
Praise God's faithfulness

Additional Reading
Song of Solomon 4:9—5:1
A love song

Hymn: Give Me Jesus, ELW 770, TFF 165

Holy God, you came to us in Jesus Christ, an act of unbridled love. Remind us of your powerful love, bring joy to our hearts again, and help us share that love with others.

Thursday, January 23, 2025
Time after Epiphany

Psalm 19
The law revives the soul

The law of the LORD is perfect,
>   reviving the soul;
the decrees of the LORD are sure,
>   making wise the simple;
the precepts of the LORD are right,
>   rejoicing the heart;
the commandment of the LORD is clear,
>   enlightening the eyes;
the fear of the LORD is pure,
>   enduring forever;
the ordinances of the LORD are true
>   and righteous altogether.
More to be desired are they than gold,
>   even much fine gold;
sweeter also than honey,
>   and drippings of the honeycomb. (Ps. 19:7-10)

Additional Readings
Isaiah 61:1-7
The spirit of God is upon me

Romans 7:1-6
The new life of the Spirit

Hymn: If You But Trust in God to Guide You, ELW 769

Life-giving God, by your hand you guided your people in the wilderness and gave them your law. Help us follow your will for us, rejoicing in the rich life we have in you.

Friday, January 24, 2025
Time after Epiphany

Romans 12:1-8
One body in Christ

For by the grace given to me I say to everyone among you not to think of yourself more highly than you ought to think, but to think with sober judgment, each according to the measure of faith that God has assigned. For as in one body we have many members, and not all the members have the same function, so we, who are many, are one body in Christ, and individually we are members one of another. We have gifts that differ according to the grace given to us: prophecy, in proportion to faith; ministry, in ministering; the teacher, in teaching; the exhorter, in exhortation; the giver, in generosity; the leader, in diligence; the compassionate, in cheerfulness. (Rom. 12:3-8)

Psalm
Psalm 19
The law revives the soul

Additional Reading:
Nehemiah 2:1-10
Nehemiah seeks the welfare of Israel

Hymn: One Bread, One Body, ELW 496, TFF 122

God of unity and peace, you have given your people many blessings and you bring us together in your one body. Strengthen us in service and encourage us in cooperation. Let our diversity and unity reflect your wholeness and love.

Saturday, January 25, 2022
Conversion of Paul

Week of Prayer for Christian Unity ends

Galatians 1:11-24

Paul receives a revelation of Christ

You have heard, no doubt, of my earlier life in Judaism. I was violently persecuting the church of God and was trying to destroy it. I advanced in Judaism beyond many among my people of the same age, for I was far more zealous for the traditions of my ancestors. But when God, who had set me apart before I was born and called me through his grace, was pleased to reveal his Son to me, so that I might proclaim him among the Gentiles, I did not confer with any human being, nor did I go up to Jerusalem to those who were already apostles before me, but I went away at once into Arabia, and afterwards I returned to Damascus. (Gal. 1:13-17)

Psalm

Psalm 67
Let all the peoples praise you, O God

Additional Readings

Acts 9:1-22
Saul is converted to Christ

Luke 21:10-19
The end times will require endurance

Hymn: We Are Called, ELW 720

O God, by the preaching of your apostle Paul you have caused the light of the gospel to shine throughout the world. Grant that we may follow his example and be witnesses to the truth of your Son, Jesus Christ, our Savior and Lord, who lives and reigns with you and the Holy Spirit, one God, now and forever.

Sunday, January 26, 2025
Third Sunday after Epiphany

Timothy, Titus, and Silas, missionaries

Luke 4:14-21

Jesus reads the prophet Isaiah

When [Jesus] came to Nazareth, where he had been brought up, he went to the synagogue on the sabbath day, as was his custom. He stood up to read, and the scroll of the prophet Isaiah was given to him. He unrolled the scroll and found the place where it was written:

"The Spirit of the Lord is upon me,

because he has anointed me

to bring good news to the poor.

He has sent me to proclaim release to the captives

and recovery of sight to the blind,

to let the oppressed go free,

to proclaim the year of the Lord's favor." (Luke 4:16-19)

Psalm

Psalm 19
The law revives the soul

Additional Readings

Nehemiah 8:1-3, 5-6, 8-10
Ezra reads the law

1 Corinthians 12:12-31a
You are the body of Christ

Hymn: Lord, Keep Us Steadfast in Your Word, ELW 517

Blessed Lord God, you have caused the holy scriptures to be written for the nourishment of your people. Grant that we may hear them, read, mark, learn, and inwardly digest them, that, comforted by your promises, we may embrace and forever hold fast to the hope of eternal life, through your Son, Jesus Christ our Lord.

Monday, January 27, 2025
Time after Epiphany

Lydia, Dorcas, and Phoebe, witnesses to the faith

Psalm 119:89-96
The law of God gives life

The LORD exists forever;
> your word is firmly fixed in heaven.
Your faithfulness endures to all generations;
> you have established the earth, and it stands fast.
By your appointment they stand today,
> for all things are your servants.
If your law had not been my delight,
> I would have perished in my misery.
I will never forget your precepts,
> for by them you have given me life. (Ps. 119:89-93)

Additional Readings
Jeremiah 36:1-10
The scroll is read in the temple

1 Corinthians 14:1-12
The assembly's gifts

Hymn: How Firm a Foundation, ELW 796

God of all creation, in your great love you have called us your own people and given us your law to guide our steps. Teach us to delight in your teachings and find joy in your promises.

Tuesday, January 28, 2025
Time after Epiphany

Thomas Aquinas, teacher, died 1274

2 Corinthians 7:2-12
Grief leads to repentance

Now I rejoice, not because you were grieved, but because your grief led to repentance; for you felt a godly grief, so that you were not harmed in any way by us. For godly grief produces a repentance that leads to salvation and brings no regret, but worldly grief produces death. For see what earnestness this godly grief has produced in you, what eagerness to clear yourselves, what indignation, what alarm, what longing, what zeal, what punishment! At every point you have proved yourselves guiltless in the matter.

So although I wrote to you, it was not on account of the one who did the wrong, nor on account of the one who was wronged, but in order that your zeal for us might be made known to you before God. (2 Cor. 7:9-12)

Psalm
Psalm 119:89-96
The law of God gives life

Additional Reading
Jeremiah 36:11-26
Jehoiakim burns the scroll

Hymn: Restore in Us, O God, ELW 328

God of forgiveness and new life, you are always more willing to forgive than we are to confess. Stir our hearts with a recognition of our sin, and comfort our consciences with the promise of your love.

Wednesday, January 29, 2025
Time after Epiphany

Jeremiah 36:27-32

Jeremiah dictates a second scroll

Now, after the king had burned the scroll with the words that Baruch wrote at Jeremiah's dictation, the word of the LORD came to Jeremiah: Take another scroll and write on it all the former words that were in the first scroll, which King Jehoiakim of Judah has burned. And concerning King Jehoiakim of Judah you shall say: Thus says the LORD, You have dared to burn this scroll, saying, Why have you written in it that the king of Babylon will certainly come and destroy this land, and will cut off from it human beings and animals? Therefore thus says the LORD concerning King Jehoiakim of Judah: He shall have no one to sit upon the throne of David, and his dead body shall be cast out to the heat by day and the frost by night. And I will punish him and his offspring and his servants for their iniquity; I will bring on them, and on the inhabitants of Jerusalem, and on the people of Judah, all the disasters with which I have threatened them—but they would not listen. (Jer. 36:27-31)

Psalm
Psalm 119:89-96
The law of God gives life

Additional Reading
Luke 4:38-44
Jesus heals and preaches in synagogues

Hymn: The Lord Now Sends Us Forth, ELW 538

God our sovereign, you are the one who guides us. Forgive our earthly leaders when their decisions do not reflect your love. Change their hearts and help them make choices that share your mercy with others.

Thursday, January 30, 2025
Time after Epiphany

Psalm 71:1-6
You have been my strength

In you, O Lord, I take refuge;
  let me never be put to shame.
In your righteousness deliver me and rescue me;
  incline your ear to me and save me.
Be to me a rock of refuge,
  a strong fortress, to save me,
  for you are my rock and my fortress.

Rescue me, O my God, from the hand of the wicked,
  from the grasp of the unjust and cruel.
For you, O Lord, are my hope,
  my trust, O Lord, from my youth. (Ps. 71:1-5)

Additional Readings
2 Chronicles 34:1-7
Youthful Josiah inaugurates reform

Acts 10:44-48
Gentiles receive the Holy Spirit

Hymn: A Mighty Fortress Is Our God, ELW 503–505, TFF 133

Holy and eternal God, you are our rock and fortress, our stability in an uncertain world. Keep us grounded in you. Bring your peace to our hearts. Help us find our rest and restored energy in you.

Friday, January 31, 2025
Time after Epiphany

2 Chronicles 35:20-27
Jeremiah laments the death of Josiah

The archers shot King Josiah; and the king said to his servants, "Take me away, for I am badly wounded." So his servants took him out of the chariot and carried him in his second chariot and brought him to Jerusalem. There he died, and was buried in the tombs of his ancestors. All Judah and Jerusalem mourned for Josiah. Jeremiah also uttered a lament for Josiah, and all the singing men and singing women have spoken of Josiah in their laments to this day. They made these a custom in Israel; they are recorded in the Laments. Now the rest of the acts of Josiah and his faithful deeds in accordance with what is written in the law of the LORD, and his acts, first and last, are written in the Book of the Kings of Israel and Judah. (2 Chron. 35:23-27)

Psalm
Psalm 71:1-6
You have been my strength

Additional Reading
Acts 19:1-10
Believers speak in tongues

Hymn: Healer of Our Every Ill, ELW 612

Creator God, you are the one who brings new life. When our hearts break, mend them. When our tears fall, wipe them away. When our minds are mixed up, calm them. Remind us of resurrection life.

Prayer List for February

Saturday, February 1, 2025
Time after Epiphany

2 Chronicles 36:11-21
Zedekiah ignores Jeremiah and Jerusalem falls

Zedekiah was twenty-one years old when he began to reign; he reigned eleven years in Jerusalem. He did what was evil in the sight of the LORD his God. He did not humble himself before the prophet Jeremiah who spoke from the mouth of the LORD. He also rebelled against King Nebuchadnezzar, who had made him swear by God; he stiffened his neck and hardened his heart against turning to the LORD, the God of Israel. All the leading priests and the people also were exceedingly unfaithful, following all the abominations of the nations; and they polluted the house of the LORD that he had consecrated in Jerusalem. (2 Chron. 36:11-14)

Psalm
Psalm 71:1-6
You have been my strength

Additional Reading
John 1:43-51
Can anything good come out of Nazareth?

Hymn: Jesus Calls Us; o'er the Tumult, ELW 696

O God of all strength and comfort, when the brokenness of the world seems too much, we are reminded of your Son and the good news of your love for each of us. Be with us as you always have been.

Sunday, February 2, 2025
Presentation of Our Lord

Luke 2:22-40

The child is brought to the temple

Simeon took [the child Jesus] in his arms and praised God, saying,
"Master, now you are dismissing your servant in peace,
according to your word;
for my eyes have seen your salvation,
which you have prepared in the presence of all peoples,
a light for revelation to the Gentiles
and for glory to your people Israel." (Luke 2:28-32)

Psalm
Psalm 84
How dear to me is your dwelling, O God

Additional Readings
Malachi 3:1-4
My messenger, a refiner and purifier

Hebrews 2:14-18
Jesus shares human flesh and sufferings

Hymn: Comfort, Comfort Now My People, ELW 256

Almighty and ever-living God, your only-begotten Son was presented this day in the temple. May we be presented to you with clean and pure hearts by the same Jesus Christ, our great high priest, who lives and reigns with you and the Holy Spirit, one God, now and forever.

Monday, February 3, 2025
Time after Epiphany

Ansgar, Bishop of Hamburg, missionary to Denmark and Sweden, died 865

1 Kings 17:8-16
The widow of Zarephath fed

Elijah said to her, "Do not be afraid; go and do as you have said; but first make me a little cake of it and bring it to me, and afterwards make something for yourself and your son. For thus says the LORD the God of Israel: The jar of meal will not be emptied and the jug of oil will not fail until the day that the LORD sends rain on the earth." She went and did as Elijah said, so that she as well as he and her household ate for many days. The jar of meal was not emptied, neither did the jug of oil fail, according to the word of the LORD that he spoke by Elijah. (1 Kings 17:13-16)

Psalm
Psalm 56
In God I trust

Additional Reading
1 Corinthians 2:6-16
Interpreting spiritual things

Hymn: Don't Be Afraid, ACS 1027

God our source, when we are fearful give us courage. Remind us that you have been our caring provider all the days of our lives and that you will continue to meet our deepest needs.

Tuesday, February 4, 2025
Time after Epiphany

Psalm 56
In God I trust

Be gracious to me, O God, for people trample on me;
> all day long foes oppress me;
my enemies trample on me all day long,
> for many fight against me.
O Most High, when I am afraid,
> I put my trust in you.
In God, whose word I praise,
> in God I trust; I am not afraid;
> what can flesh do to me? (Ps. 56:1-4)

Additional Readings
2 Kings 5:1-14
Naaman the Syrian healed

1 Corinthians 14:13-25
Interpreting tongues

Hymn: How Firm a Foundation, ELW 796

Gracious God, we place our trust in you. You hear our prayers and remind us of your love in ways we may not understand in the moment. Remind us that we are worthy in your eyes.

Wednesday, February 5, 2025
Time after Epiphany

The Martyrs of Japan, died 1597

Luke 19:41-44

Recognizing the works of God

As [Jesus] came near and saw the city, he wept over it, saying, "If you, even you, had only recognized on this day the things that make for peace! But now they are hidden from your eyes. Indeed, the days will come upon you, when your enemies will set up ramparts around you and surround you, and hem you in on every side. They will crush you to the ground, you and your children within you, and they will not leave within you one stone upon another; because you did not recognize the time of your visitation from God." (Luke 19:41-44)

Psalm

Psalm 56
In God I trust

Additional Reading

Jeremiah 1:11-19
Jeremiah warns of disaster

Hymn: Jesus Christ, When First You Came to Earth, ELW 727

Almighty God, as we celebrate this season of your Son breaking into the world, make us mindful of your creation around us. Help us to see the good news of your Spirit's work.

Thursday, February 6, 2025
Time after Epiphany

Psalm 138
I will bow toward your holy temple

I give you thanks, O LORD, with my whole heart;
> before the gods I sing your praise;
I bow down toward your holy temple
>> and give thanks to your name for your steadfast love and your
>>> faithfulness;
>> for you have exalted your name and your word
>> above everything.
On the day I called, you answered me,
> you increased my strength of soul.

All the kings of the earth shall praise you, O LORD,
> for they have heard the words of your mouth.
They shall sing of the ways of the LORD,
> for great is the glory of the LORD. (Ps. 138:1-5)

Additional Readings
Numbers 20:22-29
Eleazar succeeds Aaron

Acts 9:19b-25
Saul's call is questioned

Hymn: Look Who Gathers at Christ's Table, ACS 977

God, we give you thanks today for your steadfast love and faithfulness. As we gather around your table, help us to see the belovedness of our neighbors and the light of your Son they each carry.

Friday, February 7, 2025
Time after Epiphany

Acts 9:26-31
The apostles reluctantly welcome Saul

When [Saul] had come to Jerusalem, he attempted to join the disciples; and they were all afraid of him, for they did not believe that he was a disciple. But Barnabas took him, brought him to the apostles, and described for them how on the road he had seen the Lord, who had spoken to him, and how in Damascus he had spoken boldly in the name of Jesus. So he went in and out among them in Jerusalem, speaking boldly in the name of the Lord. He spoke and argued with the Hellenists; but they were attempting to kill him. When the believers learned of it, they brought him down to Caesarea and sent him off to Tarsus.

Meanwhile the church throughout Judea, Galilee, and Samaria had peace and was built up. Living in the fear of the Lord and in the comfort of the Holy Spirit, it increased in numbers. (Acts 9:26-31)

Psalm
Psalm 138
I will bow toward your holy temple

Additional Reading
Numbers 27:12-23
God's choice of Joshua

Hymn: Thank You, Lord, ACS 1092, TFF 296

Creator God, you look upon all people as beloved. We give you thanks for the witness of Barnabas in welcoming Saul into the community of faith and reminding us of the power of your unending mercy and grace.

Saturday, February 8, 2025
Time after Epiphany

Judges 3:7-11
God's spirit rests on Othniel

The Israelites did what was evil in the sight of the LORD, forgetting the LORD their God, and worshiping the Baals and the Asherahs. Therefore the anger of the LORD was kindled against Israel, and he sold them into the hand of King Cushan-rishathaim of Aram-naharaim; and the Israelites served Cushan-rishathaim eight years. But when the Israelites cried out to the LORD, the LORD raised up a deliverer for the Israelites, who delivered them, Othniel son of Kenaz, Caleb's younger brother. The spirit of the LORD came upon him, and he judged Israel; he went out to war, and the LORD gave King Cushan-rishathaim of Aram into his hand; and his hand prevailed over Cushan-rishathaim. So the land had rest forty years. Then Othniel son of Kenaz died. (Judg. 3:7-11)

Psalm
Psalm 138
I will bow toward your holy temple

Additional Reading
Luke 4:42-44
Jesus preaches

Hymn: Holy Spirit, Ever Dwelling, ELW 582

God of all nations, we give thanks for your loving Spirit that dwells within us. Move us in ways that work toward your peace, and keep us mindful of the ways your Spirit works through us.

Sunday, February 9, 2025
Fifth Sunday after Epiphany

Luke 5:1-11
Jesus calls the disciples to fish for people

When [the disciples had let down the nets], they caught so many fish that their nets were beginning to break. . . . But when Simon Peter saw it, he fell down at Jesus' knees, saying, "Go away from me, Lord, for I am a sinful man!" For he and all who were with him were amazed at the catch of fish that they had taken; and so also were James and John, sons of Zebedee, who were partners with Simon. Then Jesus said to Simon, "Do not be afraid; from now on you will be catching people." When they had brought their boats to shore, they left everything and followed him. (Luke 5:6, 8-11)

Psalm

Psalm 138
I will bow toward your holy temple

Additional Readings

Isaiah 6:1-8 [9-13]
Send me

1 Corinthians 15:1-11
I am the least of the apostles

Hymn: Holy, Holy, Holy, ACS 1089

Most holy God, the earth is filled with your glory, and before you angels and saints stand in awe. Enlarge our vision to see your power at work in the world, and by your grace make us heralds of your Son, Jesus Christ, our Savior and Lord.

Monday, February 10, 2025
Time after Epiphany

Psalm 115
God blesses the chosen people

May the LORD give you increase,
  both you and your children.
May you be blessed by the LORD,
  who made heaven and earth.

The heavens are the LORD's heavens,
  but the earth he has given to human beings.
The dead do not praise the LORD,
  nor do any that go down into silence.
But we will bless the LORD
  from this time on and forevermore.
Praise the LORD! (Ps. 115:14-18)

Additional Readings
Judges 5:1-11
Deborah the judge sings God's praise

1 Corinthians 14:26-40
Advice about worship

Hymn: Rise, Shine, You People! ELW 665

O God, you give blessing upon blessing to all your people. Your unending grace and mercy are steadfast, and we give thanks for the faith you have in us to be your chosen people. Walk with us always, even when we stumble.

Tuesday, February 11, 2025
Time after Epiphany

1 Samuel 9:15—10:1b
The call of Saul

When [Saul and Samuel] came down from the shrine into the town, a bed was spread for Saul on the roof, and he lay down to sleep. Then at the break of dawn Samuel called to Saul upon the roof, "Get up, so that I may send you on your way." Saul got up, and both he and Samuel went out into the street.

As they were going down to the outskirts of the town, Samuel said to Saul, "Tell the boy to go on before us, and when he has passed on, stop here yourself for a while, that I may make known to you the word of God."

Samuel took a vial of oil and poured it on his head, and kissed him; he said, "The Lord has anointed you ruler over his people Israel. You shall reign over the people of the Lord and you will save them from the hand of their enemies all around." (1 Sam. 9:25—10:1b)

Psalm
Psalm 115
God blesses the chosen people

Additional Reading
1 Timothy 3:1-9
Qualities needed by church leaders

Hymn: Come to Us, Creative Spirit, ELW 687

God, our life and our strength, just as Samuel sent Saul out into the world, you send us out as well. Help us to be the light Christ brings into the world.

Wednesday, February 12, 2025
Time after Epiphany

Luke 5:27-32
The call of Levi

Then Levi gave a great banquet for [Jesus] in his house; and there was a large crowd of tax collectors and others sitting at the table with them. The Pharisees and their scribes were complaining to his disciples, saying, "Why do you eat and drink with tax collectors and sinners?" Jesus answered, "Those who are well have no need of a physician, but those who are sick; I have come to call not the righteous but sinners to repentance." (Luke 5:29-32)

Psalm
Psalm 115
God blesses the chosen people

Additional Reading
Isaiah 8:1-15
Resisting the call

Hymn: Beloved, God's Chosen, ELW 648

Living God, in Christ you have made all things new. Send your Spirit upon us to remind us that you have claimed us as part of your body and that we are made to share your good works.

Thursday, February 13, 2025
Time after Epiphany

Psalm 1

Trees planted by streams of water

Happy are those
> who do not follow the advice of the wicked,
or take the path that sinners tread,
> or sit in the seat of scoffers;
but their delight is in the law of the LORD,
> and on his law they meditate day and night.
They are like trees
> planted by streams of water,
which yield their fruit in its season,
> and their leaves do not wither.
In all that they do, they prosper. (Ps. 1:1-3)

Additional Readings

Jeremiah 13:12-19
The threat of exile

Acts 13:26-34
God raised Jesus from the dead

Hymn: May This Church Be like a Tree, ACS 1042

Compassionate God, root us deeply in your love, like the tree that is planted along the stream. Guide us with your Spirit in the ways in which we can be good stewards of your creation.

Friday, February 14, 2025
Time after Epiphany

Cyril, monk, died 869; Methodius, bishop, died 885; missionaries to the Slavs

1 Peter 1:17—2:1
Born anew

Now that you have purified your souls by your obedience to the truth so that you have genuine mutual love, love one another deeply from the heart. You have been born anew, not of perishable but of imperishable seed, through the living and enduring word of God.
For
> "All flesh is like grass
>> and all its glory like the flower of grass.
> The grass withers,
>> and the flower falls,
> but the word of the Lord endures forever."

That word is the good news that was announced to you. (1 Peter 1:22-25)

Psalm
Psalm 1
Trees planted by streams of water

Additional Reading
Jeremiah 13:20-27
Can leopards change their spots?

Hymn: The Church's One Foundation, ELW 654

Creator, make us instruments of your peace, that by your word we hear the good news of your love for all humanity. Help us seek understanding, consoling all who call on you, in the name of your Son Jesus Christ.

Saturday, February 15, 2025
Time after Epiphany

Jeremiah 17:1-4

A heritage lost

The sin of Judah is written with an iron pen; with a diamond point it is engraved on the tablet of their hearts, and on the horns of their altars, while their children remember their altars and their sacred poles, beside every green tree, and on the high hills, on the mountains in the open country. Your wealth and all your treasures I will give for spoil as the price of your sin throughout all your territory. By your own act you shall lose the heritage that I gave you, and I will make you serve your enemies in a land that you do not know, for in my anger a fire is kindled that shall burn forever. (Jer. 17:1-4)

Psalm

Psalm 1
Trees planted by streams of water

Additional Reading

Luke 11:24-28
Blessings on those who hear the word

Hymn: Dearest Jesus, at Your Word, ELW 520

God our rock, as you were with your prophet Jeremiah in Judah, so you are with us. Engrave upon our hearts openness to your Spirit's work and remembrance of the heritage we have been given as stewards of your good creation.

Sunday, February 16, 2025
Sixth Sunday after Epiphany

Luke 6:17-26
Blessings on the poor, woes on the rich

Then [Jesus] looked up at his disciples and said:
   "Blessed are you who are poor,
      for yours is the kingdom of God.
   "Blessed are you who are hungry now,
      for you will be filled.
   "Blessed are you who weep now,
      for you will laugh.

"Blessed are you when people hate you, and when they exclude you, revile you, and defame you on account of the Son of Man. Rejoice in that day and leap for joy, for surely your reward is great in heaven; for that is what their ancestors did to the prophets." (Luke 6:20-23)

Psalm

Psalm 1
Trees planted by streams of water

Additional Readings

Jeremiah 17:5-10
Those who trust the Lord are like trees

1 Corinthians 15:12-20
Christ has been raised

Hymn: Let Streams of Living Justice, ELW 710

Living God, in Christ you make all things new. Transform the poverty of our nature by the riches of your grace, and in the renewal of our lives make known your glory, through Jesus Christ, our Savior and Lord.

Monday, February 17, 2025
Time after Epiphany

Psalm 120
Woe to me

In my distress I cry to the LORD,
    that he may answer me:
"Deliver me, O LORD,
    from lying lips,
    from a deceitful tongue."

Woe is me, that I am an alien in Meshech,
    that I must live among the tents of Kedar.
Too long have I had my dwelling
    among those who hate peace.
I am for peace;
    but when I speak,
    they are for war. (Ps. 120:1-2, 5-7)

Additional Readings
2 Kings 24:18—25:21
Woes come upon Jerusalem

1 Corinthians 15:20-34
The end time

Hymn: Earth, Earth, Awake! ACS 937

Merciful God, we give you thanks for your presence in our lives. You greet us with the hope of your Son. Be with us in moments when the brokenness of the world becomes too much.

Tuesday, February 18, 2025
Time after Epiphany

Martin Luther, renewer of the church, died 1546

2 Corinthians 1:12-19
The day of the Lord Jesus

Indeed, this is our boast, the testimony of our conscience: we have behaved in the world with frankness and godly sincerity, not by earthly wisdom but by the grace of God—and all the more toward you. For we write you nothing other than what you can read and also understand; I hope you will understand until the end—as you have already understood us in part—that on the day of the Lord Jesus we are your boast even as you are our boast. (2 Cor. 1:12-14)

Psalm
Psalm 120
Woe to me

Additional Reading
Ezra 1:1-11
Blessings return to Jerusalem

Hymn: Hail to the Lord's Anointed, ELW 311

Almighty God, through the signs and wonders of your Son we are made witnesses and instruments of your peace. We give thanks for the people in our lives who remind us of the power of your grace.

Wednesday, February 19, 2025
Time after Epiphany

Jeremiah 22:11-17
Woe to the unjust

Woe to him who builds his house by unrighteousness,
    and his upper rooms by injustice;
who makes his neighbors work for nothing,
    and does not give them their wages;
who says, "I will build myself a spacious house
    with large upper rooms,"
and who cuts out windows for it,
    paneling it with cedar,
    and painting it with vermilion.
Are you a king
    because you compete in cedar?
Did not your father eat and drink
    and do justice and righteousness?
    Then it was well with him.
He judged the cause of the poor and needy;
    then it was well. (Jer. 22:13-16)

Psalm
Psalm 120
Woe to me

Additional Reading
Luke 11:37-52
Woe to the sinners

Hymn: Before the Ancient One, Christ Stands, ACS 953

Loving God, you bring justice to those who call upon you. Inspire us to serve our neighbors and not profit off of them, even when the brokenness of the world confounds us.

Thursday, February 20, 2025
Time after Epiphany

Psalm 37:1–11, 39–40
The lowly shall possess the land

Refrain from anger, and forsake wrath.
> Do not fret—it leads only to evil.
For the wicked shall be cut off,
> but those who wait for the LORD shall inherit the land.

Yet a little while, and the wicked will be no more;
> though you look diligently for their place, they will not be there.
But the meek shall inherit the land,
> and delight themselves in abundant prosperity. (Ps. 37:8-11)

Additional Readings
Genesis 43:16–34
Joseph welcomes his brother Benjamin

Romans 8:1-11
You are one in the Spirit

Hymn: Come Down, O Love Divine, ELW 804

Everlasting God, help us to love in your name. Teach us to refrain from anger and wrath, and lead us to walk with our siblings in all times of injustice.

Friday, February 21, 2025
Time after Epiphany

1 John 2:12-17

The world and its desires are passing away

Do not love the world or the things in the world. The love of the Father is not in those who love the world; for all that is in the world—the desire of the flesh, the desire of the eyes, the pride in riches—comes not from the Father but from the world. And the world and its desire are passing away, but those who do the will of God live forever. (1 John 2:15-17)

Psalm

Psalm 37:1–11, 39–40
The lowly shall possess the land

Additional Reading

Genesis 44:1–17
Joseph detains his brother Benjamin

Hymn: O God, to You I Cry in Pain, ACS 1021

O divine Creator, we call on you in times of joy and in times of sorrow. Open our hearts to all things new and to your love that comes through your Son Jesus Christ our Lord.

Saturday, February 22, 2025
Time after Epiphany

Luke 12:57-59

Settling with your opponent

[The Lord said,] "And why do you not judge for yourselves what is right? Thus, when you go with your accuser before a magistrate, on the way make an effort to settle the case, or you may be dragged before the judge, and the judge hand you over to the officer, and the officer throw you in prison. I tell you, you will never get out until you have paid the very last penny." (Luke 12:57-59)

Psalm

Psalm 37:1-11, 39-40
The lowly shall possess the land

Additional Reading

Genesis 44:18-34
Judah offers himself in Benjamin's place

Hymn: To You All Hearts Are Open, ACS 1012

God of grace and mercy, help us open our hearts, reconciling with those we are in any conflict with. Remind us that since you loved us first, we are also called to love one another.

Sunday, February 23, 2025
Seventh Sunday after Epiphany

Polycarp, Bishop of Smyrna, martyr, died 156

Luke 6:27-38
Love your enemies

[Jesus said,] "But I say to you that listen, Love your enemies, do good to those who hate you, bless those who curse you, pray for those who abuse you. If anyone strikes you on the cheek, offer the other also; and from anyone who takes away your coat do not withhold even your shirt. Give to everyone who begs from you; and if anyone takes away your goods, do not ask for them again. Do to others as you would have them do to you." (Luke 6:27-31)

Psalm
Psalm 37:1-11, 39-40
The lowly shall possess the land

Additional Readings
Genesis 45:3-11, 15
Joseph forgives his brothers

1 Corinthians 15:35-38, 42-50
The mystery of the resurrection

Hymn: Build a Longer Table, ACS 1062

O Lord Jesus, make us instruments of your peace, that where there is hatred, we may sow love, where there is injury, pardon, and where there is despair, hope. Grant, O divine master, that we may seek to console, to understand, and to love in your name, for you live and reign with the Father and the Holy Spirit, one God, now and forever.

Monday, February 24, 2025
Time after Epiphany

Psalm 38
Confession of sin

I confess my iniquity;
    I am sorry for my sin.
Those who are my foes without cause are mighty,
    and many are those who hate me wrongfully.
Those who render me evil for good
    are my adversaries because I follow after good.

Do not forsake me, O LORD;
    O my God, do not be far from me;
make haste to help me,
    O Lord, my salvation. (Ps. 38:18-22)

Additional Readings

Genesis 33:1-17
Jacob and Esau reconcile

1 Corinthians 11:2-16
Advice for church life

Hymn: Welcome Table, ACS 969, TFF 263

O God, we gather at your welcome table. Transform our nature, prone to creating barriers for ourselves and one another, and remind us of the ways that we are connected as one body through your Son Jesus Christ.

Tuesday, February 25, 2025
Time after Epiphany

Elizabeth Fedde, deaconess, died 1921

1 Corinthians 11:17-22, 27-33
Advice concerning the Lord's supper

Now in the following instructions I do not commend you, because
when you come together it is not for the better but for the worse. For,
to begin with, when you come together as a church, I hear that there
are divisions among you; and to some extent I believe it. Indeed, there
have to be factions among you, for only so will it become clear who
among you are genuine. When you come together, it is not really to eat
the Lord's supper. For when the time comes to eat, each of you goes
ahead with your own supper, and one goes hungry and another becomes
drunk. What! Do you not have homes to eat and drink in? Or do you
show contempt for the church of God and humiliate those who have
nothing? What should I say to you? Should I commend you? In this
matter I do not commend you! (1 Cor. 11:17-22)

Psalm
Psalm 38
Confession of sin

Additional Reading
1 Samuel 24:1-22
David spares Saul's life

Hymn: Loaves Were Broken, Words Were Spoken, ACS 966

*God of all understanding, as the bread of life, your Son brings us together
around the table, uplifting and nurturing the varied gifts and talents we
each bring. May we do the same and build up our community.*

Wednesday, February 26, 2025
Time after Epiphany

Luke 17:1-4
Forgiving seven times

Jesus said to his disciples, "Occasions for stumbling are bound to come, but woe to anyone by whom they come! It would be better for you if a millstone were hung around your neck and you were thrown into the sea than for you to cause one of these little ones to stumble. Be on your guard! If another disciple sins, you must rebuke the offender, and if there is repentance, you must forgive. And if the same person sins against you seven times a day, and turns back to you seven times and says, 'I repent,' you must forgive." (Luke 17:1-4)

Psalm
Psalm 38
Confession of sin

Additional Reading
Leviticus 5:1-13
Offering for pardon

Hymn: Forgive Our Sins as We Forgive, ELW 605

God, Jesus reminds us of the ways in which we have moved further away from you and your people. Pour out your Spirit upon us, opening our hearts to moments when reconciliation and forgiveness can be had.

Thursday, February 27, 2025
Time after Epiphany

Psalm 99
Worship upon God's holy hill

The LORD is king; let the peoples tremble!
> He sits enthroned upon the cherubim; let the earth quake!
The LORD is great in Zion;
> he is exalted over all the peoples.
Let them praise your great and awesome name.
> Holy is he!
Mighty King, lover of justice,
> you have established equity;
you have executed justice
> and righteousness in Jacob.

Extol the LORD our God,
> and worship at his holy mountain;
> for the LORD our God is holy. (Ps. 99:1-4, 9)

Additional Readings

Deuteronomy 9:1-5
God's oath to Abraham, Isaac, and Jacob

Acts 3:11-16
Abraham, Isaac, and Jacob's God glorifies Jesus

Hymn: Holy, Holy, TFF 289

O God, your word brings life to the whole of your creation. When the nations rage and the earth quakes around us, fill our hearts with your unending love and compassionate justice for all.

Friday, February 28, 2025
Time after Epiphany

Acts 10:1-8
The vision of Cornelius

In Caesarea there was a man named Cornelius, a centurion of the Italian Cohort, as it was called. He was a devout man who feared God with all his household; he gave alms generously to the people and prayed constantly to God. One afternoon at about three o'clock he had a vision in which he clearly saw an angel of God coming in and saying to him, "Cornelius." He stared at him in terror and said, "What is it, Lord?" He answered, "Your prayers and your alms have ascended as a memorial before God." (Acts 10:1-4)

Psalm
Psalm 99
Worship upon God's holy hill

Additional Reading
Deuteronomy 9:6-14
Remember your rebellion in the wilderness

Hymn: Just a Closer Walk with Thee, ELW 697, TFF 253

Triune God, we lift our prayers to you because we know you hear us when we call. Guide us to walk closer to you and your reign here on earth, trusting that our lives are always in your keeping.

Prayer List for March

_____

_____

_____

_____

_____

_____

_____

_____

_____

Saturday, March 1, 2025
Time after Epiphany

George Herbert, hymnwriter, died 1633

Deuteronomy 9:15-24
Moses on the blazing mountain

So I turned and went down from the mountain, while the mountain was ablaze; the two tablets of the covenant were in my two hands. Then I saw that you had indeed sinned against the LORD your God, by casting for yourselves an image of a calf; you had been quick to turn from the way that the LORD had commanded you. So I took hold of the two tablets and flung them from my two hands, smashing them before your eyes. Then I lay prostrate before the LORD as before, forty days and forty nights; I neither ate bread nor drank water, because of all the sin you had committed, provoking the LORD by doing what was evil in his sight. For I was afraid that the anger that the LORD bore against you was so fierce that he would destroy you. But the LORD listened to me that time also. (Deut. 9:15-19)

Psalm
Psalm 99
Worship upon God's holy hill

Additional Reading
Luke 10:21-24
Blessed are the eyes that see what you see

Hymn: We Sing to You, O God, ELW 791

Liberating God, you keep your promises even as we struggle to trust you. Surprise us time and again with your mercy and steadfast love. No one else can save us; lead us to worship you alone.

Sunday, March 2, 2025
Transfiguration of Our Lord

John Wesley, died 1791; Charles Wesley, died 1788; renewers of the church

Luke 9:28-36 [37-43a]

Jesus is transfigured on the mountain

Now about eight days after these sayings Jesus took with him Peter and John and James, and went up on the mountain to pray. And while he was praying, the appearance of his face changed, and his clothes became dazzling white. Suddenly they saw two men, Moses and Elijah, talking to him. They appeared in glory and were speaking of his departure, which he was about to accomplish at Jerusalem. Now Peter and his companions were weighed down with sleep; but since they had stayed awake, they saw his glory and the two men who stood with him. (Luke 9:28-32)

Psalm

Psalm 99
Worship upon God's holy hill

Additional Readings

Exodus 34:29-35
Moses' face shone

2 Corinthians 3:12—4:2
We will be transformed

Hymn: Come with Us, O Blessed Jesus, ELW 501

Holy God, mighty and immortal, you are beyond our knowing, yet we see your glory in the face of Jesus Christ. Transform us into the likeness of your Son, who renewed our humanity so that we may share in his divinity, Jesus Christ our Lord, who lives and reigns with you and the Holy Spirit, one God, now and forever.

Monday, March 3, 2025
Time after Epiphany

Psalm 35:11-28
Do not be far from me

You have seen, O LORD; do not be silent!
    O Lord, do not be far from me!
Wake up! Bestir yourself for my defense,
    for my cause, my God and my Lord!
Vindicate me, O LORD, my God,
    according to your righteousness,
    and do not let them rejoice over me.
Do not let them say to themselves,
    "Aha, we have our heart's desire."
Do not let them say, "We have swallowed you up."

Let all those who rejoice at my calamity
    be put to shame and confusion;
let those who exalt themselves against me
    be clothed with shame and dishonor. (Ps. 35:22-26)

Additional Readings
Exodus 35:1-29
Offerings for the tent of meeting

Acts 10:9-23a
Peter's vision of what God makes clean

Hymn: There Is a Longing in Our Hearts, ACS 1078

God of our deliverance, you are attentive to our cries for justice. Our strength wanes and our voices fail, but you never cease to advocate for abundant life for all. When evil threatens to consume us, defend us from despair.

Tuesday, March 4, 2025
Time after Epiphany

Acts 10:23b-33
Cornelius and Peter

On Peter's arrival Cornelius met him, and falling at his feet, worshiped him. But Peter made him get up, saying, "Stand up; I am only a mortal." And as he talked with him, he went in and found that many had assembled; and he said to them, "You yourselves know that it is unlawful for a Jew to associate with or to visit a Gentile; but God has shown me that I should not call anyone profane or unclean." (Acts 10:25-28)

Psalm
Psalm 35:11-28
Do not be far from me

Additional Reading
Ezekiel 1:1—2:1
Ezekiel's vision of the chariot

Hymn: God Welcomes All, ACS 978

Creator God, you have revealed to us your unequivocal and enduring love for all creation. Help us to perceive our neighbors as your beloved ones; break down every barrier that divides us from one another.

Lent

Lent is a forty-day journey from Ash Wednesday to Easter. Christians enter into this time of discernment with Noah's family, sheltered by God in the ark for forty days; with the Israelites, who journeyed through the desert for forty years; and with Moses, Elijah, and Jesus, who fasted for forty days to prepare for lives of faithfulness.

During Lent Christians journey with those who are preparing for baptism at Easter. With them we all reflect on our responses to the baptismal questions: Do you renounce the forces and powers that defy and rebel against God? Do you believe in God the Father, the Son, and the Holy Spirit? (*ELW*, p. 229)

We renew our promise to live among God's people, to hear God's word and receive the Lord's supper, to proclaim in word and deed the good news, to serve others following Jesus' example, and to strive for justice and peace in all the earth (*ELW*, p. 236). In preparation for this renewal many Christians take up the traditional Lenten practices of prayer, fasting, and giving to people in need.

Table Prayer for the Season of Lent

Blessed are you, O God, giver of all.
You send us daily bread
and invite us to accompany you
in the transformation of the world.
Be present with us as we eat this meal
and share our joys and sorrows.
Send us out to be bread for others in a world hungry for your mercy.
In Jesus' name we pray. Amen.

Wednesday, March 5, 2025
Ash Wednesday

Matthew 6:1-6, 16-21
The practice of faith

[Jesus said,] "And whenever you fast, do not look dismal, like the hypocrites, for they disfigure their faces so as to show others that they are fasting. Truly I tell you, they have received their reward. But when you fast, put oil on your head and wash your face, so that your fasting may be seen not by others but by your Father who is in secret; and your Father who sees in secret will reward you." (Matt. 6:16-18)

Psalm
Psalm 51:1-17
Plea for mercy

Additional Readings
Joel 2:1-2, 12-17
Return to God

2 Corinthians 5:20b—6:10
Now is the day of salvation

Hymn: Abide, O Dearest Jesus, ELW 539

Almighty and ever-living God, you hate nothing you have made, and you forgive the sins of all who are penitent. Create in us new and honest hearts, so that, truly repenting of our sins, we may receive from you, the God of all mercy, full pardon and forgiveness through your Son, Jesus Christ, our Savior and Lord, who lives and reigns with you and the Holy Spirit, one God, now and forever.

Thursday, March 6, 2025
Week before Lent 1

Psalm 91:1-2, 9-16
God shall keep you

You who live in the shelter of the Most High,
    who abide in the shadow of the Almighty,
will say to the LORD, "My refuge and my fortress;
    my God, in whom I trust."

Because you have made the LORD your refuge,
    the Most High your dwelling place,
no evil shall befall you,
    no scourge come near your tent.

For he will command his angels concerning you
    to guard you in all your ways. (Ps. 91:1-2, 9-11)

Additional Readings

Exodus 5:10-23
Israel labors in Egypt

Acts 7:30-34
Moses, called from the burning bush to the exodus

Hymn: On Eagle's Wings, ELW 787

Sheltering God, you hold us close to your heart. You are our sanctuary and our security. When the challenges of life mount up against us, causing us to fear, assure us of your saving presence in our lives.

Friday, March 7, 2025
Week before Lent 1

Perpetua and Felicity and companions, martyrs at Carthage, died 202

Exodus 6:1-13
God promises deliverance

Then the LORD spoke to Moses, "Go and tell Pharaoh king of Egypt to let the Israelites go out of his land." But Moses spoke to the LORD, "The Israelites have not listened to me; how then shall Pharaoh listen to me, poor speaker that I am?" Thus the LORD spoke to Moses and Aaron, and gave them orders regarding the Israelites and Pharaoh king of Egypt, charging them to free the Israelites from the land of Egypt. (Exod. 6:10-13)

Psalm
Psalm 91:1-2, 9-16
God shall keep you

Additional Reading
Acts 7:35-42
The people complain to Moses

Hymn: Build Us Up, Lord, ELW 670

Persistent God, you work through us to enact freedom for your beloved children. When we doubt our ability to answer your call, remind us that we need not rely on our own power. With you, all things are possible.

Saturday, March 8, 2025
Week before Lent 1

Ecclesiastes 3:1-8

For everything a season

For everything there is a season, and a time for every matter under heaven:

> a time to be born, and a time to die;
> a time to plant, and a time to pluck up what is planted;
> a time to kill, and a time to heal;
> a time to break down, and a time to build up. (Eccles. 3:1-3)

Psalm

Psalm 91:1-2, 9-16
God shall keep you

Additional Reading

John 12:27-36
Jesus announces his passion

Hymn: Let My Spirit Always Sing, ACS 1020

When everything changes, O God, you are steady and true. As the seasons of our lives bring new opportunities and new challenges, ground us in your grace and reveal to us your purpose in all things.

Sunday, March 9, 2025
First Sunday in Lent

Luke 4:1-13

The temptation of Jesus

Jesus, full of the Holy Spirit, returned from the Jordan and was led by the Spirit in the wilderness, where for forty days he was tempted by the devil. He ate nothing at all during those days, and when they were over, he was famished. The devil said to him, "If you are the Son of God, command this stone to become a loaf of bread." Jesus answered him, "It is written, 'One does not live by bread alone.'" (Luke 4:1-4)

Psalm

Psalm 91:1-2, 9-16
God shall keep you

Additional Readings

Deuteronomy 26:1-11
Saved from Egypt

Romans 10:8b-13
You will be saved

Hymn: As Your Spirit in the Desert, ACS 923

O Lord God, you led your people through the wilderness and brought them to the promised land. Guide us now, so that, following your Son, we may walk safely through the wilderness of this world toward the life you alone can give, through Jesus Christ, our Savior and Lord, who lives and reigns with you and the Holy Spirit, one God, now and forever.

Monday, March 10, 2025
Week of Lent 1

Harriet Tubman, died 1913; Sojourner Truth, died 1883; renewers of society

Psalm 17
Prayer for protection from evil ones

I call upon you, for you will answer me, O God;
    incline your ear to me, hear my words.
Wondrously show your steadfast love,
    O savior of those who seek refuge
    from their adversaries at your right hand.

Guard me as the apple of the eye;
    hide me in the shadow of your wings. (Ps. 17:6-8)

Additional Readings
1 Chronicles 21:1-17
Satan tempts David

1 John 2:1-6
Obey God's commandments

Hymn: Golden Breaks the Dawn, ELW 852

God, you cover us with your powerful wings and warm us with your radiant love. Like newborns, we nestle into you, our savior. Shield us from danger, and open our hearts to trust you completely.

Tuesday, March 11, 2025
Week of Lent 1

Zechariah 3:1-10
Satan tempts Joshua

Then the angel of the LORD assured Joshua, saying "Thus says the LORD of hosts: If you will walk in my ways and keep my requirements, then you shall rule my house and have charge of my courts, and I will give you the right of access among those who are standing here. Now listen, Joshua, high priest, you and your colleagues who sit before you! For they are an omen of things to come: I am going to bring my servant the Branch. For on the stone that I have set before Joshua, on a single stone with seven facets, I will engrave its inscription, says the LORD of hosts, and I will remove the guilt of this land in a single day. On that day, says the LORD of hosts, you shall invite each other to come under your vine and fig tree." (Zech. 3:6-10)

Psalm
Psalm 17
Prayer for protection from evil ones

Additional Reading
2 Peter 2:4-21
Believers who fall into sin

Hymn: Beautiful Savior, ELW 838

God, without any hesitation you declare us forgiven. Give us today a vision of your promised future. Silence the voices around and within us that shame and accuse. Free us to serve our neighbors with generous hearts and radical hospitality.

Wednesday, March 12, 2025
Week of Lent 1

Gregory the Great, Bishop of Rome, died 604

Job 1:1-22
Satan tempts Job

Then Job arose, tore his robe, shaved his head, and fell on the ground and worshiped. He said, "Naked I came from my mother's womb, and naked shall I return there; the LORD gave, and the LORD has taken away; blessed be the name of the LORD."

In all this Job did not sin or charge God with wrongdoing. (Job 1:20-22)

Psalm
Psalm 17
Prayer for protection from evil ones

Additional Reading
Luke 21:34—22:6
Satan enters Judas

Hymn: God Weeps with Us Who Weep and Mourn, ACS 1054

God, you are good. In days of deepest grief and loss, when we cannot help but question why such heartache plagues us and our loved ones, assure us of your goodness and inspire us still to worship you.

Thursday, March 13, 2025
Week of Lent 1

Psalm 27
The Lord shall keep me safe

The LORD is my light and my salvation;
    whom shall I fear?
The LORD is the stronghold of my life;
    of whom shall I be afraid?

When evildoers assail me
    to devour my flesh—
my adversaries and foes—
    they shall stumble and fall.

Though an army encamp against me,
    my heart shall not fear;
though war rise up against me,
    yet I will be confident. (Ps. 27:1-3)

Additional Readings
Genesis 13:1-7, 14-18
Abram begins his pilgrimage

Philippians 3:2-12
Paul affirms the Abrahamic tradition

Hymn: Day by Day, ELW 790

Trustworthy God, you illumine our lives and embody among us your love for this world. We give thanks that you are for us; we need not fear. You are with us; we can move forward with confidence.

Friday, March 14, 2025
Week of Lent 1

Philippians 3:17-20
Our citizenship is in heaven

Brothers and sisters, join in imitating me, and observe those who live according to the example you have in us. For many live as enemies of the cross of Christ; I have often told you of them, and now I tell you even with tears. Their end is destruction; their god is the belly; and their glory is in their shame; their minds are set on earthly things. But our citizenship is in heaven, and it is from there that we are expecting a Savior, the Lord Jesus Christ. (Phil. 3:17-20)

Psalm
Psalm 27
The Lord shall keep me safe

Additional Reading
Genesis 14:17-24
Abram is blessed by Melchizedek

Hymn: Come and Seek the Ways of Wisdom, ACS 971

God of heaven and earth, the cross of Christ and his empty tomb are your stunning victory over all that seeks to destroy us. Remind us we belong to you; set our minds to love others as you love us.

Saturday, March 15, 2025
Week of Lent 1

Psalm 118:26-29
A pilgrimage song of praise

Blessed is the one who comes in the name of the LORD.
>   We bless you from the house of the LORD.
The LORD is God,
>   and he has given us light.
Bind the festal procession with branches,
>   up to the horns of the altar.

You are my God, and I will give thanks to you;
>   you are my God, I will extol you.

O give thanks to the LORD, for he is good,
>   for his steadfast love endures forever. (Ps. 118:26-29)

Psalm
Psalm 27
The Lord shall keep me safe

Additional Reading
Matthew 23:37-39
Jesus laments over Jerusalem

Hymn: Amen, We Praise Your Name, ELW 846, TFF 279

Gentle and generous God, you furnish our lives with portraits of your goodness. We lift our voices in praise of you, part of the infinite parade of those who worship you throughout the world. Continue to be our song as we journey.

Sunday, March 16, 2025
Second Sunday in Lent

Luke 13:31-35

A hen gathering her brood

At that very hour some Pharisees came and said to [Jesus], "Get away from here, for Herod wants to kill you." He said to them, "Go and tell that fox for me, 'Listen, I am casting out demons and performing cures today and tomorrow, and on the third day I finish my work. Yet today, tomorrow, and the next day I must be on my way, because it is impossible for a prophet to be killed outside of Jerusalem.' Jerusalem, Jerusalem, the city that kills the prophets and stones those who are sent to it! How often have I desired to gather your children together as a hen gathers her brood under her wings, and you were not willing! See, your house is left to you. And I tell you, you will not see me until the time comes when you say, 'Blessed is the one who comes in the name of the Lord.' " (Luke 13:31-35)

Psalm

Psalm 27
The Lord shall keep me safe

Additional Readings

Genesis 15:1-12, 17-18
The covenant with Abram

Philippians 3:17—4:1
Our citizenship is in heaven

Hymn: Thy holy wings, ELW 613

God of the covenant, in the mystery of the cross you promise everlasting life to the world. Gather all peoples into your arms, and shelter us with your mercy, that we may rejoice in the life we share in your Son, Jesus Christ, our Savior and Lord, who lives and reigns with you and the Holy Spirit, one God, now and forever.

Monday, March 17, 2025
Week of Lent 2

Patrick, bishop, missionary to Ireland, died 461

Psalm 105:1-15 [16-41] 42
God's covenant with Abraham

O give thanks to the LORD, call on his name,
　　make known his deeds among the peoples.
Sing to him, sing praises to him;
　　tell of all his wonderful works.
Glory in his holy name;
　　let the hearts of those who seek the LORD rejoice.
Seek the LORD and his strength;
　　seek his presence continually. (Ps. 105:1-4)

Additional Readings
Exodus 33:1-6
Abraham's descendants lament

Romans 4:1-12
The faith of Abraham

Hymn: O God in Heaven, ELW 748

God of every generation, you are authoring the story of a world set free from tyranny and terror. Chapter by chapter, call us to abundant life and empower us to share your story with all who need to hear it.

Tuesday, March 18, 2025
Week of Lent 2

1 Corinthians 10:1-13
God is faithful

I do not want you to be unaware, brothers and sisters, that our ancestors were all under the cloud, and all passed through the sea, and all were baptized into Moses in the cloud and in the sea, and all ate the same spiritual food, and all drank the same spiritual drink. For they drank from the spiritual rock that followed them, and the rock was Christ. Nevertheless, God was not pleased with most of them, and they were struck down in the wilderness. (1 Cor. 10:1-5)

Psalm
Psalm 105:1-15 [16-41] 42
God's covenant with Abraham

Additional Reading
Numbers 14:10b-24
Moses intercedes for the people

Hymn: Soul, Adorn Yourself with Gladness, ELW 488/489

Faithful God, like water from a rock you show up in miraculous ways and tend to our well-being. Help us to pay attention and to notice you at work, both in our lives and in the life of the world.

Wednesday, March 19, 2025
Joseph, Guardian of Jesus

Matthew 1:16, 18-21, 24a
The Lord appears to Joseph in a dream

Now the birth of Jesus the Messiah took place in this way. When his mother Mary had been engaged to Joseph, but before they lived together, she was found to be with child from the Holy Spirit. Her husband Joseph, being a righteous man and unwilling to expose her to public disgrace, planned to dismiss her quietly. But just when he had resolved to do this, an angel of the Lord appeared to him in a dream and said, "Joseph, son of David, do not be afraid to take Mary as your wife, for the child conceived in her is from the Holy Spirit. She will bear a son, and you are to name him Jesus, for he will save his people from their sins." (Matt. 1:18-21)

Psalm
Psalm 89:1-29
The Lord's steadfast love is established forever

Additional Readings
2 Samuel 7:4, 8-16
God makes a covenant with David

Romans 4:13-18
The promise to those who share Abraham's faith

Hymn: Be Thou My Vision, ELW 793

O God, from the family of your servant David you raised up Joseph to be the guardian of your incarnate Son and the husband of his blessed mother. Give us grace to imitate his uprightness of life and his obedience to your commands, through Jesus Christ, our Savior and Lord, who lives and reigns with you and the Holy Spirit, one God, now and forever.

Thursday, March 20, 2025
Week of Lent 2

Psalm 63:1-8

O God, eagerly I seek you

O God, you are my God, I seek you,
> my soul thirsts for you;
my flesh faints for you,
> as in a dry and weary land where there is no water.
So I have looked upon you in the sanctuary,
> beholding your power and glory.
Because your steadfast love is better than life,
> my lips will praise you.
So I will bless you as long as I live;
> I will lift up my hands and call on your name. (Ps. 63:1-4)

Additional Readings

Daniel 3:19-30
Servants of God vindicated

Revelation 2:8-11
Warning to the church in Smyrna

Hymn: Beneath the Cross of Jesus, ELW 338

You remain with us, O God, even as we traverse long, arduous stretches of spiritual drought. When we are weary and spent, water our wilted spirits and raise us up to verdant, flourishing life in you.

Friday, March 21, 2025
Week of Lent 2

Thomas Cranmer, Bishop of Canterbury, martyr, died 1556

Revelation 3:1-6
Warning to the church in Sardis

"And to the angel of the church in Sardis write: These are the words of him who has the seven spirits of God and the seven stars:

"I know your works; you have a name of being alive, but you are dead. Wake up, and strengthen what remains and is on the point of death, for I have not found your works perfect in the sight of my God. Remember then what you received and heard; obey it, and repent. If you do not wake up, I will come like a thief, and you will not know at what hour I will come to you. Yet you have still a few persons in Sardis who have not soiled their clothes; they will walk with me, dressed in white, for they are worthy. If you conquer, you will be clothed like them in white robes, and I will not blot your name out of the book of life; I will confess your name before my Father and before his angels." (Rev. 3:1-5)

Psalm
Psalm 63:1-8
O God, eagerly I seek you

Additional Reading
Daniel 12:1-4
God sends Michael

Hymn: Lord Jesus, Think on Me, ELW 599

God, you have shown us the way of life. Still, sin clings to our common life and injustice batters your beloved. Revive this world you love so dearly, filling our lungs with your breath. Daily turn us back to you.

Saturday, March 22, 2025
Week of Lent 2

Jonathan Edwards, teacher, missionary to American Indians, died 1758

Luke 6:43-45
A tree and its fruits

[Jesus said,] "No good tree bears bad fruit, nor again does a bad tree bear good fruit; for each tree is known by its own fruit. Figs are not gathered from thorns, nor are grapes picked from a bramble bush. The good person out of the good treasure of the heart produces good, and the evil person out of evil treasure produces evil; for it is out of the abundance of the heart that the mouth speaks." (Luke 6:43-45)

Psalm
Psalm 63:1-8
O God, eagerly I seek you

Additional Reading
Isaiah 5:1-7
The song of the vineyard

Hymn: O God beyond All Praising, ELW 880

Gardener God, you looked upon your creation and called it good. By your Spirit, we flourish and thrive. Continue to plant, feed, water, and weed our hearts so that we might yield nourishing fruit for the sake of the world.

Sunday, March 23, 2025
Third Sunday in Lent

Luke 13:1-9
The parable of the fig tree

Then [Jesus] told this parable: "A man had a fig tree planted in his vineyard; and he came looking for fruit on it and found none. So he said to the gardener, 'See here! For three years I have come looking for fruit on this fig tree, and still I find none. Cut it down! Why should it be wasting the soil?' He replied, 'Sir, let it alone for one more year, until I dig around it and put manure on it. If it bears fruit next year, well and good; but if not, you can cut it down.'" (Luke 13:6-9)

Psalm
Psalm 63:1-8
O God, eagerly I seek you

Additional Readings
Isaiah 55:1-9
Come to the water

1 Corinthians 10:1-13
Israel, baptized in cloud and seas

Hymn: Faith Begins By Letting Go, ACS 1004

Eternal God, your kingdom has broken into our troubled world through the life, death, and resurrection of your Son. Help us to hear your word and obey it, and bring your saving love to fruition in our lives, through Jesus Christ, our Savior and Lord, who lives and reigns with you and the Holy Spirit, one God, now and forever.

Monday, March 24, 2025
Week of Lent 3

Oscar Arnulfo Romero, Bishop of El Salvador, martyr, died 1980

Psalm 39
My hope is in God

"LORD, let me know my end,
>and what is the measure of my days;
>let me know how fleeting my life is.
You have made my days a few handbreadths,
>and my lifetime is as nothing in your sight.
Surely everyone stands as a mere breath.

>Surely everyone goes about like a shadow.
Surely for nothing they are in turmoil;
>they heap up, and do not know who will gather.

"And now, O Lord, what do I wait for?
>My hope is in you." (Ps. 39:4-7)

Additional Readings
Jeremiah 11:1-17
Judgment against the olive tree

Romans 2:1-11
Divine judgment applies to all

Hymn: O God, Our Help in Ages Past, ELW 632

Eternal God, you are the beginning and the end. In your Son, Jesus Christ, all things hold together. When we grow overwhelmed at how quickly our days are passing by, be our peace and our hope.

Tuesday, March 25, 2025
Annunciation of Our Lord

Luke 1:26-38
The angel greets Mary

In the sixth month the angel Gabriel was sent by God to a town in Galilee called Nazareth, to a virgin engaged to a man whose name was Joseph, of the house of David. The virgin's name was Mary. And he came to her and said, "Greetings, favored one! The Lord is with you." But she was much perplexed by his words and pondered what sort of greeting this might be. The angel said to her, "Do not be afraid, Mary, for you have found favor with God. And now, you will conceive in your womb and bear a son, and you will name him Jesus." (Luke 1:26-31)

Psalm

Psalm 45
Your name will be remembered

Additional Readings

Isaiah 7:10-14
A young woman will bear a son

Hebrews 10:4-10
The offering of Jesus' body sanctifies us

Hymn: Signs and Wonders, ELW 672

Pour your grace into our hearts, O God, that we who have known the incarnation of your Son, Jesus Christ, announced by an angel, may by his cross and passion be brought to the glory of his resurrection; for he lives and reigns with you, in the unity of the Holy Spirit, one God, now and forever.

Wednesday, March 26, 2025
Week of Lent 3

Numbers 13:17-27
The fruit of the promised land

Moses sent [men] to spy out the land of Canaan, and said to them, "Go up there into the Negeb, and go up into the hill country, and see what the land is like, and whether the people who live in it are strong or weak, whether they are few or many."

At the end of forty days they returned from spying out the land. And they came to Moses and Aaron and to all the congregation of the Israelites in the wilderness of Paran, at Kadesh; they brought back word to them and to all the congregation, and showed them the fruit of the land. And they told him, "We came to the land to which you sent us; it flows with milk and honey, and this is its fruit." (Num. 13:17-18, 25-27)

Psalm
Psalm 39
My hope is in God

Additional Reading
Luke 13:18-21
Parables of the mustard seed, yeast

Hymn: God of the Fertile Fields, ACS 1063

God of abundance, the richness of your grace is astounding. Free us from fears of scarcity, and help us notice the overflowing goodness you provide for your creation. Inspire us to share freely what you have given us so that all experience your loving care.

Thursday, March 27, 2025
Week of Lent 3

Psalm 32
Be glad, you righteous

Happy are those whose transgression is forgiven,
    whose sin is covered.
Happy are those to whom the LORD imputes no iniquity,
    and in whose spirit there is no deceit.

Be glad in the LORD and rejoice, O righteous,
    and shout for joy, all you upright in heart. (Ps. 32:1-2, 11)

Additional Readings
Joshua 4:1-13
Joshua leads the people across the Jordan

2 Corinthians 4:16—5:5
Paul comforts with a promise of glory

Hymn: I'm So Glad Jesus Lifted Me, ELW 860, TFF 191

Merciful God, through your incarnate word, Jesus Christ, you refuse to hold our failings against us. Instead, you remove our shame and deliver us from evil. Empower us to live as you intend, loving you and our neighbors wholeheartedly.

Friday, March 28, 2025
Week of Lent 3

2 Corinthians 5:6-15
Walking by faith and not by sight

So we are always confident; even though we know that while we are at home in the body we are away from the Lord— for we walk by faith, not by sight. Yes, we do have confidence, and we would rather be away from the body and at home with the Lord. So whether we are at home or away, we make it our aim to please him. For all of us must appear before the judgment seat of Christ, so that each may receive recompense for what has been done in the body, whether good or evil. Therefore, knowing the fear of the Lord, we try to persuade others; but we ourselves are well known to God, and I hope that we are also well known to your consciences.

For the love of Christ urges us on, because we are convinced that one has died for all; therefore all have died. And he died for all, so that those who live might live no longer for themselves, but for him who died and was raised for them. (2 Cor. 5:6-11, 14-15)

Psalm
Psalm 32
Be glad, you righteous

Additional Reading
Joshua 4:14-24
God's people come through the waters dry-shod

Hymn: Jesus Lives, My Sure Defense, ELW 621

God, you know us better than we know ourselves. When we struggle, you cheer us on through the love of Christ. Make us confident in your saving grace so that we might encourage others to behold your mercy.

Saturday, March 29, 2025
Week of Lent 3

Hans Nielsen Hauge, renewer of the church, died 1824

Exodus 32:7-14

Moses begs forgiveness

Moses implored the LORD his God, and said, "O LORD, why does your wrath burn hot against your people, whom you brought out of the land of Egypt with great power and with a mighty hand? Why should the Egyptians say, 'It was with evil intent that he brought them out to kill them in the mountains, and to consume them from the face of the earth'? Turn from your fierce wrath; change your mind and do not bring disaster on your people. Remember Abraham, Isaac, and Israel, your servants, how you swore to them by your own self, saying to them, 'I will multiply your descendants like the stars of heaven, and all this land that I have promised I will give to your descendants, and they shall inherit it forever.'" And the LORD changed his mind about the disaster that he planned to bring on his people. (Exod. 32:11-14)

Psalm

Psalm 32
Be glad, you righteous

Additional Reading

Luke 15:1-10
Parables of a lost sheep and a lost coin

Hymn: Chief of Sinners Though I Be, ELW 609

God, you hear our pleas for forgiveness and respond with tenderhearted compassion. You do not destroy us with condemnation but save us with your sacrificial love. Remember your promises to your people.

Sunday, March 30, 2025

Fourth Sunday in Lent

Luke 15:1-3, 11b-32

The parable of the forgiving father

[Jesus said, "The elder son] answered his father, 'Listen! For all these years I have been working like a slave for you, and I have never disobeyed your command; yet you have never given me even a young goat so that I might celebrate with my friends. But when this son of yours came back, who has devoured your property with prostitutes, you killed the fatted calf for him!'" Then the father said to him, 'Son, you are always with me, and all that is mine is yours. But we had to celebrate and rejoice, because this brother of yours was dead and has come to life; he was lost and has been found.'" (Luke 15:29-32)

Psalm

Psalm 32
Be glad, you righteous

Additional Readings

Joshua 5:9-12
Israel eats bread and grain

2 Corinthians 5:16-21
The mystery and ministry of reconciliation

Hymn: God, Be the Love to Search and Keep Me, ACS 1084

God of compassion, you welcome the wayward, and you embrace us all with your mercy. By our baptism clothe us with garments of your grace, and feed us at the table of your love, through Jesus Christ, our Savior and Lord, who lives and reigns with you and the Holy Spirit, one God, now and forever.

Monday, March 31, 2025
Week of Lent 4

John Donne, poet, died 1631

Psalm 53
Restoring our fortunes

God looks down from heaven on humankind
  to see if there are any who are wise,
  who seek after God.

They have all fallen away, they are all alike perverse;
  there is no one who does good,
  no, not one.

O that deliverance for Israel would come from Zion!
  When God restores the fortunes of his people,
  Jacob will rejoice; Israel will be glad. (Ps. 53:2-3, 6)

Additional Readings
Leviticus 23:26-41
Days for confession and celebration

Revelation 19:1-8
The marriage supper of the Lamb

Hymn: Wait for the Lord, ELW 262

God, you weep over your creation. Even as we are reckless with one another and the world, you will never reject or abandon us. Make us wise; let us seek you and do your will.

Prayer List for April

_____

_____

_____

_____

_____

_____

_____

_____

_____

Tuesday, April 1, 2025
Week of Lent 4

Revelation 19:9-10
Blessed are those invited to the marriage supper

And the angel said to me, "Write this: Blessed are those who are invited to the marriage supper of the Lamb." And he said to me, "These are true words of God." Then I fell down at his feet to worship him, but he said to me, "You must not do that! I am a fellow servant with you and your comrades who hold the testimony of Jesus. Worship God! For the testimony of Jesus is the spirit of prophecy." (Rev. 19:9-10)

Psalm
Psalm 53
Restoring our fortunes

Additional Reading
Leviticus 25:1-19
The jubilee celebration

Hymn: Oh, Happy Day When We Shall Stand, ELW 441

O God, you call us to celebration and offer us a feast of your sustaining grace. Guide our praise and direct our worship so that our mouths may be filled with your words of blessing and welcome to all.

Wednesday, April 2, 2025
Week of Lent 4

Luke 9:10-17
Jesus feeds 5000

The day was drawing to a close, and the twelve came to [Jesus] and said, "Send the crowd away, so that they may go into the surrounding villages and countryside, to lodge and get provisions; for we are here in a deserted place." But he said to them, "You give them something to eat." They said, "We have no more than five loaves and two fish—unless we are to go and buy food for all these people." For there were about five thousand men. And he said to his disciples, "Make them sit down in groups of about fifty each." They did so and made them all sit down. And taking the five loaves and the two fish, he looked up to heaven, and blessed and broke them, and gave them to the disciples to set before the crowd. And all ate and were filled. What was left over was gathered up, twelve baskets of broken pieces. (Luke 9:12-17)

Psalm
Psalm 53
Restoring our fortunes

Additional Reading
2 Kings 4:1-7
The widow saved

Hymn: Build a Longer Table, ACS 1062

God of deserted places, you draw hungry souls toward you even as others demand they be sent away. Open our ears to your clear call to join you in gathering, blessing, and feeding all who hunger.

Thursday, April 3, 2025
Week of Lent 4

Psalm 126
Sowing with tears, reaping with joy

Restore our fortunes, O LORD,
    like the watercourses in the Negeb.
May those who sow in tears
    reap with shouts of joy.
Those who go out weeping,
    bearing the seed for sowing,
shall come home with shouts of joy,
    carrying their sheaves. (Ps. 126:4-6)

Additional Readings
Isaiah 43:1-7
God will gather through fire and water

Philippians 2:19-24
Apostolic visits are promised

Hymn: As the Sun with Longer Journey, ELW 329

As spring rain marks this season's change, O God, so your grace guides us through winter's loss and sorrow. Bring your light to hearts frozen with grief so that tears may be sown as seeds for healing.

Friday, April 4, 2025
Week of Lent 4

Benedict the African, confessor, died 1589

Isaiah 43:8-15
God is Lord, Holy One, Creator, Ruler

I, I am the LORD,
    and besides me there is no savior.
I declared and saved and proclaimed,
    when there was no strange god among you;
    and you are my witnesses, says the LORD.
I am God, and also henceforth I am He;
    there is no one who can deliver from my hand;
    I work and who can hinder it?

Thus says the LORD,
    your Redeemer, the Holy One of Israel:
For your sake I will send to Babylon
    and break down all the bars,
    and the shouting of the Chaldeans will be turned to lamentation.
I am the LORD, your Holy One,
    the Creator of Israel, your King. (Isa. 43:11-15)

Psalm
Psalm 126
Sowing with tears, reaping with joy

Additional Reading
Philippians 2:25—3:1
Paul praises a co-worker

Hymn: Nothing Can Trouble, ACS 1033

Holy One, neither beside you nor before you is there any capable god who can deliver us. Turn yet again our hearts from all diversions and distractions, that we may find both refuge and freedom in you.

Saturday, April 5, 2025
Week of Lent 4

Exodus 12:21-27
Passover instituted to celebrate the exodus

Then Moses called all the elders of Israel and said to them, "Go, select lambs for your families, and slaughter the passover lamb. Take a bunch of hyssop, dip it in the blood that is in the basin, and touch the lintel and the two doorposts with the blood in the basin. None of you shall go outside the door of your house until morning. For the LORD will pass through to strike down the Egyptians; when he sees the blood on the lintel and on the two doorposts, the LORD will pass over that door and will not allow the destroyer to enter your houses to strike you down. You shall observe this rite as a perpetual ordinance for you and your children. When you come to the land that the LORD will give you, as he has promised, you shall keep this observance." (Exod. 12:21-25)

Psalm
Psalm 126
Sowing with tears, reaping with joy

Additional Reading
John 11:45-57
Plotting against Jesus during Passover

Hymn: O God, Who Gives Us Life, ACS 1086

Life-giving God, you offer yourself as the Passover lamb whose blood is the source of freedom. In all our rituals and prayer, perpetually remind us that your ultimate sacrifice refused violence so that love could truly be liberated.

Sunday, April 6, 2025
Fifth Sunday in Lent

Albrecht Dürer, died 1528; Matthias Grünewald, died 1529;
Lucas Cranach, died 1553; artists

John 12:1-8
Mary anoints Jesus for his burial

Mary took a pound of costly perfume made of pure nard, anointed Jesus' feet, and wiped them with her hair. The house was filled with the fragrance of the perfume. But Judas Iscariot, one of his disciples (the one who was about to betray him), said, "Why was this perfume not sold for three hundred denarii and the money given to the poor?" (He said this not because he cared about the poor, but because he was a thief; he kept the common purse and used to steal what was put into it.) Jesus said, "Leave her alone. She bought it so that she might keep it for the day of my burial." (John 12:3-7)

Psalm

Psalm 126
Sowing with tears, reaping with joy

Additional Readings

Isaiah 43:16-21
The Lord gives water in the wilderness

Philippians 3:4b-14
To know Christ and his resurrection

Hymn: Holy Woman, Graceful Giver (John 12), ACS 1002

Creator God, you prepare a new way in the wilderness, and your grace waters our desert. Open our hearts to be transformed by the new thing you are doing, that our lives may proclaim the extravagance of your love given to all through your Son, Jesus Christ, our Savior and Lord, who lives and reigns with you and the Holy Spirit, one God, now and forever.

Monday, April 7, 2025
Week of Lent 5

Psalm 20
Victory for God's anointed

Now I know that the LORD will help his anointed;
> he will answer him from his holy heaven
> with mighty victories by his right hand.
Some take pride in chariots, and some in horses,
> but our pride is in the name of the LORD our God.
They will collapse and fall,
> but we shall rise and stand upright.

Give victory to the king, O LORD;
> answer us when we call. (Ps. 20:6-9)

Additional Readings
Exodus 40:1-15
Anointing the holy things

Hebrews 10:19-25
Jesus, priest for the people of God

Hymn: Wash, O God, Our Sons and Daughters, ELW 445, TFF 112

Anointing God, you consecrate creation as a vessel of your living presence. Open our senses to your Spirit shining in everyone and your name whispered everywhere, so we might recognize your victorious reconciliation in every moment.

Tuesday, April 8, 2025
Week of Lent 5

1 John 2:18-28
Knowing the Son

Let what you heard from the beginning abide in you. If what you heard from the beginning abides in you, then you will abide in the Son and in the Father. And this is what he has promised us, eternal life.

I write these things to you concerning those who would deceive you. As for you, the anointing that you received from him abides in you, and so you do not need anyone to teach you. But as his anointing teaches you about all things, and is true and is not a lie, and just as it has taught you, abide in him.

And now, little children, abide in him, so that when he is revealed we may have confidence and not be put to shame before him at his coming. (1 John 2:24-28)

Psalm
Psalm 20
Victory for God's anointed

Additional Reading
Judges 9:7-15
Anointing the bramble

Hymn: Abide with Me, ELW 629

Abiding God, as we await your presence finally and fully revealed, help us to trust that you are here now. In breath and body, confidence and doubt, beginning and end: reveal your love's path as it traces the journeys of our lives.

Wednesday, April 9, 2025
Week of Lent 5

Dietrich Bonhoeffer, theologian, died 1945

Luke 18:31-34
Jesus foretells his death

Then [Jesus] took the twelve aside and said to them, "See, we are going up to Jerusalem, and everything that is written about the Son of Man by the prophets will be accomplished. For he will be handed over to the Gentiles; and he will be mocked and insulted and spat upon. After they have flogged him, they will kill him, and on the third day he will rise again." But they understood nothing about all these things; in fact, what he said was hidden from them, and they did not grasp what was said. (Luke 18:31-34)

Psalm
Psalm 20
Victory for God's anointed

Additional Reading
Habakkuk 3:2-15
God will save the anointed

Hymn: Let Streams of Living Justice, ELW 710

O God, in your suffering, you claimed victory, and your weakness overpowers every enemy. Call us again to your nonviolent way, that we too may die to all that hinders your love and rise again with your peace and justice.

Thursday, April 10, 2025
Week of Lent 5

Mikael Agricola, Bishop of Turku, died 1557

Psalm 31:9-16
I commend my spirit

B gracious to me, O L ord, for I am in distress;
> my eye wastes away from grief,
> my soul and body also.
For my life is spent with sorrow,
> and my years with sighing;
my strength fails because of my misery,
> and my bones waste away.

But I trust in you, O L ord;
> I say, "You are my God."
My times are in your hand;
> deliver me from the hand of my enemies and persecutors.
Let your face shine upon your servant;
> save me in your steadfast love. (Ps. 31:9-10, 14-16)

Additional Readings
Isaiah 53:10-12
The suffering one bears the sin of many

Hebrews 2:1-9
God's care for humankind

Hymn: O God, We Call, ACS 1075

Merciful God, you know our pain and our problems more intimately than we do ourselves. Shine your light into every lonely hollow so that even the shadows we cast might dance in your steadfast love.

Friday, April 11, 2025
Week of Lent 5

Isaiah 54:9-10
God's love is steadfast

This is like the days of Noah to me:
> Just as I swore that the waters of Noah
> would never again go over the earth,
so I have sworn that I will not be angry with you
> and will not rebuke you.
For the mountains may depart
> and the hills be removed,
but my steadfast love shall not depart from you,
> and my covenant of peace shall not be removed,
> says the LORD, who has compassion on you. (Isa. 54:9-10)

Psalm
Psalm 31:9-16
I commend my spirit

Additional Reading
Hebrews 2:10-18
Jesus' suffering binds him to humankind

Hymn: Lord Our God, with Praise We Come, ELW 730

God of firm and fierce compassion, even when mountains crumble and ecosystems collapse, you and your promise persist. May all creation find refuge on the ark of your resilient, steadfast love, and may new life abound when floodwaters finally recede.

Saturday, April 12, 2025
Week of Lent 5

Leviticus 23:1-8
Sabbath and passover

The LORD spoke to Moses, saying: Speak to the people of Israel and say to them: These are the appointed festivals of the LORD that you shall proclaim as holy convocations, my appointed festivals.

Six days shall work be done; but the seventh day is a sabbath of complete rest, a holy convocation; you shall do no work: it is a sabbath to the LORD throughout your settlements. (Lev. 23:1-3)

Psalm
Psalm 31:9-16
I commend my spirit

Additional Reading
Luke 22:1-13
Jesus prepares for Passover with his disciples

Hymn: As the Winter Days Grow Longer, ACS 924

Gracious God, you offer the rhythm of each week to help us recall your grace and rest in your deliverance. Hold us in your re-creation, renew us by your mercy, and strengthen us with your peace for these next seven holy days.

Holy Week

On the Sunday of the Passion, Christians enter into Holy Week. This day opens before the Christian community the final period of preparation before the celebration of the Three Days of the Lord's passion, death, and resurrection.

In many churches, palm branches will be given to worshipers for the procession into the worship space. Following an ancient custom, many Christians bring their palms home and place them in the household prayer center, behind a cross or sacred image, or above the indoor lintel of the entryway.

At sunset on Maundy Thursday, Lent comes to an end as the church begins the celebration of the events through which Christ has become the life and the resurrection for all who believe.

Prayer for Placing Palms in the Home

Use this blessing when placing palms in the home after the Palm Sunday liturgy.

Blessed is the One who comes in the name of the Lord!
May we who place these palms receive Christ into our midst
with the joy that marked the entrance to Jerusalem.
May we hold no betrayal in our hearts,
but peacefully welcome Christ
who lives and reigns with you and the Holy Spirit,
one God, now and forever. Amen.

Sunday, April 13, 2025
Sunday of the Passion / Palm Sunday

Luke 22:14—23:56

The passion and death of Jesus

Pilate, wanting to release Jesus, addressed [the chief priests, the leaders, and the people] again; but they kept shouting, "Crucify, crucify him!" A third time he said to them, "Why, what evil has he done? I have found in him no ground for the sentence of death; I will therefore have him flogged and then release him." But they kept urgently demanding with loud shouts that he should be crucified; and their voices prevailed. So Pilate gave his verdict that their demand should be granted. He released the man they asked for, the one who had been put in prison for insurrection and murder, and he handed Jesus over as they wished. (Luke 23:20-25)

Psalm

Psalm 31:9-16
I commend my spirit

Additional Readings

Isaiah 50:4-9a
The servant submits to suffering

Philippians 2:5-11
Death on a cross

Hymn: Sing, My Tongue, ELW 355/356

Everlasting God, in your endless love for the human race you sent our Lord Jesus Christ to take on our nature and to suffer death on the cross. In your mercy enable us to share in his obedience to your will and in the glorious victory of his resurrection, who lives and reigns with you and the Holy Spirit, one God, now and forever.

Monday, April 14, 2025
Monday in Holy Week

Psalm 36:5-11
Refuge under the shadow of your wings

Your steadfast love, O LORD, extends to the heavens,
  your faithfulness to the clouds.
Your righteousness is like the mighty mountains,
  your judgments are like the great deep;
  you save humans and animals alike, O LORD.

How precious is your steadfast love, O God!
  All people may take refuge in the shadow of your wings.
They feast on the abundance of your house,
  and you give them drink from the river of your delights.
For with you is the fountain of life;
  in your light we see light. (Ps. 36:5-9)

Additional Readings

Isaiah 42:1-9	Hebrews 9:11-15	John 12:1-11
The servant brings forth justice	*The blood of Christ redeems for eternal life*	*Mary of Bethany anoints Jesus*

Hymn: Come, Thou Fount of Every Blessing, ELW 807, TFF 108

O God, your Son chose the path that led to pain before joy and to the cross before glory. Plant his cross in our hearts, so that in its power and love we may come at last to joy and glory, through Jesus Christ, our Savior and Lord, who lives and reigns with you and the Holy Spirit, one God, now and forever.

Tuesday, April 15, 2025
Tuesday in Holy Week

Isaiah 49:1-7
The servant brings salvation to earth's ends

And now the LORD says,
>   who formed me in the womb to be his servant,
to bring Jacob back to him,
>   and that Israel might be gathered to him,
for I am honored in the sight of the LORD,
>   and my God has become my strength—
he says,
"It is too light a thing that you should be my servant
>   to raise up the tribes of Jacob
>   and to restore the survivors of Israel;
I will give you as a light to the nations,
>   that my salvation may reach to the end of the earth." (Isa. 49:5-6)

Psalm
Psalm 71:1-14
From my mother's womb you have been my strength

Additional Readings
1 Corinthians 1:18-31
The cross of Christ reveals God's power and wisdom

John 12:20-36
Jesus speaks of his death

Hymn: Jesus, I Will Ponder Now, ELW 345

Lord Jesus, you have called us to follow you. Grant that our love may not grow cold in your service, and that we may not fail or deny you in the time of trial, for you live and reign with the Father and the Holy Spirit, one God, now and forever.

Wednesday, April 16, 2025
Wednesday in Holy Week

Hebrews 12:1-3

Look to Jesus, who endured the cross

Therefore, since we are surrounded by so great a cloud of witnesses, let us also lay aside every weight and the sin that clings so closely, and let us run with perseverance the race that is set before us, looking to Jesus the pioneer and perfecter of our faith, who for the sake of the joy that was set before him endured the cross, disregarding its shame, and has taken his seat at the right hand of the throne of God.

Consider him who endured such hostility against himself from sinners, so that you may not grow weary or lose heart. (Heb. 12:1-3)

Psalm

Psalm 70
Be pleased, O God, to deliver me

Additional Readings

Isaiah 50:4-9a
The servant is vindicated by God

John 13:21-32
Jesus foretells his betrayal

Hymn: Making Their Way, ACS 979

Almighty God, your Son our Savior suffered at human hands and endured the shame of the cross. Grant that we may walk in the way of his cross and find it the way of life and peace, through Jesus Christ, our Savior and Lord, who lives and reigns with you and the Holy Spirit, one God, now and forever.

The Three Days

The Three Days begin at sunset on Maundy Thursday and end at sunset on Easter Day. For seventy-two hours, Christians prepare for and celebrate new life and love that lasts forever. Scripture proclaimed during the Three Days moves toward the baptismal font where new siblings in Christ are born of water and the Spirit, and where the baptized renew their own baptismal promises.

There are many ways to practice the Three Days at home and in the worshiping community. Forms of prayer, fasting, service, and silent reflection invite Christians to focus on the salvation story. Preparations can be made for the celebration of Easter: cleaning, coloring eggs, baking Easter breads, gathering greens or flowers to adorn crosses and sacred images. In those communities where baptisms will be celebrated, prayers may be offered for those to be received into the church.

Table Prayer for the Three Days

Blessed are you, O Lord our God.
You take away the sin of the world.
Nourish us with your promises
and strengthen us with this food,
so that we are sustained by your grace
for the journey from death to life,
through Jesus Christ our Lord. Amen.

Thursday, April 17, 2025
Maundy Thursday

Exodus 12:1-4 [5-10] 11-14
The passover of the Lord

Tell the whole congregation of Israel that on the tenth of this month they are to take a lamb for each family, a lamb for each household.

This is how you shall eat it: your loins girded, your sandals on your feet, and your staff in your hand; and you shall eat it hurriedly. It is the passover of the LORD. For I will pass through the land of Egypt that night, and I will strike down every firstborn in the land of Egypt, both human beings and animals; on all the gods of Egypt I will execute judgments: I am the LORD. The blood shall be a sign for you on the houses where you live: when I see the blood, I will pass over you, and no plague shall destroy you when I strike the land of Egypt. (Exod. 12:3, 11-13)

Psalm
Psalm 116:1-2, 12-19
The cup of salvation

Additional Readings
1 Corinthians 11:23-26
Proclaim the Lord's death

John 13:1-17, 31b-35
The service of Christ: footwashing and meal

Hymn: Three Holy Days Enfold Us Now, ACS 930

Holy God, source of all love, on the night of his betrayal, Jesus gave us a new commandment, to love one another as he loves us. Write this commandment in our hearts, and give us the will to serve others as he was the servant of all, your Son, Jesus Christ, our Savior and Lord, who lives and reigns with you and the Holy Spirit, one God, now and forever.

Friday, April 18, 2025
Good Friday

John 18:1—19:42
The passion and death of Jesus

Joseph of Arimathea, who was a disciple of Jesus, though a secret one because of his fear of the Jews, asked Pilate to let him take away the body of Jesus. Pilate gave him permission; so he came and removed his body. Nicodemus, who had at first come to Jesus by night, also came, bringing a mixture of myrrh and aloes, weighing about a hundred pounds. They took the body of Jesus and wrapped it with the spices in linen cloths, according to the burial custom of the Jews. Now there was a garden in the place where he was crucified, and in the garden there was a new tomb in which no one had ever been laid. And so, because it was the Jewish day of Preparation, and the tomb was nearby, they laid Jesus there. (John 19:38-42)

Psalm

Psalm 22
Why have you forsaken me?

Additional Readings

Isaiah 52:13—53:12
The suffering servant

Hebrews 10:16-25
The way to God is opened

Hymn: Ah, Holy Jesus, ELW 349

Almighty God, look with loving mercy on your family, for whom our Lord Jesus Christ was willing to be betrayed, to be given over to the hands of sinners, and to suffer death on the cross; who now lives and reigns with you and the Holy Spirit, one God, forever and ever.

Saturday, April 19, 2025
Resurrection of Our Lord
Vigil of Easter

Olavus Petri, priest, died 1552; Laurentius Petri, Bishop of Uppsala, died 1573;
renewers of the church

Romans 6:3-11

Dying and rising with Christ

Do you not know that all of us who have been baptized into Christ Jesus were baptized into his death? Therefore we have been buried with him by baptism into death, so that, just as Christ was raised from the dead by the glory of the Father, so we too might walk in newness of life.

For if we have been united with him in a death like his, we will certainly be united with him in a resurrection like his. (Rom. 6:3-5)

Psalm

Psalm 46
The God of Jacob is our stronghold

Additional Readings

Genesis 7:1-5, 11-18; 8:6-18; 9:8-13
Flood

John 20:1-18
Seeing the risen Christ

Hymn: O Sons and Daughters, Let Us Sing, ELW 386/387

Eternal giver of life and light, this holy night shines with the radiance of the risen Christ. Renew your church with the Spirit given us in baptism, that we may worship you in sincerity and truth and may shine as a light in the world, through your Son, Jesus Christ our Lord, who lives and reigns with you and the Holy Spirit, one God, now and forever.

Sunday, April 20, 2025
Resurrection of Our Lord
Easter Day

Luke 24:1-12
Women proclaim the resurrection

On the first day of the week, at early dawn, the women came to the tomb, taking the spices that they had prepared. They found the stone rolled away from the tomb, but when they went in, they did not find the body. While they were perplexed about this, suddenly two men in dazzling clothes stood beside them. The women were terrified and bowed their faces to the ground, but the men said to them, "Why do you look for the living among the dead? He is not here, but has risen. Remember how he told you, while he was still in Galilee, that the Son of Man must be handed over to sinners, and be crucified, and on the third day rise again." Then they remembered his words, and returning from the tomb, they told all this to the eleven and to all the rest. (Luke 24:1-9)

Psalm
Psalm 118:1-2, 14-24
On this day God has acted

Additional Readings
Acts 10:34-43
God raised Jesus on the third day

1 Corinthians 15:19-26
Christ raised from the dead

Hymn: This Joyful Eastertide, ELW 391

O God, you gave your only Son to suffer death on the cross for our redemption, and by his glorious resurrection you delivered us from the power of death. Make us die every day to sin, that we may live with him forever in the joy of the resurrection, through your Son, Jesus Christ our Lord, who lives and reigns with you and the Holy Spirit, one God, now and forever.

Easter

In the Christian church, Easter is not one day but a season of fifty days. During this time we explore the many ways God raises us up to new life. In a world where death threatens people on all sides, we declare that God is the God of life who has conquered death in Jesus Christ. We are invited to participate in Christ's death and resurrection, and to lean into our hope that one day, by God's grace, we will stand among God's resurrected people and see God face to face.

The fifty days were once called Pentecost, Greek for "fifty." We end this sacred time caught up in God's transforming Spirit that breaks down divisions and sends us out to accompany Jesus in tending and mending the world.

Table Prayer for the Season of Easter

O God, you raised Jesus to new life
by the power of your Holy Spirit.
Wherever we encounter pain or death,
send your Spirit with signs of your liberating life.
May this food we share
strengthen us to be Christ's body alive in the world.
In Jesus' name we pray. Amen.

Monday, April 21, 2025
Week of Easter 1

Anselm, Bishop of Canterbury, died 1109

Psalm 118:1-2, 14-24

On this day God has acted

I thank you that you have answered me
and have become my salvation.
The stone that the builders rejected
has become the chief cornerstone.
This is the LORD's doing;
it is marvelous in our eyes.
This is the day that the LORD has made;
let us rejoice and be glad in it. (Ps. 118:21-24)

Additional Readings

Joshua 10:16-27
Joshua defeats five kings

1 Corinthians 5:6b-8
Celebrating with sincerity and truth

Hymn: Thank You, Lord, ACS 1092, TFF 296

God of rejected stones and trauma-bearing trees, you opened death's hollow and flooded it with hope. Graft all rejected things onto the tree of your life, and reform all evil intent by your resurrection love.

Tuesday, April 22, 2025
Week of Easter 1

Revelation 12:1-12
The woman, the dragon, the child

War broke out in heaven; Michael and his angels fought against the dragon. The dragon and his angels fought back, but they were defeated, and there was no longer any place for them in heaven. The great dragon was thrown down, that ancient serpent, who is called the Devil and Satan, the deceiver of the whole world—he was thrown down to the earth, and his angels were thrown down with him. (Rev. 12:7-9)

Psalm
Psalm 118:1-2, 14-24
On this day God has acted

Additional Reading
Judges 4:17-23; 5:24-31a
Jael kills Sisera

Hymn: Before the Ancient One, Christ Stands, ACS 953

Great Deliverer, you watch over those who labor and you deliver war-torn children. Strengthen all who wait upon your protection today, that their work would not be in vain and your love would be born anew.

Wednesday, April 23, 2025
Week of Easter 1

Toyohiko Kagawa, renewer of society, died 1960

2 Samuel 6:1-15
David dances before the ark

It was told King David, "The LORD has blessed the household of Obed-edom and all that belongs to him, because of the ark of God." So David went and brought up the ark of God from the house of Obed-edom to the city of David with rejoicing; and when those who bore the ark of the LORD had gone six paces, he sacrificed an ox and a fatling. David danced before the LORD with all his might; David was girded with a linen ephod. So David and all the house of Israel brought up the ark of the LORD with shouting, and with the sound of the trumpet. (2 Sam. 6:12-15)

Psalm
Psalm 118:1-2, 14-24
On this day God has acted

Additional Reading
Luke 24:1-12
Women proclaim the resurrection

Hymn: Holy God, We Praise Your Name, ELW 414

O God, your holy presence astounds us and incites both fear and faith. Give us the courage to dance through fear, like David, so that we might rejoice in reporting your life-giving word, like the faithful women at the resurrection.

Thursday, April 24, 2025
Week of Easter 1

Psalm 150
Let everything praise the Lord

Praise the LORD!
Praise God in his sanctuary;
> praise him in his mighty firmament!
Praise him for his mighty deeds;
> praise him according to his surpassing greatness!

Praise him with trumpet sound;
> praise him with lute and harp!
Praise him with tambourine and dance;
> praise him with strings and pipe!
Praise him with clanging cymbals;
> praise him with loud clashing cymbals!
Let everything that breathes praise the LORD!
Praise the LORD! (Ps. 150:1-6)

Additional Readings

1 Samuel 17:1-23
The enemy Goliath taunts Israel

Acts 5:12-16
Signs and wonders by the apostles

Hymn: Alleluia! Voices Raise, ELW 828

God of the molecule and the Milky Way, your grace overwhelms and uplifts us. May our hearts magnify your deeds and our praise infuse each breath so that we may join all creation in celebrating your mighty deeds.

Friday, April 25, 2025
Mark, Evangelist

Mark 1:1-15
The beginning of the gospel of Jesus Christ

The beginning of the good news of Jesus Christ, the Son of God.

As it is written in the prophet Isaiah,
> "See, I am sending my messenger ahead of you,
> > who will prepare your way;
> the voice of one crying out in the wilderness:
> > 'Prepare the way of the Lord,
> > make his paths straight,' "

John the baptizer appeared in the wilderness, proclaiming a baptism of repentance for the forgiveness of sins. And people from the whole Judean countryside and all the people of Jerusalem were going out to him, and were baptized by him in the river Jordan, confessing their sins. (Mark 1:1-5)

Psalm
Psalm 57
Be merciful to me, O God

Additional Readings
Isaiah 52:7-10
The messenger announces salvation

2 Timothy 4:6-11, 18
The good fight of faith

Hymn: By All Your Saints, ELW 420, st. 1, 10, and Last

Almighty God, you have enriched your church with Mark's proclamation of the gospel. Give us grace to believe firmly in the good news of salvation and to walk daily in accord with it, through Jesus Christ, our Savior and Lord, who lives and reigns with you and the Holy Spirit, one God, now and forever.

Saturday, April 26, 2025
Week of Easter 1

1 Samuel 17:32-51
David conquers Goliath

When the Philistine drew nearer to meet David, David ran quickly toward the battle line to meet the Philistine. David put his hand in his bag, took out a stone, slung it, and struck the Philistine on his forehead; the stone sank into his forehead, and he fell face down on the ground.

So David prevailed over the Philistine with a sling and a stone, striking down the Philistine and killing him; there was no sword in David's hand. Then David ran and stood over the Philistine; he grasped his sword, drew it out of its sheath, and killed him; then he cut off his head with it.

When the Philistines saw that their champion was dead, they fled. (1 Sam. 17:48-51)

Psalm
Psalm 150
Let everything praise the Lord

Additional Reading
Luke 24:36-40
Beholding the wounds of the risen Christ

Hymn: The Strife Is O'er, the Battle Done, ELW 366

Great Wounded One, in your weakness hides a terrifying strength, as only you know how to strike down death. Slay every goliath that seeks to destroy your transformative grace, that your peace might prevail even on death's battlefield.

Sunday, April 27, 2025
Second Sunday of Easter

John 20:19-31

Beholding the wounds of the risen Christ

A week later [Jesus'] disciples were again in the house, and Thomas was with them. Although the doors were shut, Jesus came and stood among them and said, "Peace be with you." Then he said to Thomas, "Put your finger here and see my hands. Reach out your hand and put it in my side. Do not doubt but believe." Thomas answered him, "My Lord and my God!" Jesus said to him, "Have you believed because you have seen me? Blessed are those who have not seen and yet have come to believe." (John 20:26-29)

Psalm

Psalm 118:14-29
Glad songs of victory

Additional Readings

Acts 5:27-32
The God of our ancestors raised up Jesus

Revelation 1:4-8
Jesus Christ, firstborn of the dead

Hymn: Christ Has Risen While Earth Slumbers, ACS 938

O God of life, you reach out to us amid our fears with the wounded hands of your risen Son. By your Spirit's breath revive our faith in your mercy, and strengthen us to be the body of your Son, Jesus Christ, our Savior and Lord, who lives and reigns with you and the Holy Spirit, one God, now and forever.

Monday, April 28, 2025
Week of Easter 2

Psalm 122
Peace in Jerusalem

I was glad when they said to me,
> "Let us go to the house of the LORD!"
Our feet are standing
> within your gates, O Jerusalem.

Pray for the peace of Jerusalem:
> "May they prosper who love you.
Peace be within your walls,
> and security within your towers."
For the sake of my relatives and friends I will say,
> "Peace be within you." (Ps. 122:1-2, 6-8)

Additional Readings
Esther 7:1-10
Esther prevails over Haman

Revelation 1:9-20
A vision of Christ

Hymn: Jerusalem, My Happy Home, ELW 628

Bringer of peace, your presence delights to dwell in unity. Construct our lives as your home so that our hearts may be fortresses of your love, our minds towers of your mercy, and our bodies doorways to your grace.

Tuesday, April 29, 2025
Week of Easter 2

Catherine of Siena, theologian, died 1380

Esther 8:1-17
Destruction of the Jews is averted

Then Mordecai went out from the presence of the king, wearing royal robes of blue and white, with a great golden crown and a mantle of fine linen and purple, while the city of Susa shouted and rejoiced. For the Jews there was light and gladness, joy and honor. In every province and in every city, wherever the king's command and his edict came, there was gladness and joy among the Jews, a festival and a holiday. Furthermore, many of the peoples of the country professed to be Jews, because the fear of the Jews had fallen upon them. (Esther 8:15-17)

Psalm
Psalm 122
Peace in Jerusalem

Additional Reading
Revelation 2:8-11
Words to the church at Smyrna

Hymn: For Such a Time as This, ACS 1003

Gracious God, your saving word swiftly spreads with the urgency of liberating news. Carry us today by your light and gladness, your joy and honor, so that we too might share your presence and your peace wherever we go.

Wednesday, April 30, 2025
Week of Easter 2

Luke 12:4-12
The courage to confess Christ

[Jesus said,] "And I tell you, everyone who acknowledges me before others, the Son of Man also will acknowledge before the angels of God; but whoever denies me before others will be denied before the angels of God. And everyone who speaks a word against the Son of Man will be forgiven; but whoever blasphemes against the Holy Spirit will not be forgiven. When they bring you before the synagogues, the rulers, and the authorities, do not worry about how you are to defend yourselves or what you are to say; for the Holy Spirit will teach you at that very hour what you ought to say." (Luke 12:8-12)

Psalm
Psalm 122
Peace in Jerusalem

Additional Reading
Esther 9:1-5, 18-23
Purim celebrates victory

Hymn: Take My Life, That I May Be, ELW 583/685

Through trials and tears you stand always for justice and mercy, O God, and through even temptation and denial you forgive freely. Fortify our faith and surround us with grace so that we may live your love today and always.

Prayer List for May

_____

_____

_____

_____

_____

_____

_____

_____

_____

_____

Thursday, May 1, 2025
Philip and James, Apostles

Isaiah 30:18-21
The Lord will show mercy and Justice

Therefore the LORD waits to be gracious to you;
>   therefore he will rise up to show mercy to you.
For the LORD is a God of justice;
>   blessed are all those who wait for him.
Truly, O people in Zion, inhabitants of Jerusalem, you shall weep no
more. He will surely be gracious to you at the sound of your cry; when
he hears it, he will answer you. Though the Lord may give you the bread
of adversity and the water of affliction, yet your Teacher will not hide
himself any more, but your eyes shall see your Teacher. And when you
turn to the right or when you turn to the left, your ears shall hear a
word behind you, saying, "This is the way; walk in it." (Isa. 30:18-21)

Psalm
Psalm 44:1-3, 20-26
Save us for the sake of your steadfast love

Additional Readings
2 Corinthians 4:1-6
Proclaim Jesus Christ as Lord

John 14:8-14
Jesus and the Father are one

Hymn: The Word of God Is Source and Seed, ELW 506

*Almighty God, you gave to your apostles Philip and James grace and
strength to bear witness to your Son. Grant that we, remembering their victory of faith, may glorify in life and death the name of our Lord Jesus Christ,
who lives and reigns with you and the Holy Spirit, one God, now and forever.*

Friday, May 2, 2025
Week of Easter 2

Athanasius, Bishop of Alexandria, died 373

Isaiah 6:1-4

Heaven's holy, holy, holy

In the year that King Uzziah died, I saw the Lord sitting on a throne, high and lofty; and the hem of his robe filled the temple. Seraphs were in attendance above him; each had six wings: with two they covered their faces, and with two they covered their feet, and with two they flew. And one called to another and said:

"Holy, holy, holy is the LORD of hosts;
the whole earth is full of his glory."

The pivots on the thresholds shook at the voices of those who called, and the house filled with smoke. (Isa. 6:1-4)

Psalm	Additional Reading
Psalm 30	Revelation 4:1-11
My wailing turns to dancing	*Heaven's holy, holy, holy*

Hymn: As the Wind Song, ACS 943

Glorious God, our hearts reach out to you, as you reach out to us. We long for moments of wonder, curiosity, and connection. Turn us toward you each and every day of our lives.

Saturday, May 3, 2025
Week of Easter 2

Genesis 18:1-8

Abraham and Sarah's hospitality to the Lord

The LORD appeared to Abraham by the oaks of Mamre, as he sat at the entrance of his tent in the heat of the day. He looked up and saw three men standing near him. When he saw them, he ran from the tent entrance to meet them, and bowed down to the ground. He said, "My lord, if I find favor with you, do not pass by your servant. Let a little water be brought, and wash your feet, and rest yourselves under the tree. Let me bring a little bread, that you may refresh yourselves, and after that you may pass on—since you have come to your servant." So they said, "Do as you have said." (Gen. 18:1-5)

Psalm

Psalm 30
My wailing turns to dancing

Additional Reading

Luke 14:12-14
Welcome those in need to your table

Hymn: Let Us Break Bread Together, ELW 471

Compassionate God, you have taught us hospitality. Help us to welcome those who are strangers to us, trusting that there is enough to share and treating them as family. Nourish us with your word.

Sunday, May 4, 2025
Third Sunday of Easter

Monica, mother of Augustine, died 387

John 21:1-19

Jesus appears to the disciples

When [the disciples] had finished breakfast, Jesus said to Simon Peter, "Simon son of John, do you love me more than these?" He said to him, "Yes, Lord; you know that I love you." Jesus said to him, "Feed my lambs." A second time he said to him, "Simon son of John, do you love me?" He said to him, "Yes, Lord; you know that I love you." Jesus said to him, "Tend my sheep." He said to him the third time, "Simon son of John, do you love me?" Peter felt hurt because he said to him the third time, "Do you love me?" And he said to him, "Lord, you know everything; you know that I love you." Jesus said to him, "Feed my sheep. Very truly, I tell you, when you were younger, you used to fasten your own belt and to go wherever you wished. But when you grow old, you will stretch out your hands, and someone else will fasten a belt around you and take you where you do not wish to go." (He said this to indicate the kind of death by which he would glorify God.) After this he said to him, "Follow me." (John 21:15-19)

Psalm

Psalm 30
My wailing turns to dancing

Additional Readings

Acts 9:1-6 [7-20]
Paul's conversion, baptism, and preaching

Revelation 5:11-14
The song of the living creatures to the Lamb

Hymn: Lord, Let My Heart Be Good Soil, ELW 512, TFF 131

Eternal and all-merciful God, with all the angels and all the saints we laud your majesty and might. By the resurrection of your Son, show yourself to us and inspire us to follow Jesus Christ, our Savior and Lord, who lives and reigns with you and the Holy Spirit, one God, now and forever.

Psalm 121

God will preserve your life

I lift up my eyes to the hills—
> from where will my help come?
My help comes from the LORD,
> who made heaven and earth.

He will not let your foot be moved;
> he who keeps you will not slumber.

The sun shall not strike you by day,
> nor the moon by night.

The LORD will keep you from all evil;
> he will keep your life.
The LORD will keep
> your going out and your coming in
> from this time on and forevermore. (Ps. 121:1-3, 6-8)

Additional Readings

Ezekiel 1:1-25
Ezekiel's vision of four living creatures

Acts 9:19b-31
Saul joins the apostles in Jerusalem

Hymn: Creator Spirit, Heavenly Dove, ELW 578

Creator God, you have made the sun and the moon and the stars, and you have made each of us in your image. Strengthen us, protect us, and be with us in times of joy and in times of grief.

Tuesday, May 6, 2025
Week of Easter 3

Ezekiel 1:26—2:1
Ezekiel's vision of God's glory

And above the dome over their heads there was something like a throne, in appearance like sapphire; and seated above the likeness of a throne was something that seemed like a human form. Upward from what appeared like the loins I saw something like gleaming amber, something that looked like fire enclosed all around; and downward from what looked like the loins I saw something that looked like fire, and there was a splendor all around. Like the bow in a cloud on a rainy day, such was the appearance of the splendor all around. This was the appearance of the likeness of the glory of the LORD.

When I saw it, I fell on my face, and I heard the voice of someone speaking.

He said to me: O mortal, stand up on your feet, and I will speak with you. (Ezek. 1:26—2:1)

Psalm
Psalm 121
God will preserve your life

Additional Reading
Acts 26:1-18
Paul preaches before Agrippa

Hymn: Come and Seek the Ways of Wisdom, ACS 971

God of wonder, we have seen glimpses of you—in the morning frost, in the eyes of our neighbors, in singing together, and in the depths of our hearts. Shape our lives to be reflections of your love.

Wednesday, May 7, 2025
Week of Easter 3

Luke 5:1-11
Simon's catch of fish

Once while Jesus was standing beside the lake of Gennesaret, and the crowd was pressing in on him to hear the word of God, he saw two boats there at the shore of the lake; the fishermen had gone out of them and were washing their nets. He got into one of the boats, the one belonging to Simon, and asked him to put out a little way from the shore. Then he sat down and taught the crowds from the boat. When he had finished speaking, he said to Simon, "Put out into the deep water and let down your nets for a catch." Simon answered, "Master, we have worked all night long but have caught nothing. Yet if you say so, I will let down the nets." When they had done this, they caught so many fish that their nets were beginning to break. (Luke 5:1-6)

Psalm
Psalm 121
God will preserve your life

Additional Reading
Isaiah 6:1-8
Isaiah in the presence of God

Hymn: As We Gather at Your Table, ELW 522

God of abundance, you have created us to be in community, to share what we have, and to support each other. Help us know that our safety and freedom lie in our relationships with one another and with you.

Thursday, May 8, 2025
Week of Easter 3

Julian of Norwich, renewer of the church, died around 1416

Psalm 23
God our shepherd

The LORD is my shepherd, I shall not want.
>He makes me lie down in green pastures;
he leads me beside still waters;
>he restores my soul.
He leads me in right paths
>for his name's sake.

Even though I walk through the darkest valley,
>I fear no evil;
for you are with me;
>your rod and your staff—
>they comfort me. (Ps. 23:1-4)

Additional Readings
Ezekiel 11:1-25
Ezekiel prophesies against the shepherds of Israel

Revelation 5:1-10
The throne and the elders

Hymn: Deep Peace, ACS 1018

Loving God, we cry out to you from the depths. So much is uncertain and unstable. We come to you, bringing our whole selves, our whole lives. Wrap us in your love, and enfold us in your care.

Friday, May 9, 2025
Week of Easter 3

Nicolaus Ludwig von Zinzendorf, renewer of the church, hymnwriter, died 1760

Revelation 6:1—7:4
The servants of God are sealed

After this I saw four angels standing at the four corners of the earth, holding back the four winds of the earth so that no wind could blow on earth or sea or against any tree. I saw another angel ascending from the rising of the sun, having the seal of the living God, and he called with a loud voice to the four angels who had been given power to damage earth and sea, saying, "Do not damage the earth or the sea or the trees, until we have marked the servants of our God with a seal on their foreheads."

And I heard the number of those who were sealed, one hundred forty-four thousand, sealed out of every tribe of the people of Israel. (Rev. 7:1-4)

Psalm
Psalm 23
God our shepherd

Additional Reading
Ezekiel 20:39-44
God will gather the scattered people

Hymn: Spirit of Gentleness, ELW 396

God of creation, we live as interconnected beings. Turn us toward each other and toward the earth, which shelters and nourishes us. Remind us that we are part of your world, and help us slow down, breathe, and notice moments of awe.

Saturday, May 10, 2025
Week of Easter 3

Ezekiel 28:25-26
God gathers the people into safety

Thus says the Lord GOD: When I gather the house of Israel from the peoples among whom they are scattered, and manifest my holiness in them in the sight of the nations, then they shall settle on their own soil that I gave to my servant Jacob. They shall live in safety in it, and shall build houses and plant vineyards. They shall live in safety, when I execute judgments upon all their neighbors who have treated them with contempt. And they shall know that I am the LORD their God. (Ezek. 28:25-26)

Psalm
Psalm 23
God our shepherd

Additional Reading
Luke 12:29-32
Do not fear, little flock

Hymn: Come and Fill Our Hearts, ELW 528

God of shelter, we pray that all may have a home and a beloved community to share it with. Comfort those of us who lack the safety of stable housing, and remind us to embody your grace.

Sunday, May 11, 2025
Fourth Sunday of Easter

John 10:22-30

Jesus promises life to his sheep

[Jesus said,] "My sheep hear my voice. I know them, and they follow me. I give them eternal life, and they will never perish. No one will snatch them out of my hand. What my Father has given me is greater than all else, and no one can snatch it out of the Father's hand. The Father and I are one." (John 10:27-30)

Psalm

Psalm 23
God our shepherd

Additional Readings

Acts 9:36-43
Peter raises Tabitha from the dead

Revelation 7:9-17
A multitude sings before the Lamb

Hymn: Jesus, Remember Me, ELW 616

O God of peace, you brought again from the dead our Lord Jesus Christ, the great shepherd of the sheep. By the blood of your eternal covenant, make us complete in everything good that we may do your will, and work among us all that is well-pleasing in your sight, through Jesus Christ, our Savior and Lord, who lives and reigns with you and the Holy Spirit, one God, now and forever.

Monday, May 12, 2025
Week of Easter 4

Psalm 100
We are God's sheep

Make a joyful noise to the LORD, all the earth.
> Worship the LORD with gladness;
> come into his presence with singing.

Know that the LORD is God.
> It is he that made us, and we are his;
> we are his people, and the sheep of his pasture.

Enter his gates with thanksgiving,
> and his courts with praise.
> Give thanks to him, bless his name.

For the LORD is good;
> his steadfast love endures forever,
> and his faithfulness to all generations. (Ps. 100:1-5)

Additional Readings

Ezekiel 37:15-28
God will unite the flock

Revelation 15:1-4
The song of the Lamb

Hymn: O God, Whose Word Well-Planted, ACS 975

God, we sing out to you! We praise your name and lift our prayers to you like incense in the wind. We are yours. Show us again your love, grace, and compassion, and dwell with us.

Tuesday, May 13, 2025
Week of Easter 4

Acts 9:32-35
The healing of paralyzed Aeneas

Now as Peter went here and there among all the believers, he came down also to the saints living in Lydda. There he found a man named Aeneas, who had been bedridden for eight years, for he was paralyzed. Peter said to him, "Aeneas, Jesus Christ heals you; get up and make your bed!" And immediately he got up. And all the residents of Lydda and Sharon saw him and turned to the Lord. (Acts 9:32-35)

Psalm
Psalm 100
We are God's sheep

Additional Reading
Ezekiel 45:1-9
God promises a sanctuary

Hymn: Healer of Our Every Ill, ELW 612

God of restoration, comfort all who are living with chronic pain, addiction, or illness in any form. Help us to ask for and receive care, and to care for others within our capacity.

Wednesday, May 14, 2025
Matthias, Apostle

Luke 6:12-16
Jesus calls the twelve

Now during those days [Jesus] went out to the mountain to pray; and he spent the night in prayer to God. And when day came, he called his disciples and chose twelve of them, whom he also named apostles: Simon, whom he named Peter, and his brother Andrew, and James, and John, and Philip, and Bartholomew, and Matthew, and Thomas, and James son of Alphaeus, and Simon, who was called the Zealot, and Judas son of James, and Judas Iscariot, who became a traitor. (Luke 6:12-16)

Psalm
Psalm 56
I am bound by the vow I made to you

Additional Readings
Isaiah 66:1-2
Heaven is God's throne, earth is God's footstool

Acts 1:15-26
The apostles cast lots for Matthias

Hymn: Faith Begins by Letting Go, ACS 1004

Almighty God, you chose your faithful servant Matthias to be numbered among the twelve. Grant that your church may always be taught and guided by faithful and true pastors, through Jesus Christ our shepherd, who lives and reigns with you and the Holy Spirit, one God, now and forever.

Psalm 148

God's splendor is over earth and heaven

Praise the LORD!
Praise the LORD from the heavens;
>   praise him in the heights!
Praise him, all his angels;
>   praise him, all his host!

Praise him, sun and moon;
>   praise him, all you shining stars!
Praise him, you highest heavens,
>   and you waters above the heavens!

Let them praise the name of the LORD,
>   for he commanded and they were created.
He established them forever and ever;
>   he fixed their bounds, which cannot be passed. (Ps. 148:1-6)

Additional Readings

Ezekiel 2:8—3:11
Eating the scroll

Revelation 10:1-11
Eating the scroll

Hymn: Crashing Waters at Creation, ELW 455

Creator God, we wonder at your glory. You have created sunbeams, summer rain, and crisp breezes. You have placed your rainbow in the sky and given us senses to experience the world. Thank you. Fill us with awe.

Friday, May 16, 2025
Week of Easter 4

Daniel 7:13-14

An everlasting dominion is given

As I watched in the night visions,
>I saw one like a human being
>>coming with the clouds of heaven.
>And he came to the Ancient One
>>and was presented before him.
>To him was given dominion
>>and glory and kingship,
that all peoples, nations, and languages
>>should serve him.
His dominion is an everlasting dominion
>>that shall not pass away,
and his kingship is one
>>that shall never be destroyed. (Dan. 7:13-14)

Psalm

Psalm 148
God's splendor is over earth and heaven

Additional Reading

Revelation 11:15
God's reign at the end of time

Hymn: For the Fruit of All Creation, ELW 679

Merciful God, we live in an ever-changing, ever-shifting world. Help us to stay rooted in your love amid times of pain, suffering, and confusion in our lives. Strengthen us and keep us in your grace.

Saturday, May 17, 2025
Week of Easter 4

Revelation 11:16-19

God's reign at the end of time

Then the twenty-four elders who sit on their thrones before God fell on their faces and worshiped God, singing,

> "We give you thanks, Lord God Almighty,
>> who are and who were,
>
> for you have taken your great power
>> and begun to reign.
>
> The nations raged,
>> but your wrath has come,
>>
>> and the time for judging the dead,
>
> for rewarding your servants, the prophets
>> and saints and all who fear your name,
>>
>> both small and great,
>
> and for destroying those who destroy the earth." (Rev. 11:16-18)

Psalm

Psalm 148
God's splendor is over earth and heaven

Additional Reading

Daniel 7:27
A dominion for the holy ones of the Most High

Hymn: O God, Our Help in Ages Past, ELW 632

God of justice, we live among entangled systems that harm us, our neighbors, and creation. Transform us in response to your compassion. Inspire us to love and advocate for one another, as you love and care for us.

Sunday, May 18, 2025
Fifth Sunday of Easter

Erik, King of Sweden, martyr, died 1160

John 13:31-35
Love one another

When [Judas] had gone out, Jesus said, "Now the Son of Man has been glorified, and God has been glorified in him. If God has been glorified in him, God will also glorify him in himself and will glorify him at once. Little children, I am with you only a little longer. You will look for me; and as I said to the Jews so now I say to you, 'Where I am going, you cannot come.' I give you a new commandment, that you love one another. Just as I have loved you, you also should love one another. By this everyone will know that you are my disciples, if you have love for one another." (John 13:31-35)

Psalm

Psalm 148
God's splendor is over earth and heaven

Additional Readings

Acts 11:1-18
God saves the Gentiles

Revelation 21:1-6
New heaven, new earth

Hymn: God, When Human Bonds Are Broken, ELW 603

O Lord God, you teach us that without love, our actions gain nothing. Pour into our hearts your most excellent gift of love, that, made alive by your Spirit, we may know goodness and peace, through your Son, Jesus Christ, our Savior and Lord, who lives and reigns with you and the Holy Spirit, one God, now and forever.

Monday, May 19, 2025
Week of Easter 5

Psalm 133

How good it is to live in unity

How very good and pleasant it is
    when kindred live together in unity!
It is like the precious oil on the head,
    running down upon the beard,
on the beard of Aaron,
    running down over the collar of his robes.
It is like the dew of Hermon,
    which falls on the mountains of Zion.
For there the LORD ordained his blessing,
    life forevermore. (Ps. 133:1-3)

Additional Readings

1 Samuel 20:1-23, 35-42
The love of David and Jonathan

Acts 11:19-26
Christians in Antioch

Hymn: God We Gather as Your People, ACS 1038

God of relationship, we thank you for the many ways we are connected to each other. We lament ties that have frayed or broken, even when we have followed a faithful course of action. Help us always trust in your grace.

Tuesday, May 20, 2025
Week of Easter 5

Acts 11:27-30

Love embodied in care for others

At that time prophets came down from Jerusalem to Antioch. One of them named Agabus stood up and predicted by the Spirit that there would be a severe famine over all the world; and this took place during the reign of Claudius. The disciples determined that according to their ability, each would send relief to the believers living in Judea; this they did, sending it to the elders by Barnabas and Saul. (Acts 11:27-30)

Psalm

Psalm 133
How good it is to live in unity

Additional Reading

2 Samuel 1:4-27
David mourns Jonathan's death

Hymn: Come to Me, All Pilgrims Thirsty, ELW 777

God of community, you have created us to be in relationship with you and with each other. Strengthen our familial and neighborly bonds. Be with us as we learn how best to care for each other, creation, and ourselves.

Wednesday, May 21, 2025
Week of Easter 5

Helena, mother of Constantine, died around 330

Leviticus 19:9-18

Love your neighbor

You shall not hate in your heart anyone of your kin; you shall reprove your neighbor, or you will incur guilt yourself. You shall not take vengeance or bear a grudge against any of your people, but you shall love your neighbor as yourself: I am the LORD. (Lev. 19:17-18)

Psalm
Psalm 133
How good it is to live in unity

Additional Reading
Luke 10:25-28
Love your neighbor

Hymn: One Bread, One Body, ELW 496, TFF 122

Healing God, you have made each of us unique. We have different experiences, thoughts, and emotions. Open our hearts, and help us to live from a place of curiosity and kindness.

Thursday, May 22, 2025
Week of Easter 5

Psalm 67
Let the nations be glad

May God be gracious to us and bless us
    and make his face to shine upon us,
that your way may be known upon earth,
    your saving power among all nations.
Let the peoples praise you, O God;
    let all the peoples praise you.

the nations be glad and sing for joy,
    for you judge the peoples with equity
    and guide the nations upon earth.
Let the peoples praise you, O God;
    let all the peoples praise you. (Ps. 67:1-5)

Additional Readings

Proverbs 2:1-5
Knowledge of God like silver

Acts 15:36-41
Paul and Barnabas part company

Hymn: Like the Murmur of the Dove's Song, ELW 403

Holy God, we yearn for you. Remind us to notice moments of beauty, as they can be fleeting. Remind us to take time to mourn, as we experience the depths. Remind us always of your everlasting and all-encompassing love.

Friday, May 23, 2025
Week of Easter 5

Proverbs 2:6-8
God gives wisdom

For the LORD gives wisdom;
    from his mouth come knowledge and understanding;
he stores up sound wisdom for the upright;
    he is a shield to those who walk blamelessly,
guarding the paths of justice
    and preserving the way of his faithful ones. (Prov. 2:6-8)

Psalm
Psalm 67
Let the nations be glad

Additional Reading
Acts 16:1-8
Timothy accompanies Paul

Hymn: God Bestows on Every Sense, ACS 1069

God of blessing, guide us as we strive to live our lives in a way that reflects your mercy. May we take moments of quiet and stillness to listen for your guidance. Shape us, and shape our lives.

Saturday, May 24, 2025
Week of Easter 5

Nicolaus Copernicus, died 1543; Leonhard Euler, died 1783; scientists

Proverbs 2:9-15

Wisdom makes a home in your heart

Then you will understand righteousness and justice
    and equity, every good path;
for wisdom will come into your heart,
    and knowledge will be pleasant to your soul;
prudence will watch over you;
    and understanding will guard you. (Prov. 2:9-11)

Psalm

Psalm 67
Let the nations be glad

Additional Reading

Luke 19:1-10
Salvation makes a home with Zacchaeus

Hymn: Let All Things Now Living, ELW 881

Faithful God, so many things try to take our attention. We are overwhelmed with advertisements telling us we're not enough. We are surrounded by distractions that distance us from each other. Through your love, teach us another way to be.

Sunday, May 25, 2025
Sixth Sunday of Easter

John 14:23-29
The Father will send the Holy Spirit

[Jesus said,] "I have said these things to you while I am still with you. But the Advocate, the Holy Spirit, whom the Father will send in my name, will teach you everything, and remind you of all that I have said to you. Peace I leave with you; my peace I give to you. I do not give to you as the world gives. Do not let your hearts be troubled, and do not let them be afraid." (John 14:25-27)

Psalm
Psalm 67
Let the nations be glad

Additional Readings
Acts 16:9-15
Lydia and her household are baptized

Revelation 21:10, 22—22:5
The Lamb is the light of God's city

Hymn: O Living Breath of God, ELW 407

Bountiful God, you gather your people into your realm, and you promise us food from your tree of life. Nourish us with your word, that empowered by your Spirit we may love one another and the world you have made, through Jesus Christ, our Savior and Lord, who lives and reigns with you and the Holy Spirit, one God, now and forever.

Monday, May 26, 2025
Week of Easter 6

Psalm 93
God reigns above the floods

The Lord is king, he is robed in majesty;
>the Lord is robed, he is girded with strength.
He has established the world; it shall never be moved;
>your throne is established from of old;
>you are from everlasting.

The floods have lifted up, O Lord,
>the floods have lifted up their voice;
>the floods lift up their roaring.
More majestic than the thunders of mighty waters,
>more majestic than the waves of the sea,
>majestic on high is the Lord!

Your decrees are very sure;
>holiness befits your house,
>O Lord, forevermore. (Ps. 93:1-5)

Additional Readings
1 Chronicles 12:16-22
The spirit of God on Amasai

Revelation 21:5-14
Vision of the holy city

Hymn: O Blessed Spring, ELW 447

God of the cosmos, we are woven together in your creation. Protect those in the path of natural disasters. Turn us toward actions that uphold the beauty and dignity of the planet we call home, helping us all to live.

Tuesday, May 27, 2025
Week of Easter 6

John Calvin, renewer of the church, died 1564

Revelation 21:15-22
Vision of the holy city

The angel who talked to me had a measuring rod of gold to measure the city and its gates and walls. . . . The foundations of the wall of the city are adorned with every jewel; the first was jasper, the second sapphire, the third agate, the fourth emerald, the fifth onyx, the sixth carnelian, the seventh chrysolite, the eighth beryl, the ninth topaz, the tenth chrysoprase, the eleventh jacinth, the twelfth amethyst. And the twelve gates are twelve pearls, each of the gates is a single pearl, and the street of the city is pure gold, transparent as glass.

I saw no temple in the city, for its temple is the Lord God the Almighty and the Lamb. (Rev. 21:15, 19-22)

Psalm
Psalm 93
God reigns above the floods

Additional Reading
2 Chronicles 15:1-15
The spirit of God on Azariah

Hymn: The Earth Adorned in Verdant Robe, ACS 1068

Glorious God, you delight in the tiniest details of our lives. Help us treat each other with loving kindness, whether or not we share the same lived experiences. We yearn for a day when all may have enough.

Wednesday, May 28, 2025
Week of Easter 6

2 Chronicles 34:20-33
Josiah consults the prophet Huldah

[The prophet Huldah said,] "But as to the king of Judah, who sent you to inquire of the LORD, thus shall you say to him: Thus says the LORD, the God of Israel: Regarding the words that you have heard, because your heart was penitent and you humbled yourself before God when you heard his words against this place and its inhabitants, and you have humbled yourself before me, and have torn your clothes and wept before me, I also have heard you, says the LORD. I will gather you to your ancestors and you shall be gathered to your grave in peace; your eyes shall not see all the disaster that I will bring on this place and its inhabitants." (2 Chron. 34:26-28)

Psalm
Psalm 93
God reigns above the floods

Additional Reading
Luke 2:25-38
The spirit of God on Simeon and Anna

Hymn: In Deepest Night, ELW 699

God of wisdom, sometimes things don't turn out as we planned, or as we hoped. Be with us in moments of disappointment, and guide us so that we may follow the path of your love above all else.

Thursday, May 29, 2025
Ascension of Our Lord

Jiří Tranovský, hymnwriter, died 1637

Acts 1:1-11

Jesus sends the apostles

When [the disciples] had come together, they asked [Jesus], "Lord, is this the time when you will restore the kingdom to Israel?" He replied, "It is not for you to know the times or periods that the Father has set by his own authority. But you will receive power when the Holy Spirit has come upon you; and you will be my witnesses in Jerusalem, in all Judea and Samaria, and to the ends of the earth." When he had said this, as they were watching, he was lifted up, and a cloud took him out of their sight. While he was going and they were gazing up toward heaven, suddenly two men in white robes stood by them. They said, "Men of Galilee, why do you stand looking up toward heaven? This Jesus, who has been taken up from you into heaven, will come in the same way as you saw him go into heaven." (Acts 1:6-11)

Psalm

Psalm 47
God has gone up with a shout

Additional Readings

Ephesians 1:15-23
Seeing the risen and ascended Christ

Luke 24:44-53
Christ present in all times and places

Hymn: Lord, Listen to Your Children Praying, ELW 752, TFF 247

Almighty God, your only Son was taken into the heavens and in your presence intercedes for us. Receive us and our prayers for all the world, and in the end bring everything into your glory, through Jesus Christ, our Sovereign and Lord, who lives and reigns with you and the Holy Spirit, one God, now and forever.

Friday, May 30, 2025
Week of Easter 6

Psalm 97
Light dawns for the righteous

The Lord loves those who hate evil;
>   he guards the lives of his faithful;
>   he rescues them from the hand of the wicked.
Light dawns for the righteous,
>   and joy for the upright in heart.
Rejoice in the LORD, O you righteous,
>   and give thanks to his holy name! (Ps. 97:10-12)

Additional Readings
Exodus 33:12-17
Moses prays for the people

Revelation 22:6-9
A trustworthy testimony

Hymn: Holy God, Holy and Glorious, ELW 637

Loving God, protect us from evil. Heal us when we have been harmed. Guide our hearts toward compassion. Remind us of your wisdom passed down through our ancestors. Be with us, and enfold us in your grace.

Saturday, May 31, 2025
Visit of Mary to Elizabeth

Luke 1:39-57

Mary greets Elizabeth

In those days Mary set out and went with haste to a Judean town in the hill country, where she entered the house of Zechariah and greeted Elizabeth. When Elizabeth heard Mary's greeting, the child leaped in her womb. And Elizabeth was filled with the Holy Spirit and exclaimed with a loud cry, "Blessed are you among women, and blessed is the fruit of your womb." (Luke 1:39-42)

Psalm

Psalm 113
God, the helper of the needy

Additional Readings

1 Samuel 2:1-10
Hannah's thanksgiving

Romans 12:9-16b
Rejoice with those who rejoice

Hymn: Light Dawns on a Weary World, ELW 726

Mighty God, by whose grace Elizabeth rejoiced with Mary and greeted her as the mother of the Lord: look with favor on your lowly servants that, with Mary, we may magnify your holy name and rejoice to acclaim her Son as our Savior, who lives and reigns with you and the Holy Spirit, one God, now and forever.

Prayer List for June

_____

_____

_____

_____

_____

_____

_____

_____

_____

Sunday, June 1, 2025
Seventh Sunday of Easter

Justin, martyr at Rome, died around 165

John 17:20-26

Christ's prayer for his disciples

[Jesus said,] "I ask not only on behalf of these, but also on behalf of those who will believe in me through their word, that they may all be one. As you, Father, are in me and I am in you, may they also be in us, so that the world may believe that you have sent me. The glory that you have given me I have given them, so that they may be one, as we are one, I in them and you in me, that they may become completely one, so that the world may know that you have sent me and have loved them even as you have loved me. Father, I desire that those also, whom you have given me, may be with me where I am, to see my glory, which you have given me because you loved me before the foundation of the world." (John 17:20-24)

Psalm

Psalm 97
Light dawns for the righteous

Additional Readings

Acts 16:16-34
A jailer is baptized

Revelation 22:12-14, 16-17, 20-21
Blessed are those who wash their robes

Hymn: All Who Believe and Are Baptized, ELW 442

O God, form the minds of your faithful people into your one will. Make us love what you command and desire what you promise, that, amid all the changes of this world, our hearts may be fixed where true joy is found, your Son, Jesus Christ our Lord, who lives and reigns with you and the Holy Spirit, one God, now and forever.

Monday, June 2, 2025
Week of Easter 7

Psalm 29
The glory of God

Ascribe to the LORD, O heavenly beings,
  ascribe to the LORD glory and strength.
Ascribe to the LORD the glory of his name;
  worship the LORD in holy splendor.

The voice of the LORD is over the waters;
  the God of glory thunders,
  the LORD, over mighty waters.
The voice of the LORD is powerful;
  the voice of the LORD is full of majesty. (Ps. 29:1-4)

Additional Readings

Exodus 40:16-38
God's glory on the tabernacle

Acts 16:35-40
The magistrates apologize to Paul and Silas

Hymn: Thine Is the Glory, ELW 376

As we come to the altar of grace, show us your glory as you did to the people of Israel. Forgive us for the times we did not see your splendor and majesty in this world.

Tuesday, June 3, 2025
Week of Easter 7

The Martyrs of Uganda, died 1886
John XXIII, Bishop of Rome, died 1963

2 Chronicles 5:2-14
God's glory in the temple

Now when the priests came out of the holy place (for all the priests who were present had sanctified themselves, without regard to their divisions, and all the levitical singers, Asaph, Heman, and Jeduthun, their sons and kindred, arrayed in fine linen, with cymbals, harps, and lyres, stood east of the altar with one hundred twenty priests who were trumpeters). It was the duty of the trumpeters and singers to make themselves heard in unison in praise and thanksgiving to the LORD, and when the song was raised, with trumpets and cymbals and other musical instruments, in praise to the LORD,

"For he is good,
for his steadfast love endures forever,"

the house, the house of the LORD, was filled with a cloud, so that the priests could not stand to minister because of the cloud; for the glory of the LORD filled the house of God. (2 Chron. 5:11-14)

Psalm
Psalm 29
The glory of God

Additional Reading
Acts 26:19-29
Proclaim the light of the resurrection

Hymn: Hallelujah! Jesus Lives! ELW 380

O blessed God, you reveal yourself to all who come to you. May the Holy Spirit unbind us from any form of oppression and restore in us your unfailing mercy, for your steadfast love endures forever in Jesus Christ.

Wednesday, June 4, 2025
Week of Easter 7

Ezekiel 3:12-21
God's glory commissions the prophet

At the end of seven days, the word of the LORD came to me: Mortal, I have made you a sentinel for the house of Israel; whenever you hear a word from my mouth, you shall give them warning from me. If I say to the wicked, "You shall surely die," and you give them no warning, or speak to warn the wicked from their wicked way, in order to save their life, those wicked persons shall die for their iniquity; but their blood I will require at your hand. But if you warn the wicked, and they do not turn from their wickedness, or from their wicked way, they shall die for their iniquity; but you will have saved your life. (Ezek. 3:16-19)

Psalm
Psalm 29
The glory of God

Additional Reading
Luke 9:18-27
God's glory and discipleship

Hymn: Lord Jesus, You Shall Be My Song, ELW 808

Beloved God, you call us to journey with you. Help us in our call to see your presence in our siblings so that we can be better servants of your kingdom. In Christ Jesus, your only begotten Son.

Thursday, June 5, 2025
Week of Easter 7

Boniface, Bishop of Mainz, missionary to Germany, martyr, died 754

Psalm 104:24-34, 35b
Renewing the face of the earth

O Lord, how manifold are your works!
> In wisdom you have made them all;
> the earth is full of your creatures.
Yonder is the sea, great and wide,
> creeping things innumerable are there,
> living things both small and great.
There go the ships,
> and Leviathan that you formed to sport in it.

These all look to you
> to give them their food in due season;
when you give to them, they gather it up;
> when you open your hand, they are filled with good things.
(Ps. 104:24-28)

Additional Readings
Isaiah 32:11-17
The spirit poured out to renew the earth

Galatians 5:16-25
The fruit of the Spirit

Hymn: Spirit of God, Descend upon My Heart, ELW 800

Creator God, we give you thanks for the earth and all the resources we have inherited. Pour out the fruit of the Spirit in our hearts that we may be renewed to sustain, nurture, and refresh all life.

Friday, June 6, 2025
Week of Easter 7

Galatians 6:7-10

Reaping eternal life from the Spirit

Do not be deceived; God is not mocked, for you reap whatever you sow. If you sow to your own flesh, you will reap corruption from the flesh; but if you sow to the Spirit, you will reap eternal life from the Spirit. So let us not grow weary in doing what is right, for we will reap at harvest time, if we do not give up. So then, whenever we have an opportunity, let us work for the good of all, and especially for those of the family of faith. (Gal. 6:7-10)

Psalm

Psalm 104:24-34, 35b
Renewing the face of the earth

Additional Reading

Isaiah 44:1-4
The spirit poured out to renew the faithful

Hymn: Alleluia! Sing to Jesus, ELW 392

We praise you, eternal God of all creatures. Descend upon us, that we may live faithfully our calling to care for the earth. Equip us to raise our voices for change, our hands for healing, and our resources for compassion.

Saturday, June 7, 2025
Vigil of Pentecost

Seattle, chief of the Duwamish Confederacy, died 1866

John 7:37-39

Jesus, the true living water

On the last day of the festival, the great day, while Jesus was standing there, he cried out, "Let anyone who is thirsty come to me, and let the one who believes in me drink. As the scripture has said, 'Out of the believer's heart shall flow rivers of living water.'" Now he said this about the Spirit, which believers in him were to receive; for as yet there was no Spirit, because Jesus was not yet glorified. (John 7:37-39)

Psalm

Psalm 33:12-22
The Lord is our helper and our shield

Additional Readings

Exodus 19:1-9
The covenant at Sinai

Romans 8:14-17, 22-27
Praying with the Spirit

Hymn: God of Tempest, God of Whirlwind, ELW 400

Almighty and ever-living God, you fulfilled the promise of Easter by sending the gift of your Holy Spirit. Look upon your people gathered in prayer, open to receive the Spirit's flame. May it come to rest in our hearts and heal the divisions of word and tongue, that with one voice and one song we may praise your name in joy and thanksgiving; through Jesus Christ, our Savior and Lord, who lives and reigns with you and the Holy Spirit, one God, now and forever.

Pentecost

The festival of Pentecost celebrates the Spirit poured out on the people, the breath of God offering strength, peace, and the power to forgive sins. Christians trust that the Spirit is present wherever two or more are gathered in Jesus' name. The Spirit intercedes on our behalf, stirs in hearts and whole communities, and understands sighs too deep for words. This season we remember that God is still present and working through our human experiences. We pray for the Spirit to guide us in faith, hope, and love. And we ask the Spirit to show us patience and wisdom to live in peace with each other and our neighbors.

Table Prayer for Pentecost

Blessed are you, O Lord our God.
We give you thanks for this meal
and ask for the courage and compassion
to live like your abundance has the first and last word on our lives,
until all who hunger have daily bread
and all who have their fill are hungry for justice,
through Jesus Christ our Lord. Amen.

Thanksgiving for the Holy Spirit

Use this prayer during the week following Pentecost Sunday.

O Spirit of God, seek us;
Good Spirit, pray with us;
Spirit of counsel, inform us;
Spirit of might, free us;

Spirit of truth, enlighten us;
Spirit of Christ, raise us;
O Holy Spirit, dwell in us.
Amen.

Sunday, June 8, 2025
Day of Pentecost

Acts 2:1-21
Filled with the Spirit

When the day of Pentecost had come, [the believers] were all together in one place. And suddenly from heaven there came a sound like the rush of a violent wind, and it filled the entire house where they were sitting. Divided tongues, as of fire, appeared among them, and a tongue rested on each of them. All of them were filled with the Holy Spirit and began to speak in other languages, as the Spirit gave them ability. (Acts 2:1-4)

Psalm
Psalm 104:24-34, 35b
Send forth your spirit

Additional Readings
Romans 8:14-17
The Spirit makes us children of God

John 14:8-17 [25-27]
The Spirit of truth

Hymn: Gracious Spirit, Heed Our Pleading, ELW 401, TFF 103

God our creator, the resurrection of your Son offers life to all the peoples of earth. By your Holy Spirit, kindle in us the fire of your love, empowering our lives for service and our tongues for praise, through Jesus Christ, our Savior and Lord, who lives and reigns with you and the Holy Spirit, one God, now and forever.

Monday, June 9, 2025
Time after Pentecost

Columba, died 597; Aidan, died 651; Bede, died 735; renewers of the church

Psalm 48
The God of Zion

Walk about Zion, go all around it,
    count its towers,
consider well its ramparts;
    go through its citadels,
that you may tell the next generation
    that this is God,
our God forever and ever.
    He will be our guide forever. (Ps. 48:12-14)

Additional Readings
Joel 2:18-29
God's spirit poured out

1 Corinthians 2:1-11
About the Spirit of God

Hymn: Come, Gracious Spirit, Heavenly Dove, ELW 404

Spirit of God, present and powerful, fall afresh on us this day so that we continue using our voices and resources to amplify your works in this world. Empower us in the resurrected Jesus, who faithfully bore the cross.

Tuesday, June 10, 2025
Time after Pentecost

1 Corinthians 2:12-16
About the Spirit of God

Now we have received not the spirit of the world, but the Spirit that is from God, so that we may understand the gifts bestowed on us by God. And we speak of these things in words not taught by human wisdom but taught by the Spirit, interpreting spiritual things to those who are spiritual.

Those who are unspiritual do not receive the gifts of God's Spirit, for they are foolishness to them, and they are unable to understand them because they are spiritually discerned. Those who are spiritual discern all things, and they are themselves subject to no one else's scrutiny.

"For who has known the mind of the Lord
so as to instruct him?"
But we have the mind of Christ. (1 Cor. 2:12-16)

Psalm
Psalm 48
The God of Zion

Additional Reading
Ezekiel 11:14-25
God will gather the people

Hymn: O Holy Spirit, Root of Life, ELW 399

Creator God, we join with the whole of your creation in praising your name through the fragrance and melody of our lives. Drive us from sheltered comfort to care for your earth, upon whom we walk.

Wednesday, June 11, 2025
Barnabas, Apostle

Acts 11:19-30; 13:1-3
Barnabas and Saul are set apart

Now in the church at Antioch there were prophets and teachers: Barnabas, Simeon who was called Niger, Lucius of Cyrene, Manaen a member of the court of Herod the ruler, and Saul. While they were worshiping the Lord and fasting, the Holy Spirit said, "Set apart for me Barnabas and Saul for the work to which I have called them." Then after fasting and praying they laid their hands on them and sent them off. (Acts 13:1-3)

Psalm

Psalm 112
Happy are the God-fearing

Additional Readings

Isaiah 42:5-12
The Lord calls us in righteousness

Matthew 10:7-16
Jesus sends out the twelve

Hymn: The Lord Now Sends Us Forth, ELW 538

We praise you, O God, for the life of your faithful servant Barnabas, who, seeking not his own renown but the well-being of your church, gave generously of his life and possessions for the relief of the poor and the spread of the gospel. Grant that we may follow his example and by our actions give glory to you, Father, Son, and Holy Spirit, now and forever.

Thursday, June 12, 2025
Time after Pentecost

Psalm 8
Your majesty is praised above the heavens

O LORD, our Sovereign,
>how majestic is your name in all the earth!

You have set your glory above the heavens.
>Out of the mouths of babes and infants
you have founded a bulwark because of your foes,
>to silence the enemy and the avenger.

When I look at your heavens, the work of your fingers,
>the moon and the stars that you have established;
what are human beings that you are mindful of them,
>mortals that you care for them?

Yet you have made them a little lower than God,
>and crowned them with glory and honor. (Ps. 8:1-5)

Additional Readings
Proverbs 3:13-18
Wisdom is a tree of life

Ephesians 1:17-19
Wisdom in the Trinity

Hymn: Creator of the Stars of Night, ELW 245

Most gracious God, teach us to offer you a heart of thanksgiving and praise in all we do. You made us in your image and filled us with your love. Forgive us when we fail to honor others as your children.

Friday, June 13, 2025
Time after Pentecost

Ephesians 4:1-6
Life in the Trinity

I therefore, the prisoner in the Lord, beg you to lead a life worthy of the calling to which you have been called, with all humility and gentleness, with patience, bearing with one another in love, making every effort to maintain the unity of the Spirit in the bond of peace. There is one body and one Spirit, just as you were called to the one hope of your calling, one Lord, one faith, one baptism, one God and Father of all, who is above all and through all and in all. (Eph. 4:1-6)

Psalm
Psalm 8
Your majesty is praised above the heavens

Additional Reading
Proverbs 3:19-26
By wisdom God creates and preserves

Hymn: Lord, Keep Us Steadfast in Your Word, ELW 517

Unifying God, we praise your name and thank you for the gift of relationships which spring forth from the Trinity. Grant us wisdom to seek the well-being of our communities, that we may live in communion with you and our siblings.

Saturday, June 14, 2025
Time after Pentecost

Basil the Great, Bishop of Caesarea, died 379; Gregory, Bishop of Nyssa, died around 385; Gregory of Nazianzus, Bishop of Constantinople, died around 389; Macrina, teacher, died around 379

Proverbs 4:1-9
Choose God's wisdom

The beginning of wisdom is this: Get wisdom,
and whatever else you get, get insight.
Prize her highly, and she will exalt you;
she will honor you if you embrace her.
She will place on your head a fair garland;
she will bestow on you a beautiful crown. (Prov. 4:7-9)

Psalm
Psalm 8
Your majesty is praised above the heavens

Additional Reading
Luke 2:41-52
Jesus increases in wisdom

Hymn: Open Your Ears, O Faithful People, ELW 519

Builder of all things, we give you honor and praise for your creation. Grant us wisdom to use our hands and feet for the glory of the world you created, from east to west, from south to north.

Time after Pentecost
Summer

In worship during the time after Pentecost we listen to gospel stories about Jesus' teaching and healing ministry. This season is launched by the dramatic movement of the Spirit that unites young and old, people of all genders, and people who speak all the known languages of the world. The rest of the season involves learning to pay attention to the more subtle movements of God's creative Spirit in everyday life.

The time after Pentecost takes up the longest portion of the liturgical year, and we dress the church in the color green, a sign of fruitful growth around the globe. We listen to God's ancient story calling and shaping the Hebrew people of God. We overhear the correspondence sent by leaders of the early church to cultivate fruitful living. We pay attention to the story of Jesus as though our life depended upon it.

For those in the northern hemisphere, this season of spiritual growth corresponds to the time of planting and growing crops that feed all of us. For many, the rhythms of life change during the summer and provide for a more restful way of being in the world. We pray that the re-creation of this season offers us a clearer focus on who God declares us to be and on how we should live as God's people.

Table Prayer for Summer
Holy God, you gave us your good creation
and invited us to be co-creators and sustainers of its gifts with you.
Let this food grown from the earth nourish our bodies
so that we might be the body of your Son,
in whose life-giving name we pray. Amen.

Sunday, June 15, 2025
The Holy Trinity

John 16:12-15

The Spirit will guide you into the truth

[Jesus said,] "I still have many things to say to you, but you cannot bear them now. When the Spirit of truth comes, he will guide you into all the truth; for he will not speak on his own, but will speak whatever he hears, and he will declare to you the things that are to come. He will glorify me, because he will take what is mine and declare it to you. All that the Father has is mine. For this reason I said that he will take what is mine and declare it to you." (John 16:12-15)

Psalm

Psalm 8
Your majesty is praised above the heavens

Additional Readings

Proverbs 8:1-4, 22-31
Wisdom rejoices in the creation

Romans 5:1-5
God's love poured into our hearts

Hymn: Kyrie! God, Father, ELW 409

Almighty Creator and ever-living God: we worship your glory, eternal Three-in-One, and we praise your power, majestic One-in-Three. Keep us steadfast in this faith, defend us in all adversity, and bring us at last into your presence, where you live in endless joy and love, Father, Son, and Holy Spirit, one God, now and forever.

Monday, June 16, 2025
Time after Pentecost

Psalm 124
We have escaped like a bird

If it had not been the LORD who was on our side
  —let Israel now say—
if it had not been the LORD who was on our side,
  when our enemies attacked us,
then they would have swallowed us up alive,
  when their anger was kindled against us;
then the flood would have swept us away,
  the torrent would have gone over us;
then over us would have gone
  the raging waters. (Ps. 124:1-5)

Additional Readings

Proverbs 7:1-4
Wisdom is your sister

Ephesians 4:7-16
Building up the body of Christ

Hymn: Come, Join the Dance of Trinity, ELW 412

Blessed God, we put our trust in you. When doubt threatens to overwhelm us, fill us with the spirit of wisdom and disrupt the power of ignorance, the enemy that swallows our lives.

Tuesday, June 17, 2025
Time after Pentecost

Emanuel Nine, martyrs, died 2015

Ephesians 5:15-20

Living as wise ones in the Trinity

Be careful then how you live, not as unwise people but as wise, making the most of the time, because the days are evil. So do not be foolish, but understand what the will of the Lord is. Do not get drunk with wine, for that is debauchery; but be filled with the Spirit, as you sing psalms and hymns and spiritual songs among yourselves, singing and making melody to the Lord in your hearts, giving thanks to God the Father at all times and for everything in the name of our Lord Jesus Christ. (Eph. 5:15-20)

Psalm

Psalm 124
We have escaped like a bird

Additional Reading

Proverbs 8:4-21
Wisdom's riches

Hymn: Holy Spirit, Truth Divine, ELW 398

God of love and compassion, may your healing power, restoration, and goodness show in all the earth. May the Spirit of wisdom empower us to be agents of reconciliation, peace, and justice standing close to one another.

Wednesday, June 18, 2025
Time after Pentecost

Daniel 1:1-21
Daniel's wisdom

At the end of the time that the king had set for [the four young men] to be brought in, the palace master brought them into the presence of Nebuchadnezzar, and the king spoke with them. And among them all, no one was found to compare with Daniel, Hananiah, Mishael, and Azariah; therefore they were stationed in the king's court. In every matter of wisdom and understanding concerning which the king inquired of them, he found them ten times better than all the magicians and enchanters in his whole kingdom. And Daniel continued there until the first year of King Cyrus. (Dan. 1:18-21)

Psalm
Psalm 124
We have escaped like a bird

Additional Reading
Luke 1:46b-55
Mary sings of God

Hymn: My Hope Is Built on Nothing Less, ELW 596/597, TFF 192

God who makes all things new, we thank you for the gift of our voices, and we praise you for comforting our troubled hearts. Grant us courage to raise our voices in holy anger for the wholeness of all.

Thursday, June 19, 2025
Time after Pentecost

Psalm 22:19-28
I will praise you

But you, O Lord, do not be far away!
>   O my help, come quickly to my aid!
Deliver my soul from the sword,
>   my life from the power of the dog!
>   Save me from the mouth of the lion!

From the horns of the wild oxen you have rescued me.
I will tell of your name to my brothers and sisters;
>   in the midst of the congregation I will praise you:
You who fear the Lord, praise him!
>   All you offspring of Jacob, glorify him;
>   stand in awe of him, all you offspring of Israel! (Ps. 22:19-23)

Additional Readings
Isaiah 56:9-12
Israel's leaders are corrupt

Romans 2:17-29
Real circumcision is a matter of the heart

Hymn: Here Is Bread, ELW 483

God of wonder and mystery, you never turn away from the afflicted, the downtrodden, and the outcast. Raise up humble servants as instruments of your indwelling loving kindness so that the whole earth will remember and return to the way of love.

Friday, June 20, 2025
Time after Pentecost

Galatians 3:15-22
The purpose of the law

Brothers and sisters, I give an example from daily life: once a person's will has been ratified, no one adds to it or annuls it. Now the promises were made to Abraham and to his offspring; it does not say, "And to offsprings," as of many; but it says, "And to your offspring," that is, to one person, who is Christ. My point is this: the law, which came four hundred thirty years later, does not annul a covenant previously ratified by God, so as to nullify the promise. For if the inheritance comes from the law, it no longer comes from the promise; but God granted it to Abraham through the promise. (Gal. 3:15-18)

Psalm
Psalm 22:19-28
I will praise you

Additional Reading
Isaiah 57:1-13
The righteous perish and no one cares

Hymn: There Is a Balm in Gilead, ELW 614, TFF 185

To you, O Beloved, we lift our voices in thanksgiving for the promise to remain with us in your steadfast love. The heavens proclaim your righteousness, and the people behold your glory. Keep us in your unfailing grace.

Saturday, June 21, 2025
Time after Pentecost

Onesimos Nesib, translator, evangelist, died 1931

Isaiah 59:1-8
Sin creates barriers

See, the LORD's hand is not too short to save,
     nor his ear too dull to hear.
Rather, your iniquities have been barriers
     between you and your God,
and your sins have hidden his face from you
     so that he does not hear.
For your hands are defiled with blood,
     and your fingers with iniquity;
your lips have spoken lies,
     your tongue mutters wickedness. (Isa. 59:1-3)

Psalm
Psalm 22:19-28
I will praise you

Additional Reading
Matthew 9:27-34
Healing the blind, casting out a demon

Hymn: Abide, O Dearest Jesus, ELW 539

Merciful God, give us wisdom to see and hear you in the sufferings and the agony of the world. Empower us with hearts that love and lives that proclaim your steadfast love through our actions and words.

Sunday, June 22, 2025
Time after Pentecost

Luke 8:26-39
Jesus casts out demons

When the swineherds saw what had happened, they ran off and told it in the city and in the country. Then people came out to see what had happened, and when they came to Jesus, they found the man from whom the demons had gone sitting at the feet of Jesus, clothed and in his right mind. And they were afraid. Those who had seen it told them how the one who had been possessed by demons had been healed. (Luke 8:34-36)

Psalm
Psalm 22:19-28
I will praise you

Additional Readings
Isaiah 65:1-9
The prophet sent to a rebellious people

Galatians 3:23-29
Clothed with Christ in baptism

Hymn: Soli Deo Gloria, ELW 878

O Lord God, we bring before you the cries of a sorrowing world. In your mercy set us free from the chains that bind us, and defend us from everything that is evil, through Jesus Christ, our Savior and Lord.

Monday, June 23, 2025
Time after Pentecost

Psalm 64
Prayer for protection

Hear my voice, O God, in my complaint;
    preserve my life from the dread enemy.
Hide me from the secret plots of the wicked,
    from the scheming of evildoers,
who whet their tongues like swords,
    who aim bitter words like arrows,
shooting from ambush at the blameless;
    they shoot suddenly and without fear. (Ps. 64:1-4)

Additional Readings

Job 18:1-21
God will destroy the wicked

1 Corinthians 1:18-31
The power and wisdom of God

Hymn: O God beyond All Praising, ELW 880

Beloved One, through the cross you manifested your power and wisdom to the world. Grant us understanding and maturity to tell others that through you, we are weak and strong, we are nothing and something, we are broken and whole.

Tuesday, June 24, 2025
John the Baptist

Luke 1:57-67 [68-80]
The birth and naming of John

On the eighth day [Elizabeth and her neighbors and relatives] came to circumcise the child, and they were going to name him Zechariah after his father. But his mother said, "No; he is to be called John." They said to her, "None of your relatives has this name." Then they began motioning to his father to find out what name he wanted to give him. He asked for a writing tablet and wrote, "His name is John." And all of them were amazed. Immediately his mouth was opened and his tongue freed, and he began to speak, praising God. (Luke 1:59-64)

Psalm
Psalm 141
My eyes are turned to God

Additional Readings
Malachi 3:1-4
My messenger, a refiner and purifier

Acts 13:13-26
The gospel for the descendants of Abraham

Hymn: Come, Thou Almighty King, ELW 408

Almighty God, by your gracious providence your servant John the Baptist was born to Elizabeth and Zechariah. Grant to your people the wisdom to see your purpose and the openness to hear your will, that the light of Christ may increase in us, through Jesus Christ, our Savior and Lord, who lives and reigns with you and the Holy Spirit, one God, now and forever.

Wednesday, June 25, 2025
Time after Pentecost

Presentation of the Augsburg Confession, 1530

Philipp Melanchthon, renewer of the church, died 1560

Luke 9:37-43a

Jesus heals a boy with a demon

On the next day, when [Jesus, Peter, John, and James] had come down from the mountain, a great crowd met him. Just then a man from the crowd shouted, "Teacher, I beg you to look at my son; he is my only child. Suddenly a spirit seizes him, and all at once he shrieks. It convulses him until he foams at the mouth; it mauls him and will scarcely leave him. I begged your disciples to cast it out, but they could not." Jesus answered, "You faithless and perverse generation, how much longer must I be with you and bear with you? Bring your son here." While he was coming, the demon dashed him to the ground in convulsions. But Jesus rebuked the unclean spirit, healed the boy, and gave him back to his father. And all were astounded at the greatness of God. (Luke 9:37-43a)

Psalm
Psalm 64
Prayer for protection

Additional Reading
Ezekiel 32:1-10
Evil like a dragon will be destroyed

Hymn: Almighty God, Your Word Is Cast, ELW 516

Loving God, in your presence love exists. Make us thankful for your unfailing love, and grant us strength to discern the stumbling blocks that keep us from loving your creation as you love us.

Thursday, June 26, 2025
Time after Pentecost

Psalm 16
Protect me, O God

Protect me, O God, for in you I take refuge.
I say to the LORD, "You are my Lord;
> I have no good apart from you."

As for the holy ones in the land, they are the noble,
> in whom is all my delight.

Those who choose another god multiply their sorrows;
> their drink offerings of blood I will not pour out
> or take their names upon my lips.

The LORD is my chosen portion and my cup;
> you hold my lot. (Ps. 16:1-5)

Additional Readings

Leviticus 9:22—10:11
God's fire consumes Aaron's sons

2 Corinthians 13:5-10
Examine yourselves concerning the faith

Hymn: When We Are Living, ELW 639

Gracious God, we praise you and give thanks for your living and protecting presence. Draw us together into one great company so we can discern and bear witness to your love that is our birthright.

Friday, June 27, 2025
Time after Pentecost

Cyril, Bishop of Alexandria, died 444

Galatians 4:8-20

Paul reproves the hearers

Formerly, when you did not know God, you were enslaved to beings that by nature are not gods. Now, however, that you have come to know God, or rather to be known by God, how can you turn back again to the weak and beggarly elemental spirits? How can you want to be enslaved to them again? You are observing special days, and months, and seasons, and years. I am afraid that my work for you may have been wasted. (Gal. 4:8-11)

Psalm

Psalm 16
Protect me, O God

Additional Readings

2 Kings 1:1-16
God's fire consumes the king's men

Hymn: Beloved, God's Chosen, ELW 648

Holy God, you embrace all who are forgotten and unseen. Continue to protect all who are discriminated against and who feel the sting of oppression. Fill us with the power of your love.

Saturday, June 28, 2025
Time after Pentecost

Irenaeus, Bishop of Lyons, died around 202

Luke 9:21-27
Following Jesus

Then [Jesus] said to them all, "If any want to become my followers, let them deny themselves and take up their cross daily and follow me. For those who want to save their life will lose it, and those who lose their life for my sake will save it. What does it profit them if they gain the whole world, but lose or forfeit themselves?" (Luke 9:23-25)

Psalm

Psalm 16
Protect me, O God

Additional Reading

Deuteronomy 32:15-27, 39-43
God's anger like a fire

Hymn: How Clear Is Our Vocation, Lord, ELW 580

Almighty God, you call us to take up our cross and follow as you called the disciples. Grant us the courage to do so without hesitation, knowing that you are always with us, leading the way.

Sunday, June 29, 2025
Peter and Paul, Apostles

John 21:15-19

Jesus says to Peter: Tend my sheep

When [the disciples] had finished breakfast, Jesus said to Simon Peter, "Simon son of John, do you love me more than these?" He said to him, "Yes, Lord; you know that I love you." Jesus said to him, "Feed my lambs." A second time he said to him, "Simon son of John, do you love me?" He said to him, "Yes, Lord; you know that I love you." Jesus said to him, "Tend my sheep." He said to him the third time, "Simon son of John, do you love me?" Peter felt hurt because he said to him the third time, "Do you love me?" And he said to him, "Lord, you know everything; you know that I love you." Jesus said to him, "Feed my sheep. Very truly, I tell you, when you were younger, you used to fasten your own belt and to go wherever you wished. But when you grow old, you will stretch out your hands, and someone else will fasten a belt around you and take you where you do not wish to go." (John 21:15-18)

Psalm

Psalm 87:1-3, 5-7
Glorious things are spoken of you

Additional Readings

Acts 12:1-11
Peter released from prison

2 Timothy 4:6-8, 17-18
The good fight of faith

Hymn: Praise to the Lord, All of You, ELW 844

Almighty God, we praise you that your blessed apostles Peter and Paul glorified you by their martyrdoms. Grant that your church throughout the world may always be instructed by their teaching and example, be knit together in unity by your Spirit, and ever stand firm upon the one foundation who is Jesus Christ our Lord, for he lives and reigns with you and the Holy Spirit, one God, now and forever.

Monday, June 30, 2025
Time after Pentecost

1 John 2:7-11
Living in the light of love

Beloved, I am writing you no new commandment, but an old commandment that you have had from the beginning; the old commandment is the word that you have heard. Yet I am writing you a new commandment that is true in him and in you, because the darkness is passing away and the true light is already shining. Whoever says, "I am in the light," while hating a brother or sister, is still in the darkness. (1 John 2:7-9)

Psalm
Psalm 140
Prayer for deliverance

Additional Reading
Genesis 24:34-41, 50-67
Rebekah follows Abraham's servant

Hymn: O Beauty Ever Ancient, ACS 1100

Holy God, your wisdom is ancient yet ever new in our lives. Surround us with your love and help us to share it with our siblings, your beloved children.

Prayer List for July

_____

_____

_____

_____

_____

_____

_____

_____

_____

Tuesday, July 1, 2025
Time after Pentecost

Catherine Winkworth, died 1878; John Mason Neale, died 1866; hymn translators

Psalm 140
Prayer for deliverance

I say to the LORD, "You are my God;
    give ear, O LORD, to the voice of my supplications."
O LORD, my Lord, my strong deliverer,
    you have covered my head in the day of battle.
Do not grant, O LORD, the desires of the wicked;
    do not further their evil plot. (Ps. 140:6-8)

Additional Readings
Jeremiah 3:15-18
Nations cease to follow their own will

Ephesians 5:6-20
The fruit of the light

Hymn: Just a Closer Walk with Thee, ELW 697, TFF 253

God of protection, we give you thanks that you are always with us and for us. Make us aware of your presence and quick to rely on your trustworthy guidance as we navigate the challenges and opportunities of each day.

Wednesday, July 2, 2025
Time after Pentecost

Matthew 10:16-25
Sheep in the midst of wolves

[Jesus said,] "See, I am sending you out like sheep into the midst of wolves; so be wise as serpents and innocent as doves. Beware of them, for they will hand you over to councils and flog you in their synagogues; and you will be dragged before governors and kings because of me, as a testimony to them and the Gentiles. When they hand you over, do not worry about how you are to speak or what you are to say; for what you are to say will be given to you at that time; for it is not you who speak, but the Spirit of your Father speaking through you. Brother will betray brother to death, and a father his child, and children will rise against parents and have them put to death; and you will be hated by all because of my name. But the one who endures to the end will be saved." (Matt. 10:16-22)

Psalm
Psalm 140
Prayer for deliverance

Additional Reading
Jeremiah 23:16-22
Following stubborn hearts

Hymn: Lord, Speak to Us, That We May Speak, ELW 676

O God, you trust us to bring your peace into circumstances that threaten to overwhelm our purpose. Thank you for your Spirit that gives us courage and words to speak in the service of your love.

Thursday, July 3, 2024
Thomas, Apostle

John 14:1-7
Jesus, the way, the truth, the life

Thomas said to [Jesus], "Lord, we do not know where you are going. How can we know the way?" Jesus said to him, "I am the way, and the truth, and the life. No one comes to the Father except through me. If you know me, you will know my Father also. From now on you do know him and have seen him." (John 14:5-7)

Psalm
Psalm 136:1-4, 23-26
God's mercy endures forever

Additional Readings
Judges 6:36-40
God affirms Gideon's calling

Ephesians 4:11-16
The body of Christ has various gifts

Hymn: We've Come This Far by Faith, ELW 633, TFF 197

Ever-living God, you strengthened your apostle Thomas with firm and certain faith in the resurrection of your Son. Grant that we too may confess our faith in Jesus Christ, our Lord and our God, who lives and reigns with you and the Holy Spirit, one God, now and forever.

Friday, July 4, 2025
Time after Pentecost

Psalm 66:1-9
God holds our souls in life

Come and see what God has done:
>he is awesome in his deeds among mortals.
He turned the sea into dry land;
>they passed through the river on foot.
There we rejoiced in him,
>who rules by his might forever,
whose eyes keep watch on the nations—
>let the rebellious not exalt themselves.

Bless our God, O peoples,
>let the sound of his praise be heard,
who has kept us among the living,
>and has not let our feet slip. (Ps. 66:5-9)

Additional Readings
Jeremiah 51:47-58
Let Jerusalem come into your mind

2 Corinthians 8:1-7
Poverty overflows in generosity

Hymn: Holy God, We Praise Your Name, ELW 414

We celebrate you, God of freedom, and the power of your love that brings hope and inspiration. Help us to keep our eyes open for signs of your grace, and strengthen us to become accomplices of your compassion.

Saturday, July 5, 2025
Time after Pentecost

Zechariah 14:10-21
Jerusalem shall abide in security

The whole land shall be turned into a plain from Geba to Rimmon south of Jerusalem. But Jerusalem shall remain aloft on its site from the Gate of Benjamin to the place of the former gate, to the Corner Gate, and from the Tower of Hananel to the king's wine presses. And it shall be inhabited, for never again shall it be doomed to destruction; Jerusalem shall abide in security. (Zech. 14:10-11)

Psalm
Psalm 66:1-9
God holds our souls in life

Additional Reading
Luke 9:1-6
The mission of the twelve

Hymn: Light Dawns on a Weary World, ELW 726

Sometimes, God, our faith falls flat. When this happens, call us toward the peaks of new possibilities. Grant us fresh perspective to see the bigger picture of your work and to feel secure that our times are in your hands.

Sunday, July 6, 2025
Time after Pentecost

Jan Hus, martyr, died 1415

Luke 10:1-11, 16-20

Jesus sends out seventy disciples

After this the Lord appointed seventy others and sent them on ahead of him in pairs to every town and place where he himself intended to go. He said to them, "The harvest is plentiful, but the laborers are few; therefore ask the Lord of the harvest to send out laborers into his harvest. Go on your way. See, I am sending you out like lambs into the midst of wolves. Carry no purse, no bag, no sandals; and greet no one on the road. Whatever house you enter, first say, 'Peace to this house!' " (Luke 10:1-5)

Psalm

Psalm 66:1-9
God holds our souls in life

Additional Readings

Isaiah 66:10-14
Jerusalem, a nursing mother

Galatians 6:[1-6] 7-16
Do what is right now

Hymn: Oh, When the Saints Go Marching In, ACS 950, TFF 180

O God, the Father of our Lord Jesus, you are the city that shelters us, the mother who comforts us. With your Spirit accompany us on our life's journey, that we may spread your peace in all the world, through your Son, Jesus Christ, our Savior and Lord.

Monday, July 7, 2025
Time after Pentecost

Psalm 119:73-80
Living in faithfulness

Let your steadfast love become my comfort
   according to your promise to your servant.
Let your mercy come to me, that I may live;
   for your law is my delight.
Let the arrogant be put to shame,
   because they have subverted me with guile;
   as for me, I will meditate on your precepts.
Let those who fear you turn to me,
   so that they may know your decrees.
May my heart be blameless in your statutes,
   so that I may not be put to shame. (Ps. 119:76-80)

Additional Readings
Jeremiah 6:10-19
Call to faithfulness

Acts 19:21-27
Demetrius opposes Paul

Hymn: How Firm a Foundation, ELW 796

When we feel wobbly and jittery, O God, fill us with confidence in your steadfast presence. Empower us to live beyond the pull of fear, and show us how to be an expression of your peace for others.

Tuesday, July 8, 2025
Time after Pentecost

Jeremiah 8:4-13
Call to faithfulness

You shall say to them, Thus says the LORD:
When people fall, do they not get up again?
　　If they go astray, do they not turn back?
Why then has this people turned away
　　in perpetual backsliding?
They have held fast to deceit,
　　they have refused to return.
I have given heed and listened,
　　but they do not speak honestly;
no one repents of wickedness,
　　saying, "What have I done!"
All of them turn to their own course,
　　like a horse plunging headlong into battle. (Jer. 8:4-6)

Psalm
Psalm 119:73-80
Living in faithfulness

Additional Reading
Acts 19:28-41
A riot follows Paul's preaching

Hymn: When We Are Tested, ACS 922

O God, you know that our progress can be hard to plot: one step forward and two steps back. Yet we can always return to you, knowing that you welcome us to find our center and make a fresh start.

Wednesday, July 9, 2025
Time after Pentecost

Joshua 23:1-16
Joshua urges faithfulness

A long time afterward, when the LORD had given rest to Israel from all their enemies all around, and Joshua was old and well advanced in years, Joshua summoned all Israel, their elders and heads, their judges and officers, and said to them, "I am now old and well advanced in years; and you have seen all that the LORD your God has done to all these nations for your sake, for it is the LORD your God who has fought for you. I have allotted to you as an inheritance for your tribes those nations that remain, along with all the nations that I have already cut off, from the Jordan to the Great Sea in the west. The LORD your God will push them back before you, and drive them out of your sight; and you shall possess their land, as the LORD your God promised you." (Josh. 23:1-5)

Psalm
Psalm 119:73-80
Living in faithfulness

Additional Reading
Luke 10:13-16
Woe to unrepentant cities

Hymn: God Is Here! ELW 526

As we remember our spiritual ancestors, O God, help us to claim our place in the great drama of your love. And as we meet the future with faith in you, we give thanks for your faith in us.

Thursday, July 10, 2025
Time after Pentecost

Psalm 25:1-10
Show me your ways

To you, O Lord, I lift up my soul.
O my God, in you I trust;
>do not let me be put to shame;
>do not let my enemies exult over me.
Do not let those who wait for you be put to shame;
>let them be ashamed who are wantonly treacherous.

Make me to know your ways, O Lord;
>teach me your paths.
Lead me in your truth, and teach me,
>for you are the God of my salvation;
>for you I wait all day long. (Ps. 25:1-5)

Additional Readings
Genesis 41:14-36
Joseph plans to feed Egypt

James 2:14-26
Faith produces good works

Hymn: God of Grace and God of Glory, ELW 705

Lord of wisdom, we need your light! Help us to become thirsty for your insights and eager to learn your way of looking at the world. Fill us with patience as we wait for the gift of your guidance.

Friday, July 11, 2025
Time after Pentecost

Benedict of Nursia, Abbot of Monte Cassino, died around 540

Genesis 41:37-49

God saves Egypt from starvation

Joseph was thirty years old when he entered the service of Pharaoh
king of Egypt. And Joseph went out from the presence of Pharaoh, and
went through all the land of Egypt. During the seven plenteous years
the earth produced abundantly. He gathered up all the food of the seven
years when there was plenty in the land of Egypt, and stored up food in
the cities; he stored up in every city the food from the fields around it.
So Joseph stored up grain in such abundance—like the sand of the sea—
that he stopped measuring it; it was beyond measure. (Gen. 41:46-49)

Psalm
Psalm 25:1-10
Show me your ways

Additional Reading
Acts 7:9-16
Egypt's food rescues Israel

Hymn: For the Wholeness of the Earth, ACS 1067

*God of abundant life, help us to deal wisely with all that you have entrusted
to us. Nourish us as only you can, that we may grow in our relationship with
you and as servants of the common good.*

Saturday, July 12, 2025
Time after Pentecost

Nathan Söderblom, Bishop of Uppsala, died 1931

Leviticus 19:1-4, 32-37
Mercy to the alien

You shall rise before the aged, and defer to the old; and you shall fear your God: I am the LORD.

When an alien resides with you in your land, you shall not oppress the alien. The alien who resides with you shall be to you as the citizen among you; you shall love the alien as yourself, for you were aliens in the land of Egypt: I am the LORD your God. (Lev. 19:32-34)

Psalm	Additional Reading
Psalm 25:1-10	**John 3:16-21**
Show me your ways	*God's son saves the world*

Hymn: The Church of Christ in Every Age, ELW 729

Gracious Lord, show us how to love as you love. Fill us with your vision of hospitality, and empower us to demonstrate your compassion in every way possible until as it is in heaven, so may it be on earth.

Sunday, July 13, 2025
Time after Pentecost

Luke 10:25-37

The parable of the merciful Samaritan

[Jesus said,] "But a Samaritan while traveling came near [the man who had been robbed and beaten]; and when he saw him, he was moved with pity. He went to him and bandaged his wounds, having poured oil and wine on them. Then he put him on his own animal, brought him to an inn, and took care of him. The next day he took out two denarii, gave them to the innkeeper, and said, 'Take care of him; and when I come back, I will repay you whatever more you spend.' Which of these three, do you think, was a neighbor to the man who fell into the hands of the robbers?" [The lawyer] said, "The one who showed him mercy." Jesus said to him, "Go and do likewise." (Luke 10:33-37)

Psalm

Psalm 25:1-10
Show me your ways

Additional Readings

Deuteronomy 30:9-14
God delights in your fruitfulness

Colossians 1:1-14
The gospel is bearing fruit

Hymn: When Pain of the World Surrounds Us, ELW 704

O Lord God, your mercy delights us, and the world longs for your loving care. Hear the cries of everyone in need, and turn our hearts to love our neighbors with the love of your son, Jesus Christ, our Savior and Lord.

Monday, July 14, 2025
Time after Pentecost

Psalm 25:11-20
I take refuge in you, O God

Turn to me and be gracious to me,
    for I am lonely and afflicted.
Relieve the troubles of my heart,
    and bring me out of my distress.
Consider my affliction and my trouble,
    and forgive all my sins.

Consider how many are my foes,
    and with what violent hatred they hate me.
O guard my life, and deliver me;
    do not let me be put to shame, for I take refuge in you. (Ps. 25:16-20)

Additional Readings
Job 24:1-8
The needy are thrust off the road

James 2:1-7
God has chosen the poor

Hymn: Come to Me, O Weary Traveler, ACS 1017

God of goodness, everywhere we look something is going sideways. Yet everywhere we look: you! Deliver us, we pray, from being pulled this way and that by anxious thoughts. Help us to keep our focus on you and your saving power.

Tuesday, July 15, 2025
Time after Pentecost

Proverbs 19:1-17

Kindness to the poor

Laziness brings on deep sleep;
    an idle person will suffer hunger.
Those who keep the commandment will live;
    those who are heedless of their ways will die.
Whoever is kind to the poor lends to the LORD,
    and will be repaid in full. (Prov. 19:15-17)

Psalm

Psalm 25:11-20
I take refuge in you, O God

Additional Reading

1 John 3:11-17
Do not refuse one in need

Hymn: We Are Marching in the Light, ELW 866, TFF 63

God, we hear your call to step it up! Awaken in us a strong spirit of compassion and the wisdom to love well. Fill us with your energy for life so that we may reach out to others with love.

Wednesday, July 16, 2025
Time after Pentecost

Ecclesiastes 9:13-18

One bungler destroys much good

There was a little city with few people in it. A great king came against it and besieged it, building great siegeworks against it. Now there was found in it a poor wise man, and he by his wisdom delivered the city. Yet no one remembered that poor man. So I said, "Wisdom is better than might; yet the poor man's wisdom is despised, and his words are not heeded."

> The quiet words of the wise are more to be heeded
> > than the shouting of a ruler among fools.
> Wisdom is better than weapons of war,
> > but one bungler destroys much good. (Eccles. 9:14-18)

Psalm
Psalm 25:11-20
I take refuge in you, O God

Additional Reading
Matthew 25:31-46
As you did it to one of the least of these

Hymn: Ask the Complicated Questions, ACS 1005

You know, O God, that the volume has been turned up all around us. Give us the power to find you in quiet words of wisdom, where we can unclench our lives, regroup, and rest in you.

Thursday, July 17, 2025
Time after Pentecost

Bartolomé de Las Casas, missionary to the Indies, died 1566

Psalm 15
Leading a blameless life

O LORD, who may abide in your tent?
> Who may dwell on your holy hill?

Those who walk blamelessly, and do what is right,
> and speak the truth from their heart;
who do not slander with their tongue,
> and do no evil to their friends,
> nor take up a reproach against their neighbors;
in whose eyes the wicked are despised,
> but who honor those who fear the LORD;
who stand by their oath even to their hurt;
who do not lend money at interest,
> and do not take a bribe against the innocent.

Those who do these things shall never be moved. (Ps. 15:1-5)

Additional Readings
Genesis 12:10-20
Pharaoh offers hospitality to Sarai

Hebrews 5:1-6
Christ did not glorify himself

Hymn: I Want to Walk as a Child of the Light, ELW 815

Righteous God, you have shown us how to live good lives. Ground us in your grace, center us in your truth, so that we may live from a secure foundation, make great decisions, and entrust the future to you.

Friday, July 18, 2025
Time after Pentecost

Ephesians 3:14-21
The love of Christ surpasses knowledge

For this reason I bow my knees before the Father, from whom every family in heaven and on earth takes its name. I pray that, according to the riches of his glory, he may grant that you may be strengthened in your inner being with power through his Spirit, and that Christ may dwell in your hearts through faith, as you are being rooted and grounded in love. I pray that you may have the power to comprehend, with all the saints, what is the breadth and length and height and depth, and to know the love of Christ that surpasses knowledge, so that you may be filled with all the fullness of God. (Eph. 3:14-19)

Psalm
Psalm 15
Leading a blameless life

Additional Reading
Genesis 13:1-18
Abram and Lot separate peacefully

Hymn: Joyful, Joyful We Adore Thee, ELW 836

Energy of life, we pray for your healing power in every nook and cranny of our lives. Fill us with your Spirit: a full helping! And grant us the faith to follow the Spirit wherever it may lead.

Saturday, July 19, 2025
Time after Pentecost

Genesis 14:1-16
Lot is rescued

When Abram heard that his nephew had been taken captive, he led forth his trained men, born in his house, three hundred eighteen of them, and went in pursuit as far as Dan. He divided his forces against them by night, he and his servants, and routed them and pursued them to Hobah, north of Damascus. Then he brought back all the goods, and also brought back his nephew Lot with his goods, and the women and the people. (Gen. 14:14-16)

Psalm
Psalm 15
Leading a blameless life

Additional Reading
Luke 8:4-10
Jesus speaks in parables

Hymn: The Spirit Sends Us Forth to Serve, ELW 551, ACS 988

God of compassion, when we're called to put everything on the line for others, help us to do just that. Save us from balking at the cost, and keep us focused on demonstrating your care for those in need.

Sunday, July 20, 2025
Time after Pentecost

Luke 10:38-42
Choosing the better part

Now as [Jesus and his disciples] went on their way, he entered a certain village, where a woman named Martha welcomed him into her home. She had a sister named Mary, who sat at the Lord's feet and listened to what he was saying. But Martha was distracted by her many tasks; so she came to him and asked, "Lord, do you not care that my sister has left me to do all the work by myself? Tell her then to help me." But the Lord answered her, "Martha, Martha, you are worried and distracted by many things; there is need of only one thing. Mary has chosen the better part, which will not be taken away from her." (Luke 10:38-42)

Psalm
Psalm 15
Leading a blameless life

Additional Readings
Genesis 18:1-10a
The hospitality of Abraham and Sarah

Colossians 1:15-28
A hymn to Christ

Hymn: Lord, Thee I Love with All My Heart, ELW 750

Eternal God, you draw near to us in Christ, and you make yourself our guest. Amid the cares of our lives, make us attentive to your presence, that we may treasure your word above all else, through Jesus Christ, our Savior and Lord.

Monday, July 21, 2025
Time after Pentecost

Psalm 119:97-104
God's word like honey

Oh, how I love your law!
    It is my meditation all day long.
Your commandment makes me wiser than my enemies,
    for it is always with me.

How sweet are your words to my taste,
    sweeter than honey to my mouth!
Through your precepts I get understanding;
    therefore I hate every false way. (Ps. 119:97-98, 103-104)

Additional Readings
Exodus 18:1-12
Jethro's family eats before God

Colossians 1:27—2:7
To know Christ

Hymn: I Love to Tell the Story, ELW 661, TFF 228

Your words, O God, are sweet and nourishing. We are grateful that you make your truth so accessible: right at hand whenever we need guidance. May we always find great satisfaction in the sweetness of your wisdom.

Tuesday, July 22, 2025
Mary Magdalene, Apostle

John 20:1-2, 11-18
Mary Magdalene meets Jesus in the garden

Jesus said to [Mary Magdalene], "Woman, why are you weeping? Whom are you looking for?" Supposing him to be the gardener, she said to him, "Sir, if you have carried him away, tell me where you have laid him, and I will take him away." Jesus said to her, "Mary!" She turned and said to him in Hebrew, "Rabbouni!" (which means Teacher). Jesus said to her, "Do not hold on to me, because I have not yet ascended to the Father. But go to my brothers and say to them, 'I am ascending to my Father and your Father, to my God and your God.' " Mary Magdalene went and announced to the disciples, "I have seen the Lord"; and she told them that he had said these things to her. (John 20:15-18)

Psalm
Psalm 73:23-28
I will speak of all God's works

Additional Readings
Ruth 1:6-18
Ruth stays with Naomi

Acts 13:26-33a
The raising of Jesus fulfills God's promise

Hymn: For All the Faithful Women, ELW 419, st. 1, 9, and Last ; TFF 219, st. 1, 12, and 4

Almighty God, your Son first entrusted the apostle Mary Magdalene with the joyful news of his resurrection. Following the example of her witness, may we proclaim Christ as our living Lord and one day see him in glory, for he lives and reigns with you and the Holy Spirit, one God, now and forever.

Wednesday, July 23, 2025
Time after Pentecost

Birgitta of Sweden, renewer of the church, died 1373

John 6:41-51

Whoever eats this bread will live forever

[Jesus answered,] "Very truly, I tell you, whoever believes has eternal life. I am the bread of life. Your ancestors ate the manna in the wilderness, and they died. This is the bread that comes down from heaven, so that one may eat of it and not die. I am the living bread that came down from heaven. Whoever eats of this bread will live forever; and the bread that I will give for the life of the world is my flesh." (John 6:47-51)

Psalm

Psalm 119:97-104
God's word like honey

Additional Reading

Deuteronomy 12:1-12
The promise to eat before God

Hymn: Loaves Were Broken, Words Were Spoken, ACS 966

Thank you, God of abundance, that we are nourished by the vitality of Jesus. As we find direction for our lives in him, make us a source of encouragement for others who seek to live with hope.

Thursday, July 24, 2025
Time after Pentecost

Psalm 138
Your love endures forever

All the kings of the earth shall praise you, O LORD,
    for they have heard the words of your mouth.
They shall sing of the ways of the LORD,
    for great is the glory of the LORD.
For though the LORD is high, he regards the lowly;
    but the haughty he perceives from far away.

Though I walk in the midst of trouble,
    you preserve me against the wrath of my enemies;
you stretch out your hand,
    and your right hand delivers me.
The LORD will fulfill his purpose for me;
    your steadfast love, O LORD, endures forever.
    Do not forsake the work of your hands. (Ps. 138:4-8)

Additional Readings
Esther 2:19—3:6
The Jews save a king's life

Acts 1:15-20
A traitor's life ends

Hymn: In the Midst of Earthly Life, ACS 1026

God of traveling mercies, when the wheels come off the wagon, you're right there with us. With confidence in your steady accompaniment, we can navigate the ups and downs of life one faithful step at a time.

Friday, July 25, 2025
James, Apostle

Mark 10:35-45
Whoever wishes to be great must serve

James and John, the sons of Zebedee, came forward to [Jesus] and said to him, "Teacher, we want you to do for us whatever we ask of you." And he said to them, "What is it you want me to do for you?" And they said to him, "Grant us to sit, one at your right hand and one at your left, in your glory." But Jesus said to them, "You do not know what you are asking. Are you able to drink the cup that I drink, or be baptized with the baptism that I am baptized with?" They replied, "We are able." Then Jesus said to them, "The cup that I drink you will drink; and with the baptism with which I am baptized, you will be baptized; but to sit at my right hand or at my left is not mine to grant, but it is for those for whom it has been prepared." (Mark 10:35-40)

Psalm
Psalm 7:1-10
God, my shield and defense

Additional Readings
1 Kings 19:9-18
Elijah hears God in the midst of silence

Acts 11:27—12:3a
James is killed by Herod

Hymn: Lord, Whose Love in Humble Service, ELW 712

Gracious God, we remember before you today your servant and apostle James, the first among the twelve to be martyred for the name of Jesus Christ. Pour out on the leaders of your church that spirit of self-denying service which is the true mark of authority among your people, through Jesus Christ our servant, who lives and reigns with you and the Holy Spirit, one God, now and forever.

Saturday, July 26, 2025
Time after Pentecost

Esther 4:1-17
Royal dignity for such a time as this

Then Esther said in reply to Mordecai, "Go, gather all the Jews to be found in Susa, and hold a fast on my behalf, and neither eat nor drink for three days, night or day. I and my maids will also fast as you do. After that I will go to the king, though it is against the law; and if I perish, I perish." Mordecai then went away and did everything as Esther had ordered him. (Esther 4:15-17)

Psalm
Psalm 138
Your love endures forever

Additional Reading
Luke 8:22-25
Jesus' disciples cry out for safety

Hymn: Rise Up, O Saints of God! ELW 669

O God our friend, we feel your presence in the lives of those who support and encourage us. In those moments of companionship, we find courage to do your work. May we offer such friendship to others, in your name.

Sunday, July 27, 2025
Time after Pentecost

Luke 11:1-13
Jesus teaches prayer

[Jesus] was praying in a certain place, and after he had finished, one of his disciples said to him, "Lord, teach us to pray, as John taught his disciples." He said to them, "When you pray, say:

Father, hallowed be your name.
Your kingdom come.
Give us each day our daily bread.
And forgive us our sins,
for we ourselves forgive everyone indebted to us.
And do not bring us to the time of trial." (Luke 11:1-4)

Psalm
Psalm 138
Your love endures forever

Additional Readings
Genesis 18:20-32
Abraham bargains with God

Colossians 2:6-15 [16-19]
Buried with Christ in baptism

Hymn: O Beauty Ever Ancient, ACS 1100

Almighty and ever-living God, you are always more ready to hear than we are to pray, and you gladly give more than we either desire or deserve. Pour upon us your abundant mercy. Forgive us those things that weigh on our conscience, and give us those good things that come only through your Son, Jesus Christ, our Savior and Lord.

Monday, July 28, 2025
Time after Pentecost

Johann Sebastian Bach, died 1750; Heinrich Schütz, died 1672;
George Frederick Handel, died 1759; musicians

Psalm 55:16-23
Cast your burden on God

My companion laid hands on a friend
    and violated a covenant with me
with speech smoother than butter,
    but with a heart set on war;
with words that were softer than oil,
    but in fact were drawn swords.

Cast your burden on the LORD,
    and he will sustain you;
he will never permit
    the righteous to be moved.

But you, O God, will cast them down
    into the lowest pit;
the bloodthirsty and treacherous
    shall not live out half their days.
But I will trust in you. (Ps. 55:20-23)

Additional Readings
Esther 5:1-14
A banquet guest with a murderous heart

Colossians 2:16—3:1
About false regulations

Hymn: If You But Trust in God to Guide You, ELW 769

As we navigate challenging relationships, O God, we pray that you would center us in your steady presence. Liberate us from the burden of anxious thoughts, and free us to live with generous and openhearted trust in you.

Tuesday, July 29, 2025
Time after Pentecost

Mary, Martha, and Lazarus of Bethany
Olaf, King of Norway, martyr, died 1030

Romans 9:30—10:4
Christ is the end of the law

Brothers and sisters, my heart's desire and prayer to God for [Israel] is that they may be saved. I can testify that they have a zeal for God, but it is not enlightened. For, being ignorant of the righteousness that comes from God, and seeking to establish their own, they have not submitted to God's righteousness. For Christ is the end of the law so that there may be righteousness for everyone who believes. (Rom. 10:1-4)

Psalm
Psalm 55:16-23
Cast your burden on God

Additional Reading
Esther 6:1—7:6
A royal reversal of fortunes

Hymn: Commonwealth Is God's Commandment, ACS 1036

Creative God, shape our lives into the pattern of compassion that we see in Jesus. Place in our hearts a desire to be filled with his inexhaustible care for the world. Make us ambassadors of his grace and truth.

Wednesday, July 30, 2025
Time after Pentecost

Matthew 5:43-48
Pray for those who persecute you

[Jesus said,] "You have heard that it was said, 'You shall love your neighbor and hate your enemy.' But I say to you, Love your enemies and pray for those who persecute you, so that you may be children of your Father in heaven; for he makes his sun rise on the evil and on the good, and sends rain on the righteous and on the unrighteous. For if you love those who love you, what reward do you have? Do not even the tax collectors do the same? And if you greet only your brothers and sisters, what more are you doing than others? Do not even the Gentiles do the same? Be perfect, therefore, as your heavenly Father is perfect." (Matt. 5:43-48)

Psalm
Psalm 55:16-23
Cast your burden on God

Additional Reading
Esther 7:7—8:17
Esther saves her people

Hymn: God's Work, Our Hands, ACS 1000

Blessed God, your vision for us is breathtaking! Help us to believe in ourselves as you believe in us. Thank you for loving us as we are, and for loving us too much to leave us as we are.

Thursday, July 31, 2025
Time after Pentecost

Psalm 49:1-12
The folly of trust in riches

Why should I fear in times of trouble,
  when the iniquity of my persecutors surrounds me,
those who trust in their wealth
  and boast of the abundance of their riches?
Truly, no ransom avails for one's life,
  there is no price one can give to God for it.
For the ransom of life is costly,
  and can never suffice
that one should live on forever
  and never see the grave. (Ps. 49:5-9)

Additional Readings

Proverbs 23:1-11
Resist the allure of becoming rich

Romans 11:33-36
God's riches, wisdom, and knowledge

Hymn: Day by Day, ELW 790

God, help us to hear and receive that most tender of commandments, "Be not afraid." And as we embody the power of fearlessness in our lives, help us to become for others an experience of comfort and reassurance.

Prayer List for August

Friday, August 1, 2025
Time after Pentecost

Proverbs 24:1-12
By wisdom a house is built

Do not envy the wicked,
    nor desire to be with them;
for their minds devise violence,
    and their lips talk of mischief.

By wisdom a house is built,
    and by understanding it is established;
by knowledge the rooms are filled
    with all precious and pleasant riches. (Prov. 24:1-4)

Psalm
Psalm 49:1-12
The folly of trust in riches

Additional Reading
Ephesians 4:17-24
A new self in the likeness of God

Hymn: We Eat the Bread of Teaching, ELW 518

Wise and wondrous God, you fill us with your eternal wisdom and call us your holy people. May all that we think and say and do this day reflect your glory on those we encounter.

Saturday, August 2, 2025
Time after Pentecost

Ecclesiastes 1:1-11
Nothing new under the sun

What has been is what will be,
> and what has been done is what will be done;
> there is nothing new under the sun.
Is there a thing of which it is said,
> "See, this is new"?
It has already been,
> in the ages before us.
The people of long ago are not remembered,
> nor will there be any remembrance
of people yet to come
> by those who come after them. (Eccles. 1:9-11)

Psalm
Psalm 49:1-12
The folly of trust in riches

Additional Reading
Mark 10:17-22
Treasure in heaven

Hymn: Let My Spirit Always Sing, ACS 1020

O God, steadfast through the ages, you watch over us every moment of our lives. Comforted by such knowledge, may we rest happily in peace and quietness.

Sunday, August 3, 2025
Time after Pentecost

Luke 12:13-21

Be rich toward God, your treasure

Then [Jesus] told them a parable: "The land of a rich man produced abundantly. And he thought to himself, 'What should I do, for I have no place to store my crops?' Then he said, 'I will do this: I will pull down my barns and build larger ones, and there I will store all my grain and my goods. And I will say to my soul, 'Soul, you have ample goods laid up for many years; relax, eat, drink, be merry.' But God said to him, 'You fool! This very night your life is being demanded of you. And the things you have prepared, whose will they be?' So it is with those who store up treasures for themselves but are not rich toward God." (Luke 12:16-21)

Psalm

Psalm 49:1-12
The folly of trust in riches

Additional Readings

Ecclesiastes 1:2, 12-14;
2:18-23
Search out wisdom

Colossians 3:1-11
Clothed in Christ

Hymn: Soul, Adorn Yourself with Gladness, ELW 488/489

Benevolent God, you are the source, the guide, and the goal of our lives. Teach us to love what is worth loving, to reject what is offensive to you, and to treasure what is precious in your sight, through Jesus Christ, our Savior and Lord.

Monday, August 4, 2025
Time after Pentecost

Psalm 127
Unless the Lord builds the house

Unless the LORD builds the house,
　　those who build it labor in vain.
Unless the LORD guards the city,
　　the guard keeps watch in vain.
It is in vain that you rise up early
　　and go late to rest,
eating the bread of anxious toil;
　　for he gives sleep to his beloved.

Sons are indeed a heritage from the LORD,
　　the fruit of the womb a reward.
Like arrows in the hand of a warrior
　　are the sons of one's youth.
Happy is the man who has
　　his quiver full of them.
He shall not be put to shame
　　when he speaks with his enemies in the gate. (Ps. 127:1-5)

Additional Readings
Ecclesiastes 2:1-17
The fool accumulates wealth

Colossians 3:18—4:1
A household code

Hymn: Christ Is Made the Sure Foundation, ELW 645

O God, creator of the heavens and the earth, we glorify you for your divine artistry. Fill us with awe at your beauty, that our every moment may be drenched in delight.

Tuesday, August 5, 2025
Time after Pentecost

Colossians 4:2-6
Wise conduct toward outsiders

Devote yourselves to prayer, keeping alert in it with thanksgiving. At the same time pray for us as well that God will open to us a door for the word, that we may declare the mystery of Christ, for which I am in prison, so that I may reveal it clearly, as I should.

Conduct yourselves wisely toward outsiders, making the most of the time. Let your speech always be gracious, seasoned with salt, so that you may know how you ought to answer everyone. (Col. 4:2-6)

Psalm
Psalm 127
Unless the Lord builds the house

Additional Reading
Ecclesiastes 3:16—4:8
Death comes to all

Hymn: Now to the Holy Spirit Let Us Pray, ELW 743

Once again, precious Lord, we come to you in prayer. May we adore you with all our heart, confess to you all our shortcomings, thank you for all you give us, and pray constantly for all your blessed children.

Wednesday, August 6, 2025
Time after Pentecost

Ecclesiastes 12:1-8, 13-14
Remember God

Fear God, and keep his commandments; for that is the whole duty of everyone. For God will bring every deed into judgment, including every secret thing, whether good or evil. (Eccles. 12:13b-14)

Psalm

Psalm 127
Unless the Lord builds the house

Additional Reading

Luke 12:22-31
Trust in God

Hymn: My Lord, What a Morning, ELW 438, TFF 40

O vigilant God, you entrust us with your law, yearning to protect us and all creation. Time and again, we turn our backs on you, and time and again you call us back home. Lead us always to safety.

Thursday, August 7, 2025
Time after Pentecost

Psalm 33:12-22
Let your loving kindness be upon us

Our soul waits for the Lord;
  he is our help and shield.
Our heart is glad in him,
  because we trust in his holy name.
Let your steadfast love, O Lord, be upon us,
  even as we hope in you. (Ps. 33:20-22)

Additional Readings

Job 21:1-16
The rich blessed with children despise God

Romans 9:1-9
True descendants of Abraham

Hymn: Love Divine, All Loves Excelling, ELW 631

God our comforter and provider, we adore you for the grandeur you shower upon us. As we work and play, rest and pray, may we revel in your steadfastness and bask in your affection.

Friday, August 8, 2025
Time after Pentecost

Dominic, founder of the Order of Preachers (Dominicans), died 1221

Ecclesiastes 6:1-6

Those who waste life

There is an evil that I have seen under the sun, and it lies heavy upon humankind: those to whom God gives wealth, possessions, and honor, so that they lack nothing of all that they desire, yet God does not enable them to enjoy these things, but a stranger enjoys them. This is vanity; it is a grievous ill. A man may beget a hundred children, and live many years; but however many are the days of his years, if he does not enjoy life's good things, or has no burial, I say that a stillborn child is better off than he. For it comes into vanity and goes into darkness, and in darkness its name is covered; moreover it has not seen the sun or known anything; yet it finds rest rather than he. Even though he should live a thousand years twice over, yet enjoy no good—do not all go to one place? (Eccles. 6:1-6)

Psalm

Psalm 33:12-22
Let your loving kindness be upon us

Additional Reading

Acts 7:1-8
Descendants promised to Abraham

Hymn: Sometimes Our Only Song Is Weeping, ACS 1050

Bountiful God, you bestow upon us all that is essential and extraordinary. Open our eyes and ears, hands and hearts, that we might live in constant amazement of your eternal majesty.

Saturday, August 9, 2025
Time after Pentecost

Matthew 6:19-24
Treasures and masters

[Jesus said,] "Do not store up for yourselves treasures on earth, where moth and rust consume and where thieves break in and steal; but store up for yourselves treasures in heaven, where neither moth nor rust consumes and where thieves do not break in and steal. For where your treasure is, there your heart will be also." (Matt. 6:19-21)

Psalm
Psalm 33:12-22
Let your loving kindness be upon us

Additional Reading
Genesis 11:27-32
The ancestors of Abram and Sarai

Hymn: By Your Hand You Feed Your People, ELW 469

God of endless surprises, you invite us to the eternal celebration of gladness. Inspire us to treasure the simple things of bread and wine, water and word, that we might behold wonders of heaven freely and freshly lavished upon us.

Sunday, August 10, 2025
Time after Pentecost

Lawrence, deacon, martyr, died 258

Luke 12:32-40
The treasure of the kingdom

[Jesus said,] "Do not be afraid, little flock, for it is your Father's good pleasure to give you the kingdom. Sell your possessions, and give alms. Make purses for yourselves that do not wear out, an unfailing treasure in heaven, where no thief comes near and no moth destroys. For where your treasure is, there your heart will be also." (Luke 12:32-34)

Psalm

Psalm 33:12-22
Let your loving kindness be upon us

Additional Readings

Genesis 15:1-6
God's promise of a child

Hebrews 11:1-3, 8-16
Abraham's faith

Hymn: Have No Fear, Little Flock, ELW 764

Almighty God, you sent your Holy Spirit to be the life and light of your church. Open our hearts to the riches of your grace, that we may be ready to receive you wherever you appear, through Jesus Christ, our Savior and Lord.

Monday, August 11, 2025
Time after Pentecost

Clare, Abbess of San Damiano, died 1253

Psalm 89:1-18

God's covenant with David

I will sing of your steadfast love, O LORD, forever;
>   with my mouth I will proclaim your faithfulness to all generations.
I declare that your steadfast love is established forever;
>   your faithfulness is as firm as the heavens.

You said, "I have made a covenant with my chosen one,
>   I have sworn to my servant David:
'I will establish your descendants forever,
>   and build your throne for all generations.'" (Ps. 89:1-4)

Additional Readings

2 Chronicles 33:1-17
Manasseh returns to God

Hebrews 11:1-7
The ancestors' faith

Hymn: Oh, for a Thousand Tongues to Sing, ELW 886

God of beauty, to whom the angels and saints sing "Holy, holy, holy" forever: tune our souls to your melodies, that the songs we sing may draw our families, friends, and neighbors to join the choir of the heavenly host.

Tuesday, August 12, 2025
Time after Pentecost

Hebrews 11:17-28
The faith of Abraham's descendants

By faith Abraham, when put to the test, offered up Isaac. He who had received the promises was ready to offer up his only son, of whom he had been told, "It is through Isaac that descendants shall be named for you." He considered the fact that God is able even to raise someone from the dead—and figuratively speaking, he did receive him back. (Heb. 11:17-19)

Psalm
Psalm 89:1-18
God's covenant with David

Additional Reading
2 Chronicles 34:22-33
Huldah preaches the covenant

Hymn: The God of Abraham Praise, ELW 831

God of our ancestors, you rouse your people to dwell in holiness. Inspire us to walk in the footsteps of those who have gone before us, that trusting your promise, we might savor joy even while facing sickness and death.

Wednesday, August 13, 2025
Time after Pentecost

Florence Nightingale, died 1910; Clara Maass, died 1901; renewers of society

Luke 12:41-48
A parable of the slaves

Peter said, "Lord, are you telling this parable for us or for everyone?" And the Lord said, "Who then is the faithful and prudent manager whom his master will put in charge of his slaves, to give them their allowance of food at the proper time? Blessed is that slave whom his master will find at work when he arrives. Truly I tell you, he will put that one in charge of all his possessions." (Luke 12:41-44)

Psalm
Psalm 89:1-18
God's covenant with David

Additional Reading
Jeremiah 33:14-26
God remembers the covenant

Hymn: God, Whose Giving Knows No Ending, ELW 678

Lavish God, you bless us each with unique gifts and bid us to serve your name in the world. Enliven us to strive for excellence in our callings, that we might add a measure of radiance to your groaning creation.

Thursday, August 14, 2025
Time after Pentecost

Maximilian Kolbe, died 1941; Kaj Munk, died 1944; martyrs

Psalm 82
O God, rule the earth

God has taken his place in the divine council;
>   in the midst of the gods he holds judgment:
"How long will you judge unjustly
>   and show partiality to the wicked?
Give justice to the weak and the orphan;
>   maintain the right of the lowly and the destitute.
Rescue the weak and the needy;
>   deliver them from the hand of the wicked."

Rise up, O God, judge the earth;
>   for all the nations belong to you! (Ps. 82:1-4, 8)

Additional Readings
Joshua 7:1, 10-26
Achan punished

Hebrews 10:26-31
God's judgment

Hymn: When the Poor Ones, ELW 725

Compassionate God, you watch over the needy, especially those we too easily forget, shun, or have never known. Persuade us to seek all who are lost along the way. Teach us to behold your Son's face in every suffering soul.

Friday, August 15, 2022
Mary, Mother of Our Lord

Luke 1:46-55
Mary's thanksgiving

And Mary said,

> "My soul magnifies the Lord,
>> and my spirit rejoices in God my Savior,
> for he has looked with favor on the lowliness of his servant.
>> Surely, from now on all generations will call me blessed;
> for the Mighty One has done great things for me,
>> and holy is his name." (Luke 1:46-49)

Psalm

Psalm 34:1-9
O magnify the Lord with me

Additional Readings

Isaiah 61:7-11
God will cause righteousness to spring up

Galatians 4:4-7
We are no longer slaves, but children

Hymn: No Wind at the Window, ACS 906

Almighty God, in choosing the virgin Mary to be the mother of your Son, you made known your gracious regard for the poor, the lowly, and the despised. Grant us grace to receive your word in humility, and so to be made one with your Son, Jesus Christ our Savior and Lord, who lives and reigns with you and the Holy Spirit, one God, now and forever.

Saturday, August 16, 2025
Time after Pentecost

1 Samuel 6:1-16

The Philistines atone for sacrilege

Now the people of Beth-shemesh were reaping their wheat harvest in the valley. When they looked up and saw the ark, they went with rejoicing to meet it. The cart came into the field of Joshua of Beth-shemesh, and stopped there. A large stone was there; so they split up the wood of the cart and offered the cows as a burnt offering to the LORD. The Levites took down the ark of the LORD and the box that was beside it, in which were the gold objects, and set them upon the large stone. Then the people of Beth-shemesh offered burnt offerings and presented sacrifices on that day to the LORD. When the five lords of the Philistines saw it, they returned that day to Ekron. (1 Sam. 6:13-16)

Psalm

Psalm 82
O God, rule the earth

Additional Reading

Matthew 24:15-27
The desolating sacrilege

Hymn: Crown Him with Many Crowns, ELW 855

O God, you promise to be at our side all the days of our lives. Grant patience to those who wait for you amid fears, anxieties, and losses, and comfort us all with that peace which passes all understanding.

Luke 12:49-56

Jesus brings fire on earth

[Jesus said,] "I came to bring fire to the earth, and how I wish it were already kindled! I have a baptism with which to be baptized, and what stress I am under until it is completed! Do you think that I have come to bring peace to the earth? No, I tell you, but rather division! From now on five in one household will be divided, three against two and two against three; they will be divided:

father against son

and son against father,

mother against daughter

and daughter against mother,

mother-in-law against her daughter-in-law

and daughter-in-law against mother-in-law." (Luke 12:49-53)

Psalm

Psalm 82
O God, rule the earth

Additional Readings

Jeremiah 23:23-29
God's word is like fire

Hebrews 11:29—12:2
The faith of the Hebrew people

Hymn: I Heard an Old, Old Story, TFF 97

O God, judge eternal, you love justice and hate oppression, and you call us to share your zeal for truth. Give us courage to take our stand with all victims of bloodshed and greed, and, following your servants and prophets, to look to the pioneer and perfecter of our faith, your Son, Jesus Christ, our Savior and Lord.

Monday, August 18, 2025
Time after Pentecost

Psalm 32
Prayer for forgiveness

Happy are those whose transgression is forgiven,
>   whose sin is covered.
Happy are those to whom the LORD imputes no iniquity,
>   and in whose spirit there is no deceit.

While I kept silence, my body wasted away
>   through my groaning all day long.
For day and night your hand was heavy upon me;
>   my strength was dried up as by the heat of summer.

Then I acknowledged my sin to you,
>   and I did not hide my iniquity;
I said, "I will confess my transgressions to the LORD,"
>   and you forgave the guilt of my sin. (Ps. 32:1-5)

Additional Readings
Jeremiah 23:30-40
False prophets

1 John 4:1-6
False prophets are in the world

Hymn: By Gracious Power, ELW 626

God of tenderness, we come before you on bended knees, imploring you to forgive our sins. May we rejoice yet again that you free us from the wretched prisons of our trespasses and set us free into paths of righteousness.

Tuesday, August 19, 2025
Time after Pentecost

Acts 7:44-53

Our ancestors persecuted true prophets

[Stephen replied to the high priest:] "You stiff-necked people, uncircumcised in heart and ears, you are forever opposing the Holy Spirit, just as your ancestors used to do. Which of the prophets did your ancestors not persecute? They killed those who foretold the coming of the Righteous One, and now you have become his betrayers and murderers. You are the ones that received the law as ordained by angels, and yet you have not kept it." (Acts 7:51-53)

Psalm

Psalm 32
Prayer for forgiveness

Additional Reading

Jeremiah 25:15-29
The cup of God's wrath

Hymn: A Hymn of Glory Let Us Sing! ELW 393

God of the saints and martyrs, you inspire us by the bold witness of your faithful people through the ages. Inflamed by their remarkable stories, may we stand fast against every assault of the devil that dims your radiant handiwork.

Wednesday, August 20, 2025
Time after Pentecost

Bernard, Abbot of Clairvaux, died 1153

Jeremiah 25:30-38
The peaceful flock is devastated

Wail, you shepherds, and cry out;
>   roll in ashes, you lords of the flock,
for the days of your slaughter have come—and your dispersions,
>   and you shall fall like a choice vessel.
Flight shall fail the shepherds,
>   and there shall be no escape for the lords of the flock.
Hark! the cry of the shepherds,
>   and the wail of the lords of the flock!
For the LORD is despoiling their pasture,
>   and the peaceful folds are devastated,
>   because of the fierce anger of the LORD.
Like a lion he has left his covert;
>   for their land has become a waste
because of the cruel sword,
>   and because of his fierce anger. (Jer. 25:34-38)

Psalm
Psalm 32
Prayer for forgiveness

Additional Reading
Luke 19:45-48
Jesus cleanses the temple

Hymn: Lamb of God, ELW 336

O Good Shepherd, you bid us to bear your consolation to a world lost in misery. Deliver us from laziness, cowardice, and selfishness, that we might fervently seek the lost, lonely, grieving, and poor, soothing them with your healing balm.

Thursday, August 21, 2025
Time after Pentecost

Psalm 103:1-8
Crowned with mercy

Bless the LORD, O my soul,
    and all that is within me,
    bless his holy name.
Bless the LORD, O my soul,
    and do not forget all his benefits—
who forgives all your iniquity,
    who heals all your diseases,
who redeems your life from the Pit,
    who crowns you with steadfast love and mercy,
who satisfies you with good as long as you live
    so that your youth is renewed like the eagle's. (Ps. 103:1-5)

Additional Readings
Numbers 15:32-41
The severity of breaking sabbath law

Hebrews 12:3-17
Call for endurance

Hymn: When We Must Bear Persistent Pain, ACS 1014

Ever-present God, you are with us in all the seasons of life. Mend our hearts when they are broken; open our eyes when they grow dim; calm our minds when chaos threatens. Be present with us now and always.

Friday, August 22, 2025
Time after Pentecost

2 Chronicles 8:12-15
Solomon honors sabbaths

Then Solomon offered up burnt offerings to the LORD on the altar of the LORD that he had built in front of the vestibule, as the duty of each day required, offering according to the commandment of Moses for the sabbaths, the new moons, and the three annual festivals—the festival of unleavened bread, the festival of weeks, and the festival of booths. According to the ordinance of his father David, he appointed the divisions of the priests for their service, and the Levites for their offices of praise and ministry alongside the priests as the duty of each day required, and the gatekeepers in their divisions for the several gates; for so David the man of God had commanded. They did not turn away from what the king had commanded the priests and Levites regarding anything at all, or regarding the treasuries. (2 Chron. 8:12-15)

Psalm
Psalm 103:1-8
Crowned with mercy

Additional Reading
Acts 17:1-9
Paul preaches Christ on the sabbath

Hymn: Word of God, Come Down on Earth, ELW 510

How astonishing you are, O Lord, to invite each of us to proclaim the life, death, and resurrection of Jesus Christ our Lord. Fill us with gratitude for the opportunity to announce your salvation to those whose lives touch ours.

Saturday, August 23, 2025
Time after Pentecost

Nehemiah 13:15-22
Nehemiah enforces sabbath law

When it began to be dark at the gates of Jerusalem before the sabbath, I commanded that the doors should be shut and gave orders that they should not be opened until after the sabbath. And I set some of my servants over the gates, to prevent any burden from being brought in on the sabbath day. Then the merchants and sellers of all kinds of merchandise spent the night outside Jerusalem once or twice. But I warned them and said to them, "Why do you spend the night in front of the wall? If you do so again, I will lay hands on you." From that time on they did not come on the sabbath. And I commanded the Levites that they should purify themselves and come and guard the gates, to keep the sabbath day holy. Remember this also in my favor, O my God, and spare me according to the greatness of your steadfast love. (Neh. 13:19-22)

Psalm
Psalm 103:1-8
Crowned with mercy

Additional Reading
Luke 6:1-5
Picking grain on the sabbath

Hymn: Now That Daylight Fills the Sky, ACS 992

O God, wellspring of holiness, you draw near to us and speak to us. May we gladly hear your word and eagerly learn it, that our hearts may be purified and our lives may reflect your glory.

Sunday, August 24, 2025
Time after Pentecost

Bartholomew, Apostle (Transferred to August 25)

Luke 13:10-17
Jesus heals on the sabbath

And just then there appeared a woman with a spirit that had crippled her for eighteen years. She was bent over and was quite unable to stand up straight. When Jesus saw her, he called her over and said, "Woman, you are set free from your ailment." . . . But the leader of the synagogue, indignant because Jesus had cured on the sabbath, kept saying to the crowd, "There are six days on which work ought to be done; come on those days and be cured, and not on the sabbath day." But the Lord answered him and said, "You hypocrites! Does not each of you on the sabbath untie his ox or his donkey from the manger, and lead it away to give it water? And ought not this woman, a daughter of Abraham whom Satan bound for eighteen long years, be set free from this bondage on the sabbath day?" (Luke 13:11-12, 14-16)

Psalm
Psalm 103:1-8
Crowned with mercy

Additional Readings
Isaiah 58:9b-14
Do not trample the sabbath

Hebrews 12:18-29
Coming to the city of the living God

Hymn: Down Galilee's Slow Roadways, ACS 916

O God, mighty and immortal, you know that as fragile creatures surrounded by great dangers, we cannot by ourselves stand upright. Give us strength of mind and body, so that even when we suffer because of human sin, we may rise victorious through your Son, Jesus Christ, our Savior and Lord.

Monday, August 25, 2025
Bartholomew, Apostle (Transferred)

John 1:43-51
Jesus says: Follow me

When Jesus saw Nathanael coming toward him, he said of him, "Here is truly an Israelite in whom there is no deceit!" Nathanael asked him, "Where did you get to know me?" Jesus answered, "I saw you under the fig tree before Philip called you." Nathanael replied, "Rabbi, you are the Son of God! You are the King of Israel!" Jesus answered, "Do you believe because I told you that I saw you under the fig tree? You will see greater things than these." And he said to him, "Very truly, I tell you, you will see heaven opened and the angels of God ascending and descending upon the Son of Man." (John 1:47-51)

Psalm

Psalm 12
A plea for help in evil times

Additional Readings

Exodus 19:1-6
Israel is God's priestly kingdom

1 Corinthians 12:27-31a
The body of Christ

Hymn: Will You Come and Follow Me, ELW 798

Almighty and everlasting God, you gave to your apostle Bartholomew grace truly to believe and courageously to preach your word. Grant that your church may proclaim the good news to the ends of the earth, through Jesus Christ, our Savior and Lord, who lives and reigns with you and the Holy Spirit, one God, now and forever.

Tuesday, August 26, 2025
Time after Pentecost

Psalm 109:21-31
Praise for healing

Help me, O Lord my God!
>Save me according to your steadfast love.

May my accusers be clothed with dishonor;
>may they be wrapped in their own shame as in a mantle.
With my mouth I will give great thanks to the Lord;
>I will praise him in the midst of the throng.
For he stands at the right hand of the needy,
>to save them from those who would condemn them to death.
(Ps. 109:26, 29-31)

Additional Readings
Ezekiel 20:18-32
Israel become like the nations

Revelation 3:7-13
The new Jerusalem from heaven

Hymn: O God, Who Gives Us Life, ACS 1086

Consoling God, we gather before you with sighs too deep for words, longing for you to provide for our every need. When we lose the will and the way, gather us into your arms, reassuring us of your unfailing protection.

Wednesday, August 27, 2025
Time after Pentecost

Luke 6:6-11
Jesus heals on the sabbath

On another sabbath [Jesus] entered the synagogue and taught, and there was a man there whose right hand was withered. The scribes and the Pharisees watched him to see whether he would cure on the sabbath, so that they might find an accusation against him. Even though he knew what they were thinking, he said to the man who had the withered hand, "Come and stand here." He got up and stood there. Then Jesus said to them, "I ask you, is it lawful to do good or to do harm on the sabbath, to save life or to destroy it?" After looking around at all of them, he said to him, "Stretch out your hand." He did so, and his hand was restored. But they were filled with fury and discussed with one another what they might do to Jesus. (Luke 6:6-11)

Psalm
Psalm 109:21-31
Praise for healing

Additional Reading
Ezekiel 20:33-44
God restores rebellious Israel

Hymn: There's a Wideness in God's Mercy, ELW 587/588

Holy God, throughout the life of Jesus, you erred on the side of mercy, risking ridicule and death to heal the downtrodden. Inspire us, as well, to err on the side of mercy, that all might celebrate your healing power.

Thursday, August 28, 2025
Time after Pentecost

Augustine, Bishop of Hippo, died 430
Moses the Black, monk, martyr, died around 400

Psalm 112
The righteous are merciful

Praise the LORD!
> Happy are those who fear the LORD,
> who greatly delight in his commandments.
Their descendants will be mighty in the land;
> the generation of the upright will be blessed.
Wealth and riches are in their houses,
> and their righteousness endures forever. (Ps. 112:1-3)

Additional Readings
Proverbs 15:13-17
A continual feast for the poor

1 Peter 3:8-12
Repay abuse with a blessing

Hymn: How Shall I Sing That Majesty, ACS 1095

How good it is, O God, to sing praises to you. Thrill us throughout this day and night with the joy of your salvation. Grant that all creation might be made more brilliant by the songs we sing to you.

Friday, August 29, 2025
Time after Pentecost

1 Peter 4:7-11
Be hospitable to one another

The end of all things is near; therefore be serious and discipline yourselves for the sake of your prayers. Above all, maintain constant love for one another, for love covers a multitude of sins. Be hospitable to one another without complaining. Like good stewards of the manifold grace of God, serve one another with whatever gift each of you has received. Whoever speaks must do so as one speaking the very words of God; whoever serves must do so with the strength that God supplies, so that God may be glorified in all things through Jesus Christ. To him belong the glory and the power forever and ever. Amen. (1 Peter 4:7-11)

Psalm
Psalm 112
The righteous are merciful

Additional Reading
Proverbs 18:6-12
Humility precedes honor

Hymn: Where Charity and Love Prevail, ELW 359, TFF 84

Beloved God, you bestow honor on us, inviting us to love our neighbors as you love us. May we cherish every moment of life as if it were our last and glorify your name with every breath we take.

Saturday, August 30, 2025
Time after Pentecost

Proverbs 21:1-4, 24-26
The righteous give and do not hold back

The proud, haughty person, named "Scoffer,"
> acts with arrogant pride.
The craving of the lazy person is fatal,
> for lazy hands refuse to labor.
All day long the wicked covet,
> but the righteous give and do not hold back. (Prov. 21:24-26)

Psalm
Psalm 112
The righteous are merciful

Additional Reading
Matthew 20:20-28
A request for seats of honor

Hymn: Holy, Holy, Holy, ACS 1089

O extravagant God, the gifts you give to us are beyond belief. Amaze us with your generosity so freely poured out on us, that we may be cheerful givers for your sake and for the sake of the world.

Sunday, August 31, 2025

Time after Pentecost

Luke 14:1, 7-14

Invite the poor to your banquet

[Jesus] said also to the one who had invited him, "When you give a luncheon or a dinner, do not invite your friends or your brothers or your relatives or rich neighbors, in case they may invite you in return, and you would be repaid. But when you give a banquet, invite the poor, the crippled, the lame, and the blind. And you will be blessed, because they cannot repay you, for you will be repaid at the resurrection of the righteous." (Luke 14:12-14)

Psalm

Psalm 112
The righteous are merciful

Additional Readings

Proverbs 25:6-7
Do not put yourself forward

Hebrews 13:1-8, 15-16
God is with us

Hymn: Look Who Gathers at Christ's Table, ACS 977

O God, you resist those who are proud and give grace to those who are humble. Give us the humility of your Son, that we may embody the generosity of Jesus Christ, our Savior and Lord.

Prayer List for September

_____

_____

_____

_____

_____

_____

_____

_____

_____

Time after Pentecost
Autumn

The days of early autumn (September and October) herald the resumption of a more regular schedule: school begins, church education programs commence, and the steady rhythms of work are accompanied by cooling breezes and the changing colors of the landscape. During these months, various crops are harvested and appear on roadside stands and in grocery stores. In many countries the harvest days of September and October are marked with prayer, feasting, and special care for people who are poor and hungry.

Table Prayer for Autumn

We praise you and bless you, O God,
for bright autumn days
and for the gifts of this table.
Grant us grace to share your goodness
and to trust that there is more than enough for all of your people,
through Jesus Christ, who is abundance and mercy. Amen.

Monday, September 1, 2025
Time after Pentecost

Psalm 119:65-72
God blesses the humble

You have dealt well with your servant,
    O LORD, according to your word.
Teach me good judgment and knowledge,
    for I believe in your commandments.
Before I was humbled I went astray,
    but now I keep your word.
You are good and do good;
    teach me your statutes. (Ps. 119:65-68)

Additional Readings
2 Chronicles 12:1-12
King Rehoboam humbles himself

Hebrews 13:7-21
Call for faithfulness

Hymn: He Comes to Us as One Unknown, ELW 737

Gracious God, you are always good, especially to those who serve you. By your Spirit, help us keep your word, that we may live more fully in your image and likeness, and the world may be drawn to your goodness.

Tuesday, September 2, 2025
Time after Pentecost

Nikolai Frederik Severin Grundtvig, bishop, renewer of the church, died 1872

Titus 1:1-9
Humble and hospitable leaders

I left you behind in Crete for this reason, so that you should put in order what remained to be done, and should appoint elders in every town, as I directed you: someone who is blameless, married only once, whose children are believers, not accused of debauchery and not rebellious. For a bishop, as God's steward, must be blameless; he must not be arrogant or quick-tempered or addicted to wine or violent or greedy for gain; but he must be hospitable, a lover of goodness, prudent, upright, devout, and self-controlled. He must have a firm grasp of the word that is trustworthy in accordance with the teaching, so that he may be able both to preach with sound doctrine and to refute those who contradict it. (Titus 1:5-9)

Psalm
Psalm 119:65-72
God blesses the humble

Additional Reading
Isaiah 2:12-17
Pride shall be brought low

Hymn: Thy Strong Word, ELW 511

O God, you are the Holy One for whom our hearts long. Guide and protect all those who serve your people. Through their witness, may the church be inspired as stewards of your goodness and love.

Wednesday, September 3, 2025
Time after Pentecost

Isaiah 57:14-21
God blesses the humble

It shall be said,
"Build up, build up, prepare the way,
    remove every obstruction from my people's way."
For thus says the high and lofty one
    who inhabits eternity, whose name is Holy:
I dwell in the high and holy place,
    and also with those who are contrite and humble in spirit,
to revive the spirit of the humble,
    and to revive the heart of the contrite.
For I will not continually accuse,
    nor will I always be angry;
for then the spirits would grow faint before me,
    even the souls that I have made. (Isa. 57:14-16)

Psalm
Psalm 119:65-72
God blesses the humble

Additional Reading
Luke 14:15-24
God's hospitality to the humble

Hymn: By Grace We Have Been Saved, ACS 1006

Holy One, you are always ready to receive us, exactly as we are. Revive our spirits so that we may begin to see your reflection in us.

Thursday, September 4, 2025
Time after Pentecost

Psalm 1
Delight in the law

Happy are those
    who do not follow the advice of the wicked,
or take the path that sinners tread,
    or sit in the seat of scoffers;
but their delight is in the law of the LORD,
    and on his law they meditate day and night.
They are like trees
    planted by streams of water,
which yield their fruit in its season,
    and their leaves do not wither.
In all that they do, they prosper. (Ps. 1:1-3)

Additional Readings
Genesis 39:1-23
Joseph does not sin against God

Philippians 2:25-30
Welcome a faithful servant home

Hymn: Beautiful Savior, ELW 838

Lord God, we delight in you and in your ways. Help us to meditate on your love for us day and night so we may become firm in our faith and be blessed throughout our lives.

Friday, September 5, 2025
Time after Pentecost

Colossians 4:7-17

A faithful and beloved brother

Tychicus will tell you all the news about me; he is a beloved brother,
a faithful minister, and a fellow servant in the Lord. I have sent him
to you for this very purpose, so that you may know how we are and
that he may encourage your hearts; he is coming with Onesimus, the
faithful and beloved brother, who is one of you. They will tell you about
everything here. (Col. 4:7-9)

Psalm

Psalm 1
Delight in the law

Additional Reading

Deuteronomy 7:12-26
The way of obedience

Hymn: Jesus, Still Lead On, ELW 624

*Send forth your Holy Spirit to empower your servants and encourage our
hearts, O God. Help us to be faithful as we minister to one another in the
name of your Son, Jesus Christ.*

Saturday, September 6, 2025
Time after Pentecost

Deuteronomy 29:2-20

A renewed covenant

You stand assembled today, all of you, before the LORD your God—the leaders of your tribes, your elders, and your officials, all the men of Israel, your children, your women, and the aliens who are in your camp, both those who cut your wood and those who draw your water—to enter into the covenant of the LORD your God, sworn by an oath, which the LORD your God is making with you today; in order that he may establish you today as his people, and that he may be your God, as he promised you and as he swore to your ancestors, to Abraham, to Isaac, and to Jacob. (Deut. 29:10-13)

Psalm

Psalm 1
Delight in the law

Additional Reading

Matthew 10:34-42
The cost of discipleship

Hymn: Faith of Our Fathers, ELW 813

God of our ancestors, you have kept your word and have never abandoned us. Help us to more fully live into what it means to be your faithful and holy people.

Sunday, September 7, 2025
Time after Pentecost

Luke 14:25-33

Give up your possessions

[Jesus said,] "What king, going out to wage war against another king, will not sit down first and consider whether he is able with ten thousand to oppose the one who comes against him with twenty thousand? If he cannot, then, while the other is still far away, he sends a delegation and asks for the terms of peace. So therefore, none of you can become my disciple if you do not give up all your possessions." (Luke 14:31-33)

Psalm

Psalm 1
Delight in the law

Additional Readings

Deuteronomy 30:15-20
Walk in the way of life

Philemon 1-21
Paul says, Receive Onesimus

Hymn: Making Their Way, ACS 979

Direct us, O Lord God, in all our doings with your continual help, that in all our works, begun, continued, and ended in you, we may glorify your holy name; and finally, by your mercy, bring us to everlasting life, through Jesus Christ, our Savior and Lord.

Monday, September 8, 2025
Time after Pentecost

Psalm 101
Choosing God's law

I will sing of loyalty and of justice;
    to you, O LORD, I will sing.
I will study the way that is blameless.
    When shall I attain it?

I will walk with integrity of heart
    within my house;
I will not set before my eyes
    anything that is base.

I hate the work of those who fall away;
    it shall not cling to me. (Ps. 101:1-3)

Additional Readings
2 Kings 17:24-41
The Assyrians worship other gods

1 Timothy 3:14—4:5
Behavior in the church

Hymn: I'm Going on a Journey, ELW 446, TFF 115

God of life, the way of integrity is the path you have called us to walk. Help us to wholeheartedly pursue this journey of faith, that we may sing of your justice in a world often interested in other pursuits.

Tuesday, September 9, 2025
Time after Pentecost

Peter Claver, priest, missionary to Colombia, died 1654

1 Timothy 4:6-16
Being a servant of Christ

If you put these instructions before the brothers and sisters, you will be a good servant of Christ Jesus, nourished on the words of the faith and of the sound teaching that you have followed. Have nothing to do with profane myths and old wives' tales. Train yourself in godliness, for, while physical training is of some value, godliness is valuable in every way, holding promise for both the present life and the life to come. (1 Tim. 4:6-8)

Psalm
Psalm 101
Choosing God's law

Additional Reading
2 Kings 18:9-18
Transgressing the covenant

Hymn: Will You Let Me Be Your Servant, ELW 659

Nourish us with your word, O God, and give us the grace to train ourselves in godliness. Your light gives life to all. By your Spirit, shine your light through us, offering blessing and promise to those we encounter.

Wednesday, September 10, 2025
Time after Pentecost

Luke 18:18-30
The rich ruler

A certain ruler asked [Jesus], "Good Teacher, what must I do to inherit eternal life?" Jesus said to him, "Why do you call me good? No one is good but God alone. You know the commandments: 'You shall not commit adultery; You shall not murder; You shall not steal; You shall not bear false witness; Honor your father and mother.' " He replied, "I have kept all these since my youth." When Jesus heard this, he said to him, "There is still one thing lacking. Sell all that you own and distribute the money to the poor, and you will have treasure in heaven; then come, follow me." (Luke 18:18-22)

Psalm
Psalm 101
Choosing God's law

Additional Reading
2 Kings 18:19-25; 19:1-7
A king repents, the nation is saved

Hymn: Every Time I Feel the Spirit, TFF 241, ACS 942

Good and merciful God, we follow you not as we ought but as we are able. Empowered by your grace, may we be ever more willing and ready to respond to those who most need the blessings of your love.

Thursday, September 11, 2025
Time after Pentecost

Psalm 51:1-10
Have mercy upon me, O God

Have mercy on me, O God,
    according to your steadfast love;
according to your abundant mercy
    blot out my transgressions.
Wash me thoroughly from my iniquity,
    and cleanse me from my sin.

For I know my transgressions,
    and my sin is ever before me.
Against you, you alone, have I sinned,
    and done what is evil in your sight,
so that you are justified in your sentence
    and blameless when you pass judgment. (Ps. 51:1-4)

Additional Readings

Genesis 6:1-6
Sinful humanity forgets God

1 Timothy 1:1-11
About false teachers

Hymn: Beautiful Things, ACS 925

Your goodness overwhelms us, O Lord, as we wrestle with our shadows. Be our peace. Help us overcome what hinders us from enjoying rest in your steadfast love.

Friday, September 12, 2025
Time after Pentecost

Genesis 7:6-10; 8:1-5
God remembers faithful Noah

Noah was six hundred years old when the flood of waters came on the earth. And Noah with his sons and his wife and his sons' wives went into the ark to escape the waters of the flood. Of clean animals, and of animals that are not clean, and of birds, and of everything that creeps on the ground, two and two, male and female, went into the ark with Noah, as God had commanded Noah. And after seven days the waters of the flood came on the earth. (Gen. 7:6-10)

Psalm
Psalm 51:1-10
Have mercy upon me, O God

Additional Reading
2 Peter 2:1-10a
God judges and rescues

Hymn: When Our World Is Rent by Violence, ACS 1052

You are our ark of safety, Mighty God, as raging waters surround us. Inspire us to turn to you in times of trouble and remain faithful to your commands. We trust in your abundant goodness and the new life you offer.

Saturday, September 13, 2025
Time after Pentecost

John Chrysostom, Bishop of Constantinople, died 407

Genesis 8:20—9:7

A new covenant through Noah

Then Noah built an altar to the Lord, and took of every clean animal and of every clean bird, and offered burnt offerings on the altar. And when the Lord smelled the pleasing odor, the Lord said in his heart, "I will never again curse the ground because of humankind, for the inclination of the human heart is evil from youth; nor will I ever again destroy every living creature as I have done.

As long as the earth endures,
seedtime and harvest, cold and heat,
summer and winter, day and night,
shall not cease." (Gen. 8:20-22)

Psalm
Psalm 51:1-10
Have mercy upon me, O God

Additional Reading
John 10:11-21
Jesus, the good shepherd

Hymn: Waterlife, ELW 457

O Loving God, give us the courage and strength to daily die to ourselves so that we may live in Christ and Christ in us, for the sake of the kingdom and to the glory of your name.

Sunday, September 14, 2025
Holy Cross Day

John 3:13-17
The Son of Man will be lifted up

[Jesus said to Nicodemus,] "No one has ascended into heaven except the one who descended from heaven, the Son of Man. And just as Moses lifted up the serpent in the wilderness, so must the Son of Man be lifted up, that whoever believes in him may have eternal life.

"For God so loved the world that he gave his only Son, so that everyone who believes in him may not perish but may have eternal life.

"Indeed, God did not send the Son into the world to condemn the world, but in order that the world might be saved through him." (John 3:13-17)

Psalm

Psalm 98:1-4
God has done marvelous things

Additional Readings

Numbers 21:4b-9
A bronze serpent in the wilderness

1 Corinthians 1:18-24
The cross is the power of God

Hymn: Founded on Faith, ACS 1048

Almighty God, your Son Jesus Christ was lifted high upon the cross so that he might draw the whole world to himself. To those who look upon the cross, grant your wisdom, healing, and eternal life, through Jesus Christ, our Savior and Lord, who lives and reigns with you and the Holy Spirit, one God, now and forever.

Monday, September 15, 2025
Time after Pentecost

Amos 7:1-6
God relents from punishing Israel

This is what the Lord GOD showed me: he was forming locusts at the time the latter growth began to sprout (it was the latter growth after the king's mowings). When they had finished eating the grass of the land, I said,

> "O Lord GOD, forgive, I beg you!
>> How can Jacob stand?
>> He is so small!"
> The LORD relented concerning this;
>> "It shall not be," said the LORD. (Amos 7:1-3)

Psalm
Psalm 73
God is my portion

Additional Reading
1 Timothy 1:18-20
The danger of rejecting conscience

Hymn: Restore in Us, O God, ELW 328

Merciful God, we thank you that you see our frailty. You know how small we are standing before your throne. Bless us with your compassion and temper your justice with forgiveness.

Tuesday, September 16, 2025
Time after Pentecost

Cyprian, Bishop of Carthage, martyr, died around 258

Psalm 73
God is my portion

My flesh and my heart may fail,
>   but God is the strength of my heart and my portion forever.

Indeed, those who are far from you will perish;
>   you put an end to those who are false to you.
But for me it is good to be near God;
>   I have made the Lord GOD my refuge,
>   to tell of all your works. (Ps. 73:26-28)

Additional Readings

Jonah 3:1-10
God relents from punishing Nineveh

2 Peter 3:8-13
That all may come to repentance

Hymn: On Eagle's Wings, ELW 787

Living God, you are the ground of our being and the source of our joy. Give us strength to always make you our refuge. Equip us with the courage to tell of your love both with our lips and with our lives.

Wednesday, September 17, 2025
Time after Pentecost

Hildegard, Abbess of Bingen, died 1179

Job 40:6-14; 42:1-6
Job repents

Then Job answered the LORD:
"I know that you can do all things,
and that no purpose of yours can be thwarted.
'Who is this that hides counsel without knowledge?'
Therefore I have uttered what I did not understand,
things too wonderful for me, which I did not know.
'Hear, and I will speak;
I will question you, and you declare to me.'
I had heard of you by the hearing of the ear,
but now my eye sees you;
therefore I despise myself,
and repent in dust and ashes." (Job 42:1-6)

Psalm
Psalm 73
God is my portion

Additional Reading
Luke 22:31-33, 54-62
Peter denies Jesus

Hymn: Kneeling in the Dust to Form Us, ACS 1099

O God, you can do all things. You move our hearts to turn again toward you. When we miss the mark, help us remain attentive to your Spirit so that our eyes may be opened and our hearts may be changed.

Thursday, September 18, 2025
Time after Pentecost

Dag Hammarskjöld, renewer of society, died 1961

Psalm 113
Our God lifts up the poor

Who is like the LORD our God,
> who is seated on high,
who looks far down
> on the heavens and the earth?
He raises the poor from the dust,
> and lifts the needy from the ash heap,
to make them sit with princes,
> with the princes of his people. (Ps. 113:5-8)

Additional Readings

Exodus 23:1-9
Justice for all

Romans 3:1-8
The justice of God

Hymn: This Is My Song, ELW 887

You rule with justice and mercy, sovereign God. Manifest your reign through us, that the voices of those on the margins of society may be brought to the center, for the sake of your kingdom.

Friday, September 19, 2025
Time after Pentecost

Romans 8:31-39
It is God who justifies

What then are we to say about these things? If God is for us, who is against us? He who did not withhold his own Son, but gave him up for all of us, will he not with him also give us everything else? Who will bring any charge against God's elect? It is God who justifies. Who is to condemn? It is Christ Jesus, who died, yes, who was raised, who is at the right hand of God, who indeed intercedes for us. (Rom. 8:31-34)

Psalm
Psalm 113
Our God lifts up the poor

Additional Reading
Ezekiel 22:17-31
Israel becomes dross to God

Hymn: Jesus, Remember Me, ELW 616

Saving God, throughout time you have been for us. You've redeemed us by your Son, and you have judged us righteous. Hear the cries of our hearts and attend to those most in need of your mercy and love.

Saturday, September 20, 2025
Time after Pentecost

Mark 12:41-44
A widow's offering

[Jesus] sat down opposite the treasury, and watched the crowd putting money into the treasury. Many rich people put in large sums. A poor widow came and put in two small copper coins, which are worth a penny. Then he called his disciples and said to them, "Truly I tell you, this poor widow has put in more than all those who are contributing to the treasury. For all of them have contributed out of their abundance; but she out of her poverty has put in everything she had, all she had to live on." (Mark 12:41-44)

Psalm
Psalm 113
Our God lifts up the poor

Additional Reading
Isaiah 5:8-23
Calling evil good and good evil

Hymn: Take My Life, That I May Be, ELW 583

You receive us as we are, O God. Thank you for the abundance of your love. Help us to contribute everything we have and all that we are to your kingdom.

Sunday, September 21, 2025
Time after Pentecost

Matthew, Apostle and Evangelist (Transferred to September 22)

Luke 16:1-13
Serving God or wealth

[Jesus said,] "Whoever is faithful in a very little is faithful also in much; and whoever is dishonest in a very little is dishonest also in much. If then you have not been faithful with the dishonest wealth, who will entrust to you the true riches? And if you have not been faithful with what belongs to another, who will give you what is your own? No slave can serve two masters; for a slave will either hate the one and love the other, or be devoted to the one and despise the other. You cannot serve God and wealth." (Luke 16:10-13)

Psalm

Psalm 113
Our God lifts up the poor

Additional Readings

Amos 8:4-7
Those who trample the needy

1 Timothy 2:1-7
One God, one mediator

Hymn: The Spirit Sends Us Forth to Serve, ELW 551, ACS 988

God among us, we gather in the name of your Son to learn love for one another. Keep our feet from evil paths. Turn our minds to your wisdom and our hearts to the grace revealed in your Son, Jesus Christ, our Savior and Lord.

Monday, September 22, 2025
Matthew, Apostle and Evangelist (Transferred)

Matthew 9:9-13

Jesus calls to Matthew: Follow me

As Jesus was walking along, he saw a man called Matthew sitting at the tax booth; and he said to him, "Follow me." And he got up and followed him.

And as he sat at dinner in the house, many tax collectors and sinners came and were sitting with him and his disciples. When the Pharisees saw this, they said to his disciples, "Why does your teacher eat with tax collectors and sinners?" But when he heard this, he said, "Those who are well have no need of a physician, but those who are sick. Go and learn what this means, 'I desire mercy, not sacrifice.' For I have come to call not the righteous but sinners." (Matt. 9:9-13)

Psalm

Psalm 119:33-40
Give me understanding

Additional Readings

Ezekiel 2:8—3:11
A prophet to the house of Israel

Ephesians 2:4-10
By grace you have been saved

Hymn: Great God, Your Love Has Called Us, ELW 358

Almighty God, your Son our Savior called a despised tax collector to become one of his apostles. Help us, like Matthew, to respond to the transforming call of Jesus Christ, who lives and reigns with you and the Holy Spirit, one God, now and forever.

Tuesday, September 23, 2025
Time after Pentecost

Psalm 12
Help for the poor

"Because the poor are despoiled, because the needy groan,
    I will now rise up," says the LORD;
        "I will place them in the safety for which they long."
The promises of the LORD are promises that are pure,
        silver refined in a furnace on the ground,
        purified seven times.

You, O LORD, will protect us;
        you will guard us from this generation forever. (Ps. 12:5-7)

Additional Readings
Proverbs 17:1-5   **1 Corinthians 9:19-23**
Oppressing the poor   *A servant of the gospel*

Hymn: Canticle of the Turning, ELW 723

Lord, you promise your eternal presence and love. By your mercy and grace, refine and renew us all. Help us rise up so that we may reflect your goodness and serve creation.

Wednesday, September 24, 2025
Time after Pentecost

Proverbs 21:10-16
Ears closed to the cry of the poor

The souls of the wicked desire evil;
>   their neighbors find no mercy in their eyes.
When a scoffer is punished, the simple become wiser;
>   when the wise are instructed, they increase in knowledge.
The Righteous One observes the house of the wicked;
>   he casts the wicked down to ruin.
If you close your ear to the cry of the poor,
>   you will cry out and not be heard. (Prov. 21:10-13)

Psalm
Psalm 12
Help for the poor

Additional Reading
Luke 20:45—21:4
The rich versus the poor

Hymn: Lord, Whose Love in Humble Service, ELW 712

Righteous One, you hear the cries of the poor. Empower us by your Spirit to serve all of creation, especially those most in need. Bolster our efforts with passion for your work.

Thursday, September 25, 2025
Time after Pentecost

Psalm 146
Justice to the oppressed

Happy are those whose help is the God of Jacob,
      whose hope is in the LORD their God,
who made heaven and earth,
      the sea, and all that is in them;
who keeps faith forever;
      who executes justice for the oppressed;
      who gives food to the hungry. (Ps. 146:5-7a)

Additional Readings
Proverbs 22:2-16
The rich versus the poor

2 Corinthians 8:8-15
Christ became poor

Hymn: O Splendor of God's Glory Bright, ELW 559

Eternal God, your goodness shines with each new morning. Open our eyes today to signs of your presence everywhere, that all may know the radiance of your love and that our hearts may be glad.

Friday, September 26, 2025
Time after Pentecost

Proverbs 28:3-10
The rich versus the poor

Better to be poor and walk in integrity
    than to be crooked in one's ways even though rich.
Those who keep the law are wise children,
    but companions of gluttons shame their parents.
One who augments wealth by exorbitant interest
    gathers it for another who is kind to the poor. (Prov. 28:6-8)

Psalm
Psalm 146
Justice to the oppressed

Additional Reading
Ephesians 2:1-10
God is rich in mercy

Hymn: Be Not Afraid, ELW 388

God, you call us to journey together with your Son, Jesus, in the way of integrity. Be our companion and our source of strength as we strive to follow him.

Saturday, September 27, 2025
Time after Pentecost

Proverbs 28:11-28
Helpers of the poor lack nothing

The greedy person stirs up strife,
> but whoever trusts in the Lord will be enriched.
Those who trust in their own wits are fools;
> but those who walk in wisdom come through safely.
Whoever gives to the poor will lack nothing,
> but one who turns a blind eye will get many a curse.
When the wicked prevail, people go into hiding;
> but when they perish, the righteous increase. (Prov. 28:25-28)

Psalm
Psalm 146
Justice to the oppressed

Additional Reading
Luke 9:43b-48
Welcoming little ones

Hymn: Lord, Thee I Love with All My Heart, ELW 750

Gentle God, you enrich the hearts of those who seek after you. We thank you for the love you show. May we remember that when we trust in your ways, our joy shall increase.

Sunday, September 28, 2025
Time after Pentecost

Luke 16:19-31
Poor Lazarus and the rich man

[Jesus said,] "There was a rich man who was dressed in purple and fine linen and who feasted sumptuously every day. And at his gate lay a poor man named Lazarus, covered with sores, who longed to satisfy his hunger with what fell from the rich man's table; even the dogs would come and lick his sores. The poor man died and was carried away by the angels to be with Abraham. The rich man also died and was buried. In Hades, where he was being tormented, he looked up and saw Abraham far away with Lazarus by his side." (Luke 16:19-23)

Psalm
Psalm 146
Justice to the oppressed

Additional Readings
Amos 6:1a, 4-7
Warnings to the wealthy

1 Timothy 6:6-19
Pursuing God's justice

Hymn: You Satisfy the Hungry Heart, ELW 484

O God, rich in mercy, you look with compassion on this troubled world. Feed us with your grace, and grant us the treasure that comes only from you, through Jesus Christ, our Savior and Lord.

Monday, September 29, 2025
Michael and All Angels

Revelation 12:7-12
Michael defeats Satan in a cosmic battle

War broke out in heaven; Michael and his angels fought against the dragon. The dragon and his angels fought back, but they were defeated, and there was no longer any place for them in heaven. The great dragon was thrown down, that ancient serpent, who is called the Devil and Satan, the deceiver of the whole world—he was thrown down to the earth, and his angels were thrown down with him. (Rev. 12:7-9)

Psalm
Psalm 103:1-5, 20-22
Bless the Lord, you angels

Additional Readings
Daniel 10:10-14; 12:1-3
Michael shall arise

Luke 10:17-20
Jesus gives his followers authority

Hymn: A Mighty Fortress Is Our God, ELW 503–505, TFF 133

Everlasting God, you have wonderfully established the ministries of angels and mortals. Mercifully grant that as Michael and the angels contend against the cosmic forces of evil, so by your direction they may help and defend us here on earth, through your Son, Jesus Christ our Lord, who lives and reigns with you and the Holy Spirit, one God whom we worship and praise with angels and archangels and all the company of heaven, now and forever.

Tuesday, September 30, 2025
Time after Pentecost

Jerome, translator, teacher, died 420

Psalm 62
I wait on God

For God alone my soul waits in silence,
    for my hope is from him.
He alone is my rock and my salvation,
    my fortress; I shall not be shaken.
On God rests my deliverance and my honor;
    my mighty rock, my refuge is in God. (Ps. 62:5-7)

Additional Readings
Hosea 10:9-15
Reaping injustice

James 5:1-6
Riches that rot

Hymn: In God Alone, ACS 1031

God, you are the rock upon which our lives are built. We know we can rely on your love. Be our refuge when our lives are shaken and our faith threatened. Help us to sing of your glory and might.

Prayer List for October

_____

_____

_____

_____

_____

_____

_____

_____

_____

_____

Wednesday, October 1, 2025
Time after Pentecost

Hosea 12:2-14
I have gained wealth for myself

The LORD has an indictment against Judah,
    and will punish Jacob according to his ways,
    and repay him according to his deeds.
In the womb he tried to supplant his brother,
    and in his manhood he strove with God.
He strove with the angel and prevailed,
    he wept and sought his favor;
he met him at Bethel,
    and there he spoke with him.
The LORD the God of hosts,
    the LORD is his name!
But as for you, return to your God,
    hold fast to love and justice,
    and wait continually for your God. (Hosea 12:2-6)

Psalm
Psalm 62
I wait on God

Additional Reading
Matthew 19:16-22
Treasure in heaven

Hymn: The Lord Is My Light, TFF 61

Living and loving God, we wait on you. While we wait, lead us to notice your realm of love and justice unfolding so that we can join in your good works when you call us to follow.

Thursday, October 2, 2025
Time after Pentecost

Psalm 37:1-9
Commit your way to the Lord

Commit your way to the LORD;
>   trust in him, and he will act.
He will make your vindication shine like the light,
>   and the justice of your cause like the noonday.

Be still before the LORD, and wait patiently for him;
>   do not fret over those who prosper in their way,
>   over those who carry out evil devices.

Refrain from anger, and forsake wrath.
>   Do not fret—it leads only to evil.
For the wicked shall be cut off,
>   but those who wait for the LORD shall inherit the land. (Ps. 37:5-9)

Additional Readings
2 Kings 18:1-8, 28-36
King Hezekiah trusts in God

Revelation 2:8-11
Be faithful until death

Hymn: Come, We That Love the Lord, ELW 625, TFF 135

O steadfast God, you have delivered us. You have been with us in times of light and shadow. Help us to remember your faithfulness so that we may not worry, but have hope in your promise.

Friday, October 3, 2025
Time after Pentecost

2 Kings 19:8-20, 35-37
God saves the people

And Hezekiah prayed before the LORD, and said: "O LORD the God of Israel, who are enthroned above the cherubim, you are God, you alone, of all the kingdoms of the earth; you have made heaven and earth. Incline your ear, O LORD, and hear; open your eyes, O LORD, and see; hear the words of Sennacherib, which he has sent to mock the living God. Truly, O LORD, the kings of Assyria have laid waste the nations and their lands, and have hurled their gods into the fire, though they were no gods but the work of human hands—wood and stone—and so they were destroyed. So now, O LORD our God, save us, I pray you, from his hand, so that all the kingdoms of the earth may know that you, O LORD, are God alone." (2 Kings 19:15-19)

Psalm
Psalm 37:1-9
Commit your way to the Lord

Additional Reading
Revelation 2:12-29
Call to faithfulness

Hymn: Out of the Depths I Cry to You, ELW 600

O God of grace, we are grateful that you can hear us. We are grateful that you can see us. Help us know that we are in your hands daily. Comfort us in knowing we are not alone.

Saturday, October 4, 2025
Time after Pentecost

Francis of Assisi, renewer of the church, died 1226

Theodor Fliedner, renewer of society, died 1864

See page 420 for a blessing of pets and animals, often used on or near the October 4 commemoration of Francis of Assisi.

Matthew 20:29-34
Mercy on persistent blind men

As [Jesus and the disciples] were leaving Jericho, a large crowd followed him. There were two blind men sitting by the roadside. When they heard that Jesus was passing by, they shouted, "Lord, have mercy on us, Son of David!" The crowd sternly ordered them to be quiet; but they shouted even more loudly, "Have mercy on us, Lord, Son of David!" Jesus stood still and called them, saying, "What do you want me to do for you?" They said to him, "Lord, let our eyes be opened." Moved with compassion, Jesus touched their eyes. Immediately they regained their sight and followed him. (Matt. 20:29-34)

Psalm
Psalm 37:1-9
Commit your way to the Lord

Additional Reading
Isaiah 7:1-9
Standing firm in faith

Hymn: Total Praise, ACS 1080

Merciful God, help us to be moved to compassion like you. When someone asks for help, let us respond with loving listening and give without judgment so that your vision is fulfilled.

Sunday, October 5, 2025
Time after Pentecost

Luke 17:5-10
Faith the size of a mustard seed

The apostles said to the Lord, "Increase our faith!" The Lord replied, "If you had faith the size of a mustard seed, you could say to this mulberry tree, 'Be uprooted and planted in the sea,' and it would obey you." (Luke 17:5-6)

Psalm

Psalm 37:1-9
Commit your way to the Lord

Additional Readings

Habakkuk 1:1-4; 2:1-4
The wicked surround the righteous

2 Timothy 1:1-14
Guard the treasure entrusted to you

Hymn: We've Come This Far by Faith, ELW 633, TFF 197

Benevolent, merciful God: When we are empty, fill us. When we are weak in faith, strengthen us. When we are cold in love, warm us, that with fervor we may love our neighbors and serve them for the sake of your Son, Jesus Christ, our Savior and Lord.

Monday, October 6, 2025
Time after Pentecost

William Tyndale, translator, martyr, died 1536

Psalm 3

Deliverance comes from God

I lie down and sleep;
>I wake again, for the LORD sustains me.

I am not afraid of ten thousands of people
>who have set themselves against me all around.

Rise up, O LORD!
>Deliver me, O my God!

For you strike all my enemies on the cheek;
>you break the teeth of the wicked.

Deliverance belongs to the LORD;
>may your blessing be on your people! (Ps. 3:5-8)

Additional Readings

Habakkuk 1:5-17
The wicked swallow the righteous

James 1:2-11
Faith produces endurance

Hymn: Lord, Listen to Your Children Praying, ELW 752, TFF 247

God of deliverance, we delight in your blessings! God, you have given us all we need. Help us to know that we have enough so we can let go of our fears and deep anxieties to have your promised peace.

Tuesday, October 7, 2025
Time after Pentecost

Henry Melchior Muhlenberg, pastor in North America, died 1787

1 John 5:1-5, 13-21
Faith overcomes the world

Everyone who believes that Jesus is the Christ has been born of God, and everyone who loves the parent loves the child. By this we know that we love the children of God, when we love God and obey his commandments. For the love of God is this, that we obey his commandments. And his commandments are not burdensome, for whatever is born of God conquers the world. And this is the victory that conquers the world, our faith. Who is it that conquers the world but the one who believes that Jesus is the Son of God? (1 John 5:1-5)

Psalm
Psalm 3
Deliverance comes from God

Additional Reading
Habakkuk 2:5-11
Those who heap up what is not theirs

Hymn: I Want to Walk as a Child of the Light, ELW 815

Holy Parent, you delight in us. You did not send your Child into the world to condemn it but to love it. Let us act with love. Let your law of love become evident through us to all whom we encounter.

Wednesday, October 8, 2025
Time after Pentecost

Habakkuk 2:12-20
Knowledge of the glory of God

"Alas for you who build a town by bloodshed,
    and found a city on iniquity!"
Is it not from the LORD of hosts
    that peoples labor only to feed the flames,
    and nations weary themselves for nothing?
But the earth will be filled
    with the knowledge of the glory of the LORD,
    as the waters cover the sea. (Hab. 2:12-14)

Psalm
Psalm 3
Deliverance comes from God

Additional Reading
Mark 11:12-14, 20-24
Faith that moves mountains

Hymn: Earth Is Full of Wit and Wisdom, ACS 1064

God, your spirit is humility. We dominate creation. We exploit each other for material gain. Open our minds to understand your peaceable world so that we can live in the way Jesus taught us.

Thursday, October 9, 2025
Time after Pentecost

Psalm 111
I give thanks with my whole heart

Praise the LORD!
I will give thanks to the LORD with my whole heart,
> in the company of the upright, in the congregation.
Great are the works of the LORD,
> studied by all who delight in them.
Full of honor and majesty is his work,
> and his righteousness endures forever. (Ps. 111:1-3)

Additional Readings

Leviticus 14:33-53
Cleansing a leprous house

2 Timothy 1:13-18
Paul in prison

Hymn: Praise, Praise, Praise the Lord, ELW 875, TFF 278

O God, we thank you. You are at work in the world. We see your justice unfolding every time there is mercy given. We feel your love every time there is grace given and received. In your name, we praise!

Friday, October 10, 2025
Time after Pentecost

Numbers 4:34—5:4
A census and the exclusion of lepers

The LORD spoke to Moses, saying: Command the Israelites to put out of the camp everyone who is leprous, or has a discharge, and everyone who is unclean through contact with a corpse; you shall put out both male and female, putting them outside the camp; they must not defile their camp, where I dwell among them. The Israelites did so, putting them outside the camp; as the LORD had spoken to Moses, so the Israelites did. (Num. 5:1-4)

Psalm
Psalm 111
I give thanks with my whole heart

Additional Reading
2 Timothy 2:1-7
Share in suffering

Hymn: May God Bless Us, ACS 986, TFF 162

God, sometimes we do not understand your plan; however, we know you are ever present. In those times of disconnection, help us to know you better. In the reconnecting, help us become your hands and feet.

Saturday, October 11, 2025
Time after Pentecost

Luke 5:12-16
A leper healed

Once, when [Jesus] was in one of the cities, there was a man covered with leprosy. When he saw Jesus, he bowed with his face to the ground and begged him, "Lord, if you choose, you can make me clean." Then Jesus stretched out his hand, touched him, and said, "I do choose. Be made clean." Immediately the leprosy left him. And he ordered him to tell no one. "Go," he said, "and show yourself to the priest, and, as Moses commanded, make an offering for your cleansing, for a testimony to them." But now more than ever the word about Jesus spread abroad; many crowds would gather to hear him and to be cured of their diseases. But he would withdraw to deserted places and pray. (Luke 5:12-16)

Psalm
Psalm 111
I give thanks with my whole heart

Additional Reading
Numbers 12:1-15
Miriam contracts leprosy

Hymn: O God, to You I Cry in Pain, ACS 1021

Loving God, we are grateful that you have healed us with your death and resurrection. We proclaim this good news of salvation to the world. Fulfill your promise of abundant life for all.

Sunday, October 12, 2025
Time after Pentecost

Luke 17:11-19
One leper gives thanks to God

As [Jesus] entered a village, ten lepers approached him. Keeping their distance, they called out, saying, "Jesus, Master, have mercy on us!" When he saw them, he said to them, "Go and show yourselves to the priests." And as they went, they were made clean. Then one of them, when he saw that he was healed, turned back, praising God with a loud voice. He prostrated himself at Jesus' feet and thanked him. And he was a Samaritan. (Luke 17:12-16)

Psalm

Psalm 111
I give thanks with my whole heart

Additional Readings

2 Kings 5:1-3, 7-15c
Naaman is cleansed

2 Timothy 2:8-15
We will live with Christ

Hymn: Cradling Children in His Arm, ELW 444

Almighty and most merciful God, your bountiful goodness fills all creation. Keep us safe from all that may hurt us, that, whole and well in body and spirit, we may with grateful hearts accomplish all that you would have us do, through Jesus Christ, our Savior and Lord.

Monday, October 13, 2025
Time after Pentecost

Day of Thanksgiving (Canada)

A reading and prayer for Thanksgiving Day is provided on page 361.

Psalm 61
Prayer for a long life

Hear my cry, O God;
> listen to my prayer.
From the end of the earth I call to you,
> when my heart is faint.

Lead me to the rock
> that is higher than I;
for you are my refuge,
> a strong tower against the enemy.

Let me abide in your tent forever,
> find refuge under the shelter of your wings. (Ps. 61:1-4)

Additional Readings
2 Kings 5:15-19a
Naaman seeks to repay Elisha

Acts 26:24-29
Except for these chains

Hymn: Nothing Can Trouble, ACS 1033

O God, you are our rock when we are weary. Let not our hearts be troubled with the useless fear of people we perceive as our enemies. Enable us to trust in you and the goodness of your creation.

Tuesday, October 14, 2025
Time after Pentecost

Ephesians 6:10-20
An ambassador in chains

Finally, be strong in the Lord and in the strength of his power. Put on the whole armor of God, so that you may be able to stand against the wiles of the devil. For our struggle is not against enemies of blood and flesh, but against the rulers, against the authorities, against the cosmic powers of this present darkness, against the spiritual forces of evil in the heavenly places. (Eph. 6:10-12)

Psalm
Psalm 61
Prayer for a long life

Additional Reading
2 Kings 5:19b-27
Greed brings leprosy to Gehazi

Hymn: Commonwealth Is God's Commandment, ACS 1036

God of wisdom, help us to remember not to fight each other but rather to fight the systems that exploit and destroy your good creation. Give us endurance when it is easier to give up.

Wednesday, October 15, 2025
Time after Pentecost

Teresa of Avila, teacher, renewer of the church, died 1582

Matthew 10:5-15

Cure without payment

These twelve Jesus sent out with the following instructions: "Go nowhere among the Gentiles, and enter no town of the Samaritans, but go rather to the lost sheep of the house of Israel. As you go, proclaim the good news, 'The kingdom of heaven has come near.' Cure the sick, raise the dead, cleanse the lepers, cast out demons. You received without payment; give without payment." (Matt. 10:5-8)

Psalm

Psalm 61
Prayer for a long life

Additional Reading

2 Kings 15:1-7
A leprous king lives in isolation

Hymn: What Is the World Like, ACS 1047

O God, open our ears, open our eyes, and open our hearts to experience your good news. Help us to proclaim that your realm is real, your realm is here, and your realm is yet to be.

Thursday, October 16, 2025
Time after Pentecost

Psalm 121
My help is from the Lord

I lift up my eyes to the hills—
    from where will my help come?
My help comes from the LORD,
    who made heaven and earth.

He will not let your foot be moved;
    he who keeps you will not slumber.
He who keeps Israel
    will neither slumber nor sleep. (Ps. 121:1-4)

Additional Readings
Isaiah 54:11-17
God will vindicate the faithful

Acts 17:22-34
God has fixed a day of judgment

Hymn: Sing Praise to God, the Highest Good, ELW 871

God of protection during our rest, we thank you for the gift of rest and sabbath. Help us to likewise give these gifts to each other and restore adherence to your commandment.

Friday, October 17, 2025
Time after Pentecost

Ignatius, Bishop of Antioch, martyr, died around 115

2 Timothy 2:14-26
About the Christian life

Do your best to present yourself to God as one approved by him, a worker who has no need to be ashamed, rightly explaining the word of truth. Avoid profane chatter, for it will lead people into more and more impiety, and their talk will spread like gangrene. Among them are Hymenaeus and Philetus, who have swerved from the truth by claiming that the resurrection has already taken place. They are upsetting the faith of some. But God's firm foundation stands, bearing this inscription: "The Lord knows those who are his," and, "Let everyone who calls on the name of the Lord turn away from wickedness." (2 Tim. 2:15-19)

Psalm
Psalm 121
My help is from the Lord

Additional Reading
Genesis 31:43—32:2
Laban and Jacob make a covenant

Hymn: As Saints of Old, ELW 695

God of labor, we thank you for our jobs and vocations. Help us to have wise livelihoods that care for all people and the natural world so that your will be done on earth.

Saturday, October 18, 2025
Luke, Evangelist

Luke 1:1-4; 24:44-53
Luke witnesses to the ministry of Jesus

Since many have undertaken to set down an orderly account of the events that have been fulfilled among us, just as they were handed on to us by those who from the beginning were eyewitnesses and servants of the word, I too decided, after investigating everything carefully from the very first, to write an orderly account for you, most excellent Theophilus, so that you may know the truth concerning the things about which you have been instructed. (Luke 1:1-4)

Psalm
Psalm 124
Our help is in God

Additional Readings
Isaiah 43:8-13
You are my witnesses

2 Timothy 4:5-11
The good fight of faith

Hymn: Forgive Our Sins as We Forgive, ELW 605

Almighty God, you inspired your servant Luke to reveal in his gospel the love and healing power of your Son. Give your church the same love and power to heal, and to proclaim your salvation among the nations to the glory of your name, through Jesus Christ, your Son, our healer, who lives and reigns with you and the Holy Spirit, one God, now and forever.

Sunday, October 19, 2025
Time after Pentecost

Luke 18:1-8
A widow begs for justice

Then Jesus told them a parable about their need to pray always and not to lose heart. He said, "In a certain city there was a judge who neither feared God nor had respect for people. In that city there was a widow who kept coming to him and saying, 'Grant me justice against my opponent.' For a while he refused; but later he said to himself, 'Though I have no fear of God and no respect for anyone, yet because this widow keeps bothering me, I will grant her justice, so that she may not wear me out by continually coming.'" (Luke 18:1-5)

Psalm

Psalm 121
My help is from the Lord

Additional Readings

Genesis 32:22-31
Jacob's struggle with the angel

2 Timothy 3:14—4:5
Christ the judge

Hymn: Here I Am, Lord, ELW 574, TFF 230

O Lord God, tireless guardian of your people, you are always ready to hear our cries. Teach us to rely day and night on your care. Inspire us to seek your enduring justice for all this suffering world, through Jesus Christ, our Savior and Lord.

Monday, October 20, 2025
Time after Pentecost

Psalm 57
Vindication from God

Be merciful to me, O God, be merciful to me,
>   for in you my soul takes refuge;
in the shadow of your wings I will take refuge,
>   until the destroying storms pass by.
I cry to God Most High,
>   to God who fulfills his purpose for me.
He will send from heaven and save me,
>   he will put to shame those who trample on me.
God will send forth his steadfast love and his faithfulness. (Ps. 57:1-3)

Additional Readings

1 Samuel 25:2-22
David judges against Nabal

1 Corinthians 6:1-11
You are washed and sanctified

Hymn: Awake, My Soul, and with the Sun, ELW 557

O God of our refuge, we are restored by your grace. Help us to be merciful to others as you have been to us so that your reign of justice and love will continue to expand.

Tuesday, October 21, 2025
Time after Pentecost

James 5:7-12
The Judge standing at the doors

Be patient, therefore, beloved, until the coming of the Lord. The farmer waits for the precious crop from the earth, being patient with it until it receives the early and the late rains. You also must be patient. Strengthen your hearts, for the coming of the Lord is near. Beloved, do not grumble against one another, so that you may not be judged. See, the Judge is standing at the doors! As an example of suffering and patience, beloved, take the prophets who spoke in the name of the Lord. Indeed we call blessed those who showed endurance. You have heard of the endurance of Job, and you have seen the purpose of the Lord, how the Lord is compassionate and merciful.

Above all, my beloved, do not swear, either by heaven or by earth or by any other oath, but let your "Yes" be yes and your "No" be no, so that you may not fall under condemnation. (James 5:7-12)

Psalm
Psalm 57
Vindication from God

Additional Reading
1 Samuel 25:23-35
Abigail pleads for life

Hymn: When We Must Bear Persistent Pain, ACS 1014

O loving God of truth, you have called us to live with integrity. Give us the courage to say no to unhealthy ways of living. Give us the wisdom to say yes to your ways of goodness.

Wednesday, October 22, 2025
Time after Pentecost

Luke 22:39-46
Jesus prays for life

[Jesus] came out and went, as was his custom, to the Mount of Olives; and the disciples followed him. When he reached the place, he said to them, "Pray that you may not come into the time of trial." Then he withdrew from them about a stone's throw, knelt down, and prayed, "Father, if you are willing, remove this cup from me; yet, not my will but yours be done." (Luke 22:39-42)

Psalm
Psalm 57
Vindication from God

Additional Reading
1 Samuel 25:36-42
David welcomes Abigail as wife

Hymn: Go to Dark Gethsemane, ELW 347

Abba God, guide us in times of shadow and pain. Help us to stop, pray, and take comfort in your Spirit. Help us to be reassured in your promise. Encourage us to pray like Jesus, our deliverer, friend, and sibling.

Thursday, October 23, 2025
Time after Pentecost

James of Jerusalem, martyr, died around 62

Psalm 84:1-7

Happy are they whose strength is in you

How lovely is your dwelling place,
    O Lord of hosts!
My soul longs, indeed it faints
    for the courts of the Lord;
my heart and my flesh sing for joy
    to the living God.

Even the sparrow finds a home,
    and the swallow a nest for herself,
    where she may lay her young,
at your altars, O Lord of hosts,
    my King and my God.
Happy are those who live in your house,
    ever singing your praise. (Ps. 84:1-4)

Additional Readings

Jeremiah 9:1-16
Israel refuses to know God

2 Timothy 3:1-9
Godlessness

Hymn: Blessed Assurance, ELW 638, TFF 118

O God of delight and joy, you have given us all that we need. Help us to realize and to be reassured of this truth each and every day so that we may delight in the gift of your creation.

Friday, October 24, 2025
Time after Pentecost

Jeremiah 9:17-26
Israel uncircumcised in heart

Thus says the LORD: Do not let the wise boast in their wisdom, do not let the mighty boast in their might, do not let the wealthy boast in their wealth; but let those who boast boast in this, that they understand and know me, that I am the LORD; I act with steadfast love, justice, and righteousness in the earth, for in these things I delight, says the LORD.

The days are surely coming, says the LORD, when I will attend to all those who are circumcised only in the foreskin: Egypt, Judah, Edom, the Ammonites, Moab, and all those with shaven temples who live in the desert. For all these nations are uncircumcised, and all the house of Israel is uncircumcised in heart. (Jer. 9:23-26)

Psalm
Psalm 84:1-7
Happy are they whose strength is in you

Additional Reading
2 Timothy 3:10-15
The persecution of the godly

Hymn: Return to God, ACS 921

O living God of steadfast love and justice, we are so grateful that you are a God of mercy and grace. We rejoice in this knowledge. Help us to keep it always before us so that your will may be done.

Saturday, October 25, 2025
Time after Pentecost

Jeremiah 14:1-6
A drought portends destruction

The word of the LORD that came to Jeremiah concerning the drought:

> Judah mourns
>> and her gates languish;
> they lie in gloom on the ground,
>> and the cry of Jerusalem goes up.
> Her nobles send their servants for water;
>> they come to the cisterns,
> they find no water,
>> they return with their vessels empty. . . .
>> Because there has been no rain on the land
> the farmers are dismayed;
>> they cover their heads. (Jer. 14:1-4)

Psalm
Psalm 84:1-7
Happy are they whose strength is in you

Additional Reading
Luke 1:46-55
Mary's song

Hymn: My Soul Does Magnify the Lord, ELW 882, TFF 168

O God, you reveal yourself to us during times of fear, drought, and destruction. We plead with you to give us wisdom so that we can act in these troubled times with loving care for your creation.

Sunday, October 26, 2025
Time after Pentecost

Philipp Nicolai, died 1608; Johann Heermann, died 1647;
Paul Gerhardt, died 1676; hymnwriters

Luke 18:9-14
A Pharisee and tax collector pray

[Jesus said,] "Two men went up to the temple to pray, one a Pharisee and the other a tax collector. The Pharisee, standing by himself, was praying thus, 'God, I thank you that I am not like other people: thieves, rogues, adulterers, or even like this tax collector. I fast twice a week; I give a tenth of all my income.' But the tax collector, standing far off, would not even look up to heaven, but was beating his breast and saying, 'God, be merciful to me, a sinner!' I tell you, this man went down to his home justified rather than the other; for all who exalt themselves will be humbled, but all who humble themselves will be exalted." (Luke 18:10-14)

Psalm
Psalm 84:1-7
Happy are they whose strength is in you

Additional Readings
Jeremiah 14:7-10, 19-22
Jerusalem will be defeated

2 Timothy 4:6-8, 16-18
The good fight of faith

Hymn: Jesus, the Light of the World, ACS 914, TFF 59

Holy God, our righteous judge, daily your mercy surprises us with everlasting forgiveness. Strengthen our hope in you, and grant that all the peoples of the earth may find their glory in you, through Jesus Christ, our Savior and Lord.

Monday, October 27, 2025
Time after Pentecost

Psalm 84:8-12
A doorkeeper in God's house

O LORD God of hosts, hear my prayer;
   give ear, O God of Jacob!
Behold our shield, O God;
   look on the face of your anointed.

For a day in your courts is better
   than a thousand elsewhere.
I would rather be a doorkeeper in the house of my God
   than live in the tents of wickedness. (Ps. 84:8-10)

Additional Readings
1 Samuel 2:1-10
Hannah's song

1 Peter 4:12-19
The suffering of the righteous

Hymn: What a Fellowship, What a Joy Divine, ELW 774, TFF 220

O God, better is one day in your house than all the time or riches in the world. Use all our senses to understand that your goodness far exceeds the material goods we currently possess. Let us delight in the fellowship of your creation.

Tuesday, October 28, 2025
Simon and Jude, Apostles

John 14:21-27

Those who love Jesus will keep his word

[Jesus said,] "They who have my commandments and keep them are those who love me; and those who love me will be loved by my Father, and I will love them and reveal myself to them." Judas (not Iscariot) said to him, "Lord, how is it that you will reveal yourself to us, and not to the world?" Jesus answered him, "Those who love me will keep my word, and my Father will love them, and we will come to them and make our home with them. Whoever does not love me does not keep my words; and the word that you hear is not mine, but is from the Father who sent me." (John 14:21-24)

Psalm

Psalm 11
Take refuge in God

Additional Readings

Jeremiah 26:[1-6]
7-16
Jeremiah promises the judgment of God

1 John 4:1-6
Do not believe every spirit of this world

Hymn: Go, My Children, with My Blessing, ELW 543, TFF 161

O God, we thank you for the glorious company of the apostles, and especially on this day for Simon and Jude. We pray that, as they were faithful and zealous in your mission, so we may with ardent devotion make known the love and mercy of our Savior Jesus Christ, who lives and reigns with you and the Holy Spirit, one God, now and forever.

Wednesday, October 29, 2025
Time after Pentecost

Matthew 21:28-32
Faith of tax collectors and prostitutes

[Jesus said,] "What do you think? A man had two sons; he went to the first and said, 'Son, go and work in the vineyard today.' He answered, 'I will not'; but later he changed his mind and went. The father went to the second and said the same; and he answered, 'I go, sir'; but he did not go. Which of the two did the will of his father?" They said, "The first." Jesus said to them, "Truly I tell you, the tax collectors and the prostitutes are going into the kingdom of God ahead of you. For John came to you in the way of righteousness and you did not believe him, but the tax collectors and the prostitutes believed him; and even after you saw it, you did not change your minds and believe him." (Matt. 21:28-32)

Psalm
Psalm 84:8-12
A doorkeeper in God's house

Additional Reading
Daniel 5:13-31
Daniel urges humility

Hymn: God's Work, Our Hands, ACS 1000

God of the holy and sacred covenant, you have kept your promises to us. Help us to keep the promises we have made to you—to be your faithful people trusting in and acting on your word of love.

Thursday, October 30, 2025
Time after Pentecost

Psalm 32:1-7
Praying in time of trouble

Therefore let all who are faithful
  offer prayer to you;
at a time of distress, the rush of mighty waters
  shall not reach them.
You are a hiding place for me;
  you preserve me from trouble;
  you surround me with glad cries of deliverance. (Ps. 32:6-7)

Additional Readings
Proverbs 15:8-11, 24-33
God welcomes the righteous

2 Corinthians 1:1-11
Shared suffering, unshaken hope

Hymn: God, My Lord, My Strength, ELW 795

Faithful God, you are steadfast with love and grace. God, you share in our suffering and pain. We hope in you. Fulfill our hope that joy will come in the morning after nights of sorrow.

Friday, October 31, 2025
Reformation Day

Romans 3:19-28
Justified by God's grace as a gift

But now, apart from law, the righteousness of God has been disclosed, and is attested by the law and the prophets, the righteousness of God through faith in Jesus Christ for all who believe. For there is no distinction, since all have sinned and fall short of the glory of God; they are now justified by his grace as a gift, through the redemption that is in Christ Jesus, whom God put forward as a sacrifice of atonement by his blood, effective through faith. He did this to show his righteousness, because in his divine forbearance he had passed over the sins previously committed; it was to prove at the present time that he himself is righteous and that he justifies the one who has faith in Jesus. (Rom. 3:21-26)

Psalm
Psalm 46
The God of Jacob is our stronghold

Additional Readings
Jeremiah 31:31-34
I will write my law in their hearts

John 8:31-36
The truth will set you free

Hymn: Go to the World, ACS 991

Almighty God, gracious Lord, we thank you that your Holy Spirit renews the church in every age. Pour out your Holy Spirit on your faithful people. Keep them steadfast in your word, protect and comfort them in times of trial, defend them against all enemies of the gospel, and bestow on the church your saving peace, through Jesus Christ, our Savior and Lord, who lives and reigns with you and the Holy Spirit, one God, now and forever.

Prayer List for November

_____

_____

_____

_____

_____

_____

_____

_____

_____

Time after Pentecost
November

We begin November by remembering the people who have died in Christ on All Saints Day. We speak their names and grieve their absence. But we also know that they are entrusted into the hands of God. The One who holds them also holds us, and seeks to hold our attention long enough that hope for the future is born in us. We learn to trust in the support offered by the communion of saints, the faithful witnesses to the God of grace claimed by Jesus Christ.

November's Sunday and daily readings resonate with the harvests that happen during the fall in the northern hemisphere. The liturgical year ends with a relatively new Christian holiday, Christ the King or Reign of Christ Sunday. Pope Pius XI began this celebration in 1925. His hope was that Christians might cling to Jesus' way of ruling the world rather than offering their allegiance to earthly rulers.

As we get ready for the new church year, our celebration of Christ culminates by lifting up his transformative way of being in the world. We pledge our allegiance to the One who identifies with people who are hungry, thirsty, strangers, naked, sick, and imprisoned. We follow the One who was taunted as a king when he hung upon a cross. We live in the hope inspired by the crucified Christ, whom God raised from the dead by the power of the Holy Spirit.

Table Prayer for November
Make yourself known to us, God of life,
as we share the bounty of this food and drink.

We give you thanks for those who have gone before us in faith,
revealing to us your gracious reign.
Feed those who hunger,
and give us all a hunger for justice and peace.
We ask this through Christ our Lord. Amen.

Remembering Those Who Have Died

Use this prayer in the home or at the grave.

O God, our help in ages past and our hope for years to come:
We give you thanks for all your faithful people
who have followed the guiding light of your word throughout the
centuries, into our time and place.
Here individual names may be spoken.

As we remember these people,
strengthen us to follow Christ through this world
until we are carried into the harvest of eternal life,
where suffering and death will be no more.
Hear our prayer in the name of the good and gracious shepherd,
Jesus Christ, our Savior and Lord. Amen.

or

With reverence and affection we remember before you,
O everlasting God,
all our departed friends and relatives.
Keep us in union with them here
through faith and love toward you,
that hereafter we may enter into your presence
and be numbered with those who serve you
and look upon your face in glory everlasting,
through your Son, Jesus Christ our Lord. Amen.

Saturday, November 1, 2025
All Saints Day

Luke 6:20-31
Jesus speaks blessings and woes

Then [Jesus] looked up at his disciples and said:

"Blessed are you who are poor,

for yours is the kingdom of God.

"Blessed are you who are hungry now,

for you will be filled.

"Blessed are you who weep now,

for you will laugh.

"Blessed are you when people hate you, and when they exclude you, revile you, and defame you on account of the Son of Man. Rejoice in that day and leap for joy, for surely your reward is great in heaven; for that is what their ancestors did to the prophets." (Luke 6:20-23)

Psalm

Psalm 149
Sing praise for God's goodness

Additional Readings

Daniel 7:1-3, 15-18
The holy ones of the Most High

Ephesians 1:11-23
God made Christ head over all

Hymn: Death Be Never Last, ACS 1030

Almighty God, you have knit your people together in one communion in the mystical body of your Son, Jesus Christ our Lord. Grant us grace to follow your blessed saints in lives of faith and commitment, and to know the inexpressible joys you have prepared for those who love you, through Jesus Christ, our Savior and Lord, who lives and reigns with you and the Holy Spirit, one God, now and forever.

Sunday, November 2, 2025
Time after Pentecost

Luke 19:1-10
Zacchaeus climbs high to see Jesus

When Jesus came to [Jericho], he looked up and said to [Zacchaeus],
"Zacchaeus, hurry and come down; for I must stay at your house today."
So he hurried down and was happy to welcome him. All who saw it
began to grumble and said, "He has gone to be the guest of one who is a
sinner." Zacchaeus stood there and said to the Lord, "Look, half of my
possessions, Lord, I will give to the poor; and if I have defrauded anyone
of anything, I will pay back four times as much." Then Jesus said to
him, "Today salvation has come to this house, because he too is a son
of Abraham. For the Son of Man came to seek out and to save the lost."
(Luke 19:5-10)

Psalm
Psalm 32:1-7
Praying in time of trouble

Additional Readings
Isaiah 1:10-18
Learn to do good

2 Thessalonians 1:1-4, 11-12
Faith and love amid adversity

Hymn: Take My Life That I May Be, ELW 583/685

*Merciful God, gracious and benevolent, through your Son you invite all the
world to a meal of mercy. Grant that we may eagerly follow his call, and
bring us with all your saints into your life of justice and joy, through Jesus
Christ, our Savior and Lord.*

Monday, November 3, 2025
Time after Pentecost

Martín de Porres, renewer of society, died 1639

Psalm 50
A sacrifice of thanksgiving

The mighty one, God the Lord,
> speaks and summons the earth
> from the rising of the sun to its setting.
Out of Zion, the perfection of beauty,
> God shines forth.

Our God comes and does not keep silence,
> before him is a devouring fire,
> and a mighty tempest all around him.
He calls to the heavens above
> and to the earth, that he may judge his people:
"Gather to me my faithful ones,
> who made a covenant with me by sacrifice!"
The heavens declare his righteousness,
> for God himself is judge. (Ps. 50:1-6)

Additional Readings
Nehemiah 13:1-3, 23-31
Israel separates from foreigners

1 Corinthians 5:9-13
Drive out the wicked

Hymn: For the Beauty of the Earth, ELW 879

Speaking God, at your word creation came into existence, and by your word you create beauty that greets us on every side. Keep us aware, attentive, and obedient to your life-giving proclamation as it takes on flesh among us.

Tuesday, November 4, 2025
Time after Pentecost

Jude 5-21
Warning against sinners

But you, beloved, must remember the predictions of the apostles of our Lord Jesus Christ; for they said to you, "In the last time there will be scoffers, indulging their own ungodly lusts." It is these worldly people, devoid of the Spirit, who are causing divisions. But you, beloved, build yourselves up on your most holy faith; pray in the Holy Spirit; keep yourselves in the love of God; look forward to the mercy of our Lord Jesus Christ that leads to eternal life. (Jude 17-21)

Psalm
Psalm 50
A sacrifice of thanksgiving

Additional Reading
Zechariah 7:1-14
Fasting versus justice and mercy

Hymn: Where Charity and Love Are Shown, ACS 931

Merciful God, you send forth your Spirit and we find ourselves trusting in your love. Let us see one another as siblings in Christ, that we might live into the united family you desire us to be.

Wednesday, November 5, 2025
Time after Pentecost

Amos 5:12-24
God desires justice, not offerings

I hate, I despise your festivals,
    and I take no delight in your solemn assemblies.
Even though you offer me your burnt offerings and grain offerings,
    I will not accept them;
and the offerings of well-being of your fatted animals
    I will not look upon.
Take away from me the noise of your songs;
    I will not listen to the melody of your harps.
But let justice roll down like waters,
    and righteousness like an ever-flowing stream. (Amos 5:21-24)

Psalm
Psalm 50
A sacrifice of thanksgiving

Additional Reading
Luke 19:11-27
The parable of the pounds

Hymn: Let Justice Flow like Streams, ELW 717, TFF 48

God of justice, you call your people to let shalom pour down and water the earth. Forgive us when we have neglected our neighbors and attended only to the human traditions we ourselves have created. Teach us to walk rightly.

Thursday, November 6, 2025
Time after Pentecost

Psalm 17:1-9

Keep me as the apple of your eye

I call upon you, for you will answer me, O God;
>   incline your ear to me, hear my words.
Wondrously show your steadfast love,
>   O savior of those who seek refuge
>   from their adversaries at your right hand.

Guard me as the apple of the eye;
>   hide me in the shadow of your wings,
from the wicked who despoil me,
>   my deadly enemies who surround me. (Ps. 17:6-9)

Additional Readings

Deuteronomy 25:5-10
Instructions for levirate marriage

Acts 22:22—23:11
Paul confronts religious leaders

Hymn: O Lord, Hear My Prayer, ELW 751

How delightful it is, gracious God, that you incline your ears and listen to our joys and sorrows. Remind us of your vigilant attention. In your care we have a Savior in whom we can trust.

Friday, November 7, 2025
Time after Pentecost

John Christian Frederick Heyer, died 1873; Bartholomaeus Ziegenbalg, died 1719;
Ludwig Nommensen, died 1918; missionaries

Acts 24:10-23
Paul testifies to the resurrection

When the governor motioned to him to speak, Paul replied:
"I cheerfully make my defense, knowing that for many years you
have been a judge over this nation. As you can find out, it is not more
than twelve days since I went up to worship in Jerusalem. They did
not find me disputing with anyone in the temple or stirring up a crowd
either in the synagogues or throughout the city. Neither can they prove
to you the charge that they now bring against me. But this I admit to
you, that according to the Way, which they call a sect, I worship the
God of our ancestors, believing everything laid down according to the
law or written in the prophets. I have a hope in God—a hope that they
themselves also accept—that there will be a resurrection of both the
righteous and the unrighteous." (Acts 24:10-15)

Psalm
Psalm 17:1-9
Keep me as the apple of your eye

Additional Reading
Genesis 38:1-26
Tamar and levirate marriage

Hymn: Be Not Afraid, ELW 388

*God of life, you work wonders beyond our imagining. You take in your
hands what is dead, and it lives again. When death surround us on all sides,
inspire us to trust that resurrection will come with the dawn.*

Saturday, November 8, 2025
Time after Pentecost

Exodus 3:13-20
God appears to Moses

Moses said to God, "If I come to the Israelites and say to them, 'The God of your ancestors has sent me to you,' and they ask me, 'What is his name?' what shall I say to them?" God said to Moses, "I AM WHO I AM." He said further, "Thus you shall say to the Israelites, 'I AM has sent me to you.' " God also said to Moses, "Thus you shall say to the Israelites, 'The LORD, the God of your ancestors, the God of Abraham, the God of Isaac, and the God of Jacob, has sent me to you':

This is my name forever,
and this my title for all generations." (Exod. 3:13-15)

Psalm
Psalm 17:1-9
Keep me as the apple of your eye

Additional Reading
Luke 20:1-8
Jesus' teaching authority

Hymn: Guide My Feet, ACS 987, TFF 153

On the mountain with Moses, you revealed your name as the great I AM. Let us walk forward with courage and faith, trusting in your promise, "I AM going with you, even to the ends of the earth."

Sunday, November 9, 2025
Time after Pentecost

Luke 20:27-38

Jesus speaks of the resurrection

Jesus said to [the Sadducees], "Those who belong to this age marry and are given in marriage; but those who are considered worthy of a place in that age and in the resurrection from the dead neither marry nor are given in marriage. Indeed they cannot die anymore, because they are like angels and are children of God, being children of the resurrection. And the fact that the dead are raised Moses himself showed, in the story about the bush, where he speaks of the Lord as the God of Abraham, the God of Isaac, and the God of Jacob. Now he is God not of the dead, but of the living; for to him all of them are alive." (Luke 20:34-38)

Psalm

Psalm 17:1-9
Keep me as the apple of your eye

Additional Readings

Job 19:23-27a
I know that my Redeemer lives

2 Thessalonians 2:1-5, 13-17
The coming of Christ Jesus

Hymn: Sing with All the Saints in Glory, ELW 426

O God, our eternal redeemer, by the presence of your Spirit you renew and direct our hearts. Keep always in our mind the end of all things and the day of judgment. Inspire us for a holy life here, and bring us to the joy of the resurrection, through Jesus Christ, our Savior and Lord.

Monday, November 10, 2025
Time after Pentecost

Psalm 123
Our eyes look to God

To you I lift up my eyes,
    O you who are enthroned in the heavens!
As the eyes of servants
    look to the hand of their master,
as the eyes of a maid
    to the hand of her mistress,
so our eyes look to the LORD our God,
    until he has mercy upon us.

Have mercy upon us, O LORD, have mercy upon us,
    for we have had more than enough of contempt.
Our soul has had more than its fill
    of the scorn of those who are at ease,
    of the contempt of the proud. (Ps. 123:1-4)

Additional Readings

Job 20:1-11
Mortals fly away like a dream

2 Peter 1:16-21
Prophecy comes not by human will

Hymn: Come, Bring Your Burdens to God, ACS 1009

Turn our gaze to you, O God, so that we might see how you look on us with love and know that the scorn of others does not define us. You have named and claimed us. We are precious in your sight.

Tuesday, November 11, 2025
Time after Pentecost

Martin, Bishop of Tours, died 397
Søren Aabye Kierkegaard, teacher, died 1855

2 John 1-13
Be on your guard

Many deceivers have gone out into the world, those who do not confess that Jesus Christ has come in the flesh; any such person is the deceiver and the antichrist! Be on your guard, so that you do not lose what we have worked for, but may receive a full reward. Everyone who does not abide in the teaching of Christ, but goes beyond it, does not have God; whoever abides in the teaching has both the Father and the Son. Do not receive into the house or welcome anyone who comes to you and does not bring this teaching; for to welcome is to participate in the evil deeds of such a person. (2 John 7-11)

Psalm
Psalm 123
Our eyes look to God

Additional Reading
Job 21:1, 17-34
Poor and rich lie down in the dust

Hymn: Each Winter as the Year Grows Older, ELW 252

Holy God, you so loved this world that you sent your Son to live in the flesh among us. Assure us that as he has come to be fully with us, we shall come to live fully with you.

Wednesday, November 12, 2025
Time after Pentecost

John 5:19-29
The authority of the Son

[Jesus said,] "Very truly, I tell you, the hour is coming, and is now here, when the dead will hear the voice of the Son of God, and those who hear will live. For just as the Father has life in himself, so he has granted the Son also to have life in himself; and he has given him authority to execute judgment, because he is the Son of Man. Do not be astonished at this; for the hour is coming when all who are in their graves will hear his voice and will come out—those who have done good, to the resurrection of life, and those who have done evil, to the resurrection of condemnation." (John 5:25-29)

Psalm
Psalm 123
Our eyes look to God

Additional Reading
Job 25:1—26:14
Even Sheol is naked before God

Hymn: The Day of Resurrection, ACS 936

Resurrecting God, you are the death of death, transforming it into life. Keep us awake so that we may embrace you at your arrival. Let us not be a people of condemnation but of life.

Thursday, November 13, 2025
Time after Pentecost

Psalm 98
God judges the world

Let the sea roar, and all that fills it;
> the world and those who live in it.
Let the floods clap their hands;
> let the hills sing together for joy
at the presence of the LORD, for he is coming
> to judge the earth.
He will judge the world with righteousness,
> and the peoples with equity. (Ps. 98:7-9)

Additional Readings
1 Samuel 28:3-19
Saul warned of God's judgment

Romans 1:18-25
The revealing of God's wrath

Hymn: As Rivers Flow from a Distant Spring, ACS 1046

Inspire us to join all creation in your praise, O God. For this we have been created: to confess your wonders and glorify you forever. Let our song be true.

Friday, November 14, 2025
Time after Pentecost

2 Thessalonians 1:3-12
God's judgment

This is evidence of the righteous judgment of God, and is intended to make you worthy of the kingdom of God, for which you are also suffering. For it is indeed just of God to repay with affliction those who afflict you, and to give relief to the afflicted as well as to us, when the Lord Jesus is revealed from heaven with his mighty angels in flaming fire, inflicting vengeance on those who do not know God and on those who do not obey the gospel of our Lord Jesus. (2 Thess. 1:5-8)

Psalm
Psalm 98
God judges the world

Additional Reading
2 Samuel 21:1-14
Violence comes on Saul's household

Hymn: For the Troubles and the Sufferings, ACS 1051

Lord of all the earth, reveal your righteousness to us, and transform us so that we live in its light. Bring comfort to those who suffer, and transform us who have looked the other way in the face of injustice.

Saturday, November 15, 2025
Time after Pentecost

Luke 17:20-37
The judgment coming

Then [Jesus] said to the disciples, "The days are coming when you will long to see one of the days of the Son of Man, and you will not see it. They will say to you, 'Look there!' or 'Look here!' Do not go, do not set off in pursuit. For as the lightning flashes and lights up the sky from one side to the other, so will the Son of Man be in his day." (Luke 17:22-24)

Psalm
Psalm 98
God judges the world

Additional Reading
Ezekiel 10:1-19
God's glory leaves Jerusalem

Hymn: Wait for the Lord, ELW 262

True and living God, many come in your name, claiming that their deceit is your truth. Grant your people clarity in our discernment, that we might know when it is you who draws near to us with good news.

Sunday, November 16, 2025
Time after Pentecost

Luke 21:5-19
Suffering for Jesus' sake

[Jesus said,] "You will be betrayed even by parents and brothers, by relatives and friends; and they will put some of you to death. You will be hated by all because of my name. But not a hair of your head will perish. By your endurance you will gain your souls." (Luke 21:16-19)

Psalm
Psalm 98
God judges the world

Additional Readings
Malachi 4:1-2a
A day of healing for the righteous

2 Thessalonians 3:6-13
Do what is right

Hymn: Lead Me, Guide Me, ELW 768, TFF 70

O God, the protector of all who trust in you, without you nothing is strong, nothing is holy. Embrace us with your mercy, that with you as our ruler and guide, we may live through what is temporary without losing what is eternal, through Jesus Christ, our Savior and Lord.

Monday, November 17, 2025
Time after Pentecost

Elizabeth of Hungary, renewer of society, died 1231

Psalm 141
God is my refuge

But my eyes are turned toward you, O GOD, my Lord;
　　in you I seek refuge; do not leave me defenseless.
Keep me from the trap that they have laid for me,
　　and from the snares of evildoers.
Let the wicked fall into their own nets,
　　while I alone escape. (Ps. 141:8-10)

Additional Readings

Ezekiel 11:14-25
Judgment and promised restoration

Ephesians 4:25—5:2
Be imitators of God

Hymn: The King of Love My Shepherd Is, ELW 502

Help us, you whose name is Mercy, for traps lie around us and within us: fear, hatred, despair, greed. But you are our safety. With you, we may be led on paths of righteousness for your name's sake.

Tuesday, November 18, 2025
Time after Pentecost

1 Corinthians 10:23—11:1
Do all to the glory of God

So, whether you eat or drink, or whatever you do, do everything for the glory of God. Give no offense to Jews or to Greeks or to the church of God, just as I try to please everyone in everything I do, not seeking my own advantage, but that of many, so that they may be saved. Be imitators of me, as I am of Christ. (1 Cor. 10:31—11:1)

Psalm
Psalm 141
God is my refuge

Additional Reading
Ezekiel 39:21—40:4
Mercy on the house of Israel

Hymn: To Be Your Presence, ELW 546

Compassionate God, you sent your Son to walk among us, revealing the God-shaped life. Conform our lives to Jesus' life, that good news and liberating power might be unleashed for all—those near to us now and those far off.

Wednesday, November 19, 2025
Time after Pentecost

Ezekiel 43:1-12
Divine glory returns to the temple

As for you, mortal, describe the temple to the house of Israel, and let them measure the pattern; and let them be ashamed of their iniquities. When they are ashamed of all that they have done, make known to them the plan of the temple, its arrangement, its exits and its entrances, and its whole form—all its ordinances and its entire plan and all its laws; and write it down in their sight, so that they may observe and follow the entire plan and all its ordinances. This is the law of the temple: the whole territory on the top of the mountain all around shall be most holy. This is the law of the temple. (Ezek. 43:10-12)

Psalm
Psalm 141
God is my refuge

Additional Reading
Matthew 23:37—24:14
The last things

Hymn: You Are Holy, ELW 525

Forgive us, Lord, when we act in shameless ways and do not comprehend our misdeeds. Make us into your holy, whole people, that we might be a witness to your goodness and graciousness.

Thursday, November 20, 2025
Time after Pentecost

Psalm 46
The God of Jacob is our stronghold

There is a river whose streams make glad the city of God,
>   the holy habitation of the Most High.
God is in the midst of the city; it shall not be moved;
>   God will help it when the morning dawns.
The nations are in an uproar, the kingdoms totter;
>   he utters his voice, the earth melts.
The LORD of hosts is with us;
>   the God of Jacob is our refuge. (Ps. 46:4-7)

Additional Readings
2 Chronicles 18:12-22
Sheep without a shepherd

Hebrews 9:23-28
Christ has appeared once for all

Hymn: When Peace like a River, ELW 785, TFF 194

In you, Creator of all, we find a refuge; you restore us to live in your kindness and mercy. Refresh your people with the water of life, that our lives might flow in your currents.

1 Peter 1:3-9

An imperishable inheritance

Blessed be the God and Father of our Lord Jesus Christ! By his great mercy he has given us a new birth into a living hope through the resurrection of Jesus Christ from the dead, and into an inheritance that is imperishable, undefiled, and unfading, kept in heaven for you, who are being protected by the power of God through faith for a salvation ready to be revealed in the last time. In this you rejoice, even if now for a little while you have had to suffer various trials, so that the genuineness of your faith—being more precious than gold that, though perishable, is tested by fire—may be found to result in praise and glory and honor when Jesus Christ is revealed. (1 Peter 1:3-7)

Psalm

Psalm 46
The God of Jacob is our stronghold

Additional Reading

Zechariah 11:1-17
Shepherds who desert the flock

Hymn: Blessed Be the Name, ELW 797

Lord of all hopefulness, you are the midwife who brings us into new birth. In you are all things good and enduring. Let our borning cry be a sign of your deliverance, a cry awakening the world to your trustworthiness.

Saturday, November 22, 2025
Time after Pentecost

Luke 18:15-17
Receiving the kingdom of God

People were bringing even infants to [Jesus] that he might touch them; and when the disciples saw it, they sternly ordered them not to do it. But Jesus called for them and said, "Let the little children come to me, and do not stop them; for it is to such as these that the kingdom of God belongs. Truly I tell you, whoever does not receive the kingdom of God as a little child will never enter it." (Luke 18:15-17)

Psalm
Psalm 46
The God of Jacob is our stronghold

Additional Reading
Jeremiah 22:18-30
The wind shepherds the shepherds

Hymn: God Welcomes All, ACS 978

Welcoming God, you have called us to become like children, trusting your blessing, delighting in your presence. May we run with abandon into your open arms and thus become signs of your kingdom come on earth among us.

Sunday, November 23, 2025
Christ the King

Clement, Bishop of Rome, died around 100
Miguel Agustín Pro, martyr, died 1927

Luke 23:33-43
Jesus crucified with two thieves

When they came to the place that is called The Skull, they crucified Jesus there with the criminals, one on his right and one on his left. [[Then Jesus said, "Father, forgive them; for they do not know what they are doing."]] And they cast lots to divide his clothing. And the people stood by, watching; but the leaders scoffed at him, saying, "He saved others; let him save himself if he is the Messiah of God, his chosen one!" The soldiers also mocked him, coming up and offering him sour wine, and saying, "If you are the King of the Jews, save yourself!" (Luke 23:33-37)

Psalm

Psalm 46
The God of Jacob is our stronghold

Additional Readings

Jeremiah 23:1-6
Coming of the shepherd

Colossians 1:11-20
A hymn to Christ, firstborn of all creation

Hymn: In the Cross of Christ I Glory, ELW 324

O God, our true life, to serve you is freedom, and to know you is unending joy. We worship you, we glorify you, we give thanks to you for your great glory. Abide with us, reign in us, and make this world into a fit habitation for your divine majesty, through Jesus Christ, our Savior and Lord, who lives and reigns with you and the Holy Spirit, one God, now and forever.

Monday, November 24, 2025
Time after Pentecost

Justus Falckner, died 1723; Jehu Jones, died 1852; William Passavant, died 1894; pastors in North America

Psalm 24
The King of glory comes

Lift up your heads, O gates!
> and be lifted up, O ancient doors!
> that the King of glory may come in.

Who is the King of glory?
> The LORD, strong and mighty,
> the LORD, mighty in battle.

Lift up your heads, O gates!
> and be lifted up, O ancient doors!
> that the King of glory may come in.

Who is this King of glory?
> The LORD of hosts,
> he is the King of glory. (Ps. 24:7-10)

Additional Readings

Jeremiah 46:18-28
God will save Israel

Revelation 21:5-27
God reigns in the holy city

Hymn: God Is Here! ELW 526

We know no greater gift than you entering through our gates. Lift up our heads, O God, so that we relish the wide and wonderful mystery of your coming to be with us and for us.

Tuesday, November 25, 2025
Time after Pentecost

Isaac Watts, hymnwriter, died 1748

Revelation 22:8-21

Surely, I am coming soon

"See, I am coming soon; my reward is with me, to repay according to everyone's work. I am the Alpha and the Omega, the first and the last, the beginning and the end."

Blessed are those who wash their robes, so that they will have the right to the tree of life and may enter the city by the gates. (Rev. 22:12-14)

Psalm

Psalm 24
The King of glory comes

Additional Reading

Isaiah 33:17-22
Our God rules

Hymn: Tree of Life and Awesome Mystery, ELW 334

Source of all, our beginning and our final resting place, you hold all of creation in your spacious heart. Warm us with your promise of eternal life. We long for the day when we will see you as you are!

Isaiah 60:8-16

The forsaken become majestic

The descendants of those who oppressed you
>	shall come bending low to you,
and all who despised you
>	shall bow down at your feet;
they shall call you the City of the LORD,
>	the Zion of the Holy One of Israel.
Whereas you have been forsaken and hated,
>	with no one passing through,
I will make you majestic forever,
>	a joy from age to age.
You shall suck the milk of nations,
>	you shall suck the breasts of kings;
and you shall know that I, the LORD, am your Savior
>	and your Redeemer, the Mighty One of Jacob. (Isa. 60:14-16)

Psalm

Psalm 24
The King of glory comes

Additional Reading

Luke 1:1-4
That you may know the truth

Hymn: Canticle of the Turning, ELW 723

Redeemer of the world, we know that your reign of righteousness will come even without our petitions, but we pray today that it might come even to us and that we might be filled with graciousness like yours.

On Thanksgiving Day

Today we practice trusting God's provision like the Israelites in Exodus 16. When they saw a flaky white substance on the ground, they wondered what it was.

Moses said to them, "It is the bread that the Lord has given you to eat. This is what the Lord has commanded: 'Gather as much of it as each of you needs, . . ., all providing for those in their own tents.'" The Israelites did so, some gathering more, some less. But when they measured it with an omer, those who gathered much had nothing over, and those who gathered little had no shortage; they gathered as much as each of them needed. (Exod. 16:15-18)

On the heels of harvest, we give thanks for the labor, land, and seasons that prepare our food. We honor the wild and dormant places, the fruitful and fallow places. We remember that we are stewards of the earth and we are called to care for every living thing. We honor Indigenous peoples, generations past, present, and future, who care for creation with traditional wisdom.

We also acknowledge the ways we have failed to share the gifts of creation and have mistrusted God's promise of enough. We recognize the harm caused by those who colonized Indigenous peoples and forcefully occupied land in the name of God. We who are descendants of settlers confess that we benefit from broken promises and lies about who is valuable and what is enough. God calls us to turn and recognize that all people and all creation are precious in God's sight. In God's abundance there is enough for us all.

Let us pray.
God who provides, your dreams for the world are revealed when communities are fed, promises are kept, and the vulnerable have what they need. May the tables we set in your name honor the fullness of your creation and your wide welcome. May your blessings move freely through us as delight that flows like rivers and waterways, signs of new life. Amen.

Thursday, November 27, 2025
Time after Pentecost

Day of Thanksgiving (USA)

Psalm 122
Gladness in God's house

I was glad when they said to me,
    "Let us go to the house of the LORD!"
Our feet are standing
    within your gates, O Jerusalem.

Jerusalem—built as a city
    that is bound firmly together.
To it the tribes go up,
    the tribes of the LORD,
as was decreed for Israel,
    to give thanks to the name of the LORD.
For there the thrones for judgment were set up,
    the thrones of the house of David. (Ps. 122:1-5)

Additional Readings
Daniel 9:15-19
A plea for forgiveness

James 4:1-10
A plea for God's grace and human humility

Hymn: Now Thank We All Our God, ELW 839, 840

We come before you, giving God, with thankfulness for the dwellings where you shelter us. Teach us to make thriving communities where your presence is witnessed to faithfully. Let our lives ever be a thanksgiving to you.

Friday, November 28, 2025
Time after Pentecost

Hebrews 11:1-7

Noah acts in faith

By faith Abel offered to God a more acceptable sacrifice than Cain's. Through this he received approval as righteous, God himself giving approval to his gifts; he died, but through his faith he still speaks. By faith Enoch was taken so that he did not experience death; and "he was not found, because God had taken him." For it was attested before he was taken away that "he had pleased God." And without faith it is impossible to please God, for whoever would approach him must believe that he exists and that he rewards those who seek him. By faith Noah, warned by God about events as yet unseen, respected the warning and built an ark to save his household; by this he condemned the world and became an heir to the righteousness that is in accordance with faith. (Heb. 11:4-7)

Psalm

Psalm 122
Gladness in God's house

Additional Reading

Genesis 6:1-10
Humankind's wickedness, Noah's righteousness

Hymn: Founded on Faith, ACS 1048

Steadfast God, you come among us and create trust in our hearts. Let our faith move forward with confidence, trusting in your promises, serving in your reign. Let our voices join with those of our ancestors, announcing the gospel.

Saturday, November 29, 2025
Time after Pentecost

Genesis 6:11-22

The command to build an ark: Noah's obedience

Now the earth was corrupt in God's sight, and the earth was filled with violence. And God saw that the earth was corrupt; for all flesh had corrupted its ways upon the earth. And God said to Noah, "I have determined to make an end of all flesh, for the earth is filled with violence because of them; now I am going to destroy them along with the earth....

"But I will establish my covenant with you; and you shall come into the ark, you, your sons, your wife, and your sons' wives with you. And of every living thing, of all flesh, you shall bring two of every kind into the ark, to keep them alive with you; they shall be male and female." (Gen. 6:11-13, 18-19)

Psalm

Psalm 122
Gladness in God's house

Additional Reading

Matthew 24:1-22
The day of the Lord is coming

Hymn: Thy Holy Wings, ELW 613

The call to violence seduces us, Lord, and so the earth is filled with it. Guide us as we treasure signs of salvation so that the world might choose the ever more excellent way of peace.

Advent

In the days of Advent, Christians prepare to celebrate the presence of God's Word among us in our own day. During these four weeks, we pray that the reign of God, which Jesus preached and lived, would come among us. We pray that God's justice would flourish in our land, that the people of the earth would live in peace, and that those who are weak, sick, or hungry would be strengthened, healed, and fed with God's merciful presence.

During the last days of Advent, Christians welcome Christ with names inspired by the prophets: wisdom, liberator of the enslaved, mighty power, radiant dawn and sun of justice, the keystone of the arch of humanity, and Emmanuel—God with us.

The Advent Wreath

One of the best-known customs for the season is the Advent wreath. The wreath and winter candle-lighting in the midst of growing darkness strengthen some of the Advent images found in the Bible. The unbroken circle of greens is an image of everlasting life, a victory wreath, the crown of Christ, or the wheel of time itself. Christians use the wreath as a sign that Christ reaches into our time to lead us to the light of everlasting life. The four candles mark the progress of the four weeks of Advent and our growing expectation. Sometimes the wreath is embellished with natural dried flowers or fruit. Its evergreen branches lead the household and the congregation to the evergreen Christmas tree. In many homes, the family gathers for prayer around the wreath.

An Evening Service of Candlelight for Advent

This brief order may be used on any evening during the season of Advent. If the household has an Advent wreath (one candle for each of the four weeks of Advent), it may be lighted during this service. Alternatively, one simple candle (perhaps a votive candle) may be lighted instead.

Lighting the Advent Wreath

May this candle/these candles be a sign of the coming of Christ, our morning star.

One or more candles may be lighted.

Use this blessing when lighting the first candle.

Blessed are you, God of Jacob, for you promise to transform weapons of war into implements of planting and harvest and to teach us your way of peace; you promise that our night of sin is far gone and that your day of salvation is dawning.

As we light the first candle on this wreath, wake us from our sleep, wrap us in your warmth, empower us to live honorably, and guide us along your path of peace.

O house of Jacob, come,
let us walk in the light of the Lord. Amen.

Blessings for the second, third, and fourth weeks of Advent are provided on pages 377, 385, and 393, respectively.

Reading

Read one or more of the scripture passages appointed for the day in the dated pages that follow.

Hymn

One of the following, or the hymn suggested for the day, may be sung.

Light One Candle to Watch for Messiah, ELW 240
Come Now, O Prince of Peace/*Ososŏ, ososŏ*, ELW 247
People, Look East, ELW 248
My Soul Proclaims Your Greatness, ELW 251

During the final seven days of the Advent season (beginning on December 17), the hymn "O Come, O Come, Emmanuel" (ELW 257) is particularly appropriate. The stanzas of that hymn are also referred to as the "O Antiphons." The first stanza of the hymn could be sung each day during the final days before Christmas in addition to the stanza that is specifically appointed for the day.

First stanza

O come, O come, Emmanuel,
and ransom captive Israel,
that mourns in lonely exile here
until the Son of God appear.
Refrain   Rejoice! Rejoice! Emmanuel shall come to you, O Israel.

December 17

O come, O Wisdom from on high,
embracing all things far and nigh:
in strength and beauty come and stay;
teach us your will and guide our way.   *Refrain*

December 18

O come, O come, O Lord of might,
as to your tribes on Sinai's height
in ancient times you gave the law
in cloud, and majesty, and awe.   *Refrain*

December 19

O come, O Branch of Jesse, free
your own from Satan's tyranny;
from depths of hell your people save,
and give them vict'ry o'er the grave.   *Refrain*

December 20

O come, O Key of David, come,
and open wide our heav'nly home;
make safe the way that leads on high,
and close the path to misery.   *Refrain*

December 21

O come, O Dayspring, come and cheer;
O Sun of justice, now draw near.
Disperse the gloomy clouds of night,
and death's dark shadow put to flight.   *Refrain*

December 22

O come, O King of nations, come,
O Cornerstone that binds in one:
refresh the hearts that long for you;
restore the broken, make us new.   *Refrain*

December 23

O come, O come, Emmanuel,
and ransom captive Israel,
that mourns in lonely exile here
until the Son of God appear.   *Refrain*

Text: *Psalteriolum Cantionum Catholicarum*, Köln, 1710; tr. composite
Text sts. 2, 6, 7 © 1997 Augsburg Fortress

Table Prayer for Advent

For use when a meal follows.

Blessed are you, O Lord our God,
the one who is, who was, and who is to come.
At this table you fill us with good things.
May these gifts strengthen us
to share with the hungry and all those in need,
as we wait and watch for your coming among us
in Jesus Christ our Lord. Amen.

Candles may be extinguished now or after the meal, if one is to follow.

Sunday, November 30, 2025
First Sunday of Advent

Andrew, Apostle (Transferred to December 1)

Matthew 24:36-44
The sudden coming of salvation

[Jesus said,] "But about that day and hour no one knows, neither the angels of heaven, nor the Son, but only the Father. For as the days of Noah were, so will be the coming of the Son of Man. For as in those days before the flood they were eating and drinking, marrying and giving in marriage, until the day Noah entered the ark, and they knew nothing until the flood came and swept them all away, so too will be the coming of the Son of Man." (Matt. 24:36-39)

Psalm

Psalm 122
Gladness in God's house

Additional Readings

Isaiah 2:1-5
War transformed into peace

Romans 13:11-14
Salvation is near; wake from sleep

Hymn: Come Now, O God, ACS 902

Stir up your power, Lord Christ, and come. By your merciful protection save us from the threatening dangers of our sins, and enlighten our walk in the way of your salvation, for you live and reign with the Father and the Holy Spirit, one God, now and forever.

Prayer List for December

_____

_____

_____

_____

_____

_____

_____

_____

_____

_____

Monday, December 1, 2025
Andrew, Apostle (Transferred)

John 1:35-42
Jesus calls Andrew

One of the two who heard John speak and followed him was Andrew, Simon Peter's brother. He first found his brother Simon and said to him, "We have found the Messiah" (which is translated Anointed). He brought Simon to Jesus, who looked at him and said, "You are Simon son of John. You are to be called Cephas" (which is translated Peter). (John 1:40-42)

Psalm

Psalm 19:1-6
The heavens declare God's glory

Additional Readings

Ezekiel 3:16-21
A sentinel for the house of Israel

Romans 10:10-18
Faith comes from the word of Christ

Hymn: Will You Come and Follow Me, ELW 798

Almighty God, you gave your apostle Andrew the grace to obey the call of your Son and to bring his brother to Jesus. Give us also, who are called by your holy word, grace to follow Jesus without delay and to bring into his presence those who are near to us, for he lives and reigns with you and the Holy Spirit, one God, now and forever.

Tuesday, December 2, 2025
Week of Advent 1

Psalm 124
We have escaped like a bird

Blessed be the LORD,
>who has not given us
>as prey to their teeth.

We have escaped like a bird
>from the snare of the fowlers;

the snare is broken,
>and we have escaped.

Our help is in the name of the LORD,
>who made heaven and earth. (Ps. 124:6-8)

Additional Readings

Genesis 9:1-17
Command to be fruitful; sign of the rainbow

Hebrews 11:32-40
The heroes of faith

Hymn: Come to Be Our Hope, O Jesus, ACS 904

Blessed are you O God. You accompany your people and protect your creation in every age. Deepen our faith in your eternal covenant and reveal signs of your everlasting mercy, that we may rest in the knowledge of your love.

Wednesday, December 3, 2025
Week of Advent 1

Francis Xavier, missionary to Asia, died 1552

Isaiah 54:1-10
God will save the people

Sing, O barren one who did not bear;
>   burst into song and shout, you who have not been in labor!
For the children of the desolate woman will be more
>   than the children of her that is married, says the Lord.
Enlarge the site of your tent,
>   and let the curtains of your habitations be stretched out;
do not hold back; lengthen your cords
>   and strengthen your stakes.
For you will spread out to the right and to the left,
>   and your descendants will possess the nations
>   and will settle the desolate towns.

Do not fear, for you will not be ashamed;
>   do not be discouraged, for you will not suffer disgrace; . . .
the Holy One of Israel is your Redeemer,
>   the God of the whole earth he is called. (Isa. 54:1-5)

Psalm
Psalm 124
We have escaped like a bird

Additional Reading
Matthew 24:23-35
The end is coming

Hymn: Baptized and Set Free, ELW 453

Holy One, heaven and earth will pass away, but your word endures forever. Fulfill your promise to redeem your people, that, freed from shame and fear, we may offer our lives to you and to our neighbor.

Thursday, December 4, 2025
Week of Advent 1

John of Damascus, theologian and hymnwriter, died around 749

Psalm 72:1-7, 18-19
The righteous shall flourish

Give the king your justice, O God,
    and your righteousness to a king's son.
May he judge your people with righteousness,
    and your poor with justice.
May the mountains yield prosperity for the people,
    and the hills, in righteousness.
May he defend the cause of the poor of the people,
        give deliverance to the needy,
        and crush the oppressor. (Ps. 72:1-4)

Additional Readings
Isaiah 4:2-6
God's promised glory for the survivors in Zion

Acts 1:12-17, 21-26
Beginnings of the apostolic ministry

Hymn: When the Poor Ones, ELW 725

O God, you command us to defend the poor and deliver the needy. Anoint us and send us into the world as apostles of mercy and justice. Make your church a shade, a refuge, and a shelter for all people.

Friday, December 5, 2025
Week of Advent 1

Isaiah 30:19-26
God's promise to be gracious to Zion

Truly, O people in Zion, inhabitants of Jerusalem, you shall weep no more. He will surely be gracious to you at the sound of your cry; when he hears it, he will answer you. Though the Lord may give you the bread of adversity and the water of affliction, yet your Teacher will not hide himself any more, but your eyes shall see your Teacher. And when you turn to the right or when you turn to the left, your ears shall hear a word behind you, saying, "This is the way; walk in it." (Isa. 30:19-21)

Psalm
Psalm 72:1-7, 18-19
The righteous shall flourish

Additional Reading
Acts 13:16-25
Paul's testimony concerning John the Baptist

Hymn: O Christ, Your Heart, Compassionate, ELW 722

God of our weary years, God of our silent tears, you have promised that we shall see you and weep no more. Grant us the grace to hear your words and walk in your ways.

Saturday, December 6, 2025
Week of Advent 1

Nicholas, Bishop of Myra, died around 342

Isaiah 40:1-11
A voice crying in the wilderness

A voice cries out:
"In the wilderness prepare the way of the LORD,
    make straight in the desert a highway for our God.
Every valley shall be lifted up,
    and every mountain and hill be made low;
the uneven ground shall become level,
    and the rough places a plain.
Then the glory of the LORD shall be revealed,
    and all people shall see it together,
    for the mouth of the LORD has spoken." (Isa. 40:3-5)

Psalm
Psalm 72:1-7, 18-19
The righteous shall flourish

Additional Reading
John 1:19-28
John the Baptist concerning his own ministry

Hymn: Hark, the Glad Sound! ELW 239

Comforting God, your voice echoes through the wilderness of the world, calling us to prepare the way for your Beloved. May your Spirit level the uneven ground of our hearts as we receive Jesus Christ, our Savior.

Lighting the Advent Wreath

Use this blessing when lighting the first two candles.

Blessed are you, God of hope, for you promise to bring forth a shoot from the stump of Jesse who will bring justice to the poor, who will deliver the needy and crush the oppressor, who will stand as a signal of hope for all people.

As we light these candles, turn our wills to bear the fruit of repentance, transform our hearts to live in justice and harmony with one another, and fix our eyes on the root of Jesse, Jesus Christ, the hope of all nations.

O people of hope, come,
let us rejoice in the faithfulness of the Lord. Amen.

Sunday, December 7, 2025
Second Sunday of Advent

Ambrose, Bishop of Milan, died 397

Matthew 3:1-12

Prepare the way of the Lord

In those days John the Baptist appeared in the wilderness of Judea, proclaiming, "Repent, for the kingdom of heaven has come near." This is the one of whom the prophet Isaiah spoke when he said,

"The voice of one crying out in the wilderness:

'Prepare the way of the Lord,

make his paths straight.'" (Matt. 3:1-3)

Psalm
Psalm 72:1-7, 18-19
The righteous shall flourish

Additional Readings
Isaiah 11:1-10
A ruler brings justice and peace

Romans 15:4-13
Living in harmony

Hymn: There's a Voice in the Wilderness, ELW 255

Stir up our hearts, Lord God, to prepare the way of your only Son. By his coming nurture our growth as people of repentance and peace; through Jesus Christ, our Savior and Lord, who lives and reigns with you and the Holy Spirit, one God, now and forever.

Monday, December 8, 2025
Week of Advent 2

Psalm 21
God comes with judgment and strength

In your strength the king rejoices, O LORD,
> and in your help how greatly he exults!

For the king trusts in the LORD,
> and through the steadfast love of the Most High he shall not be
> moved.

Your hand will find out all your enemies;
> your right hand will find out those who hate you. (Ps. 21:1, 7-8)

Additional Readings
Isaiah 24:1-16a
Judgment is coming, but glorify God

1 Thessalonians 4:1-12
Live in holiness and love one another

Hymn: Jesu, Jesu, Fill Us with Your Love, ELW 708, TFF 83

Holy God, you command us to love our neighbor. Let the heart of Christ beat in our own hearts, and may the mind of Christ guide our lives toward loving and serving every person and every being.

Tuesday, December 9, 2025
Week of Advent 2

Romans 15:14-21
Gentiles are also called to the obedience of faith

I myself feel confident about you, my brothers and sisters, that you yourselves are full of goodness, filled with all knowledge, and able to instruct one another. Nevertheless on some points I have written to you rather boldly by way of reminder, because of the grace given me by God to be a minister of Christ Jesus to the Gentiles in the priestly service of the gospel of God, so that the offering of the Gentiles may be acceptable, sanctified by the Holy Spirit. (Rom. 15:14-16)

Psalm
Psalm 21
God comes with judgment and strength

Additional Reading
Isaiah 41:14-20
God will not forget the poor of Israel

Hymn: Freedom Is Coming, ACS 903, TFF 46

God of abundant grace, draw us to you. Teach us your ways. Fill us with the power of your Holy Spirit, that proclaiming your good news in words and deeds, we become signs of your presence in the world.

Wednesday, December 10, 2025
Week of Advent 2

Genesis 15:1-18
God's covenant with Abram

As the sun was going down, a deep sleep fell upon Abram, and a deep and terrifying darkness descended upon him. Then the LORD said to Abram, "Know this for certain, that your offspring shall be aliens in a land that is not theirs, and shall be slaves there, and they shall be oppressed for four hundred years; but I will bring judgment on the nation that they serve, and afterward they shall come out with great possessions. As for yourself, you shall go to your ancestors in peace; you shall be buried in a good old age. And they shall come back here in the fourth generation; for the iniquity of the Amorites is not yet complete." (Gen. 15:12-16)

Psalm
Psalm 21
God comes with judgment and strength

Additional Reading
Matthew 12:33-37
A good tree bears good fruit

Hymn: Come to Me, O Weary Traveler, ACS 1017

Gracious God, you call us out of exile. Empower us to welcome one another as Christ welcomes us, especially immigrants, refugees, and asylum seekers, that they find welcome, healing, and belonging, through Jesus Christ, our one true home.

Thursday, December 11, 2022
Week of Advent 2

Psalm 146:5-10
God lifts up those bowed down

Happy are those whose help is the God of Jacob,
> whose hope is in the LORD their God,
who made heaven and earth,
> the sea, and all that is in them;
who keeps faith forever;
> who executes justice for the oppressed;
> who gives food to the hungry.

The LORD sets the prisoners free;
> the LORD opens the eyes of the blind.
The LORD lifts up those who are bowed down;
> the LORD loves the righteous.
The LORD watches over the strangers;
> he upholds the orphan and the widow,
> but the way of the wicked he brings to ruin. (Ps. 146:5-9)

Additional Readings
Ruth 1:6-18
Ruth's fidelity toward Naomi and her people

2 Peter 3:1-10
The promise of the Lord's coming

Hymn: Praise the Almighty! ELW 877

Sovereign God, we praise you for your magnificent creation and place all our hope in the power of your salvation. Send your Spirit upon your whole church, that we may enact your justice, share your abundance, and welcome strangers home.

Friday, December 12, 2025
Week of Advent 2

2 Peter 3:11-18
Prepare for the Lord's coming

Therefore, beloved, while you are waiting for these things, strive to be found by [God] at peace, without spot or blemish; and regard the patience of our Lord as salvation. So also our beloved brother Paul wrote to you according to the wisdom given him, speaking of this as he does in all his letters. There are some things in them hard to understand, which the ignorant and unstable twist to their own destruction, as they do the other scriptures. You therefore, beloved, since you are forewarned, beware that you are not carried away with the error of the lawless and lose your own stability. But grow in the grace and knowledge of our Lord and Savior Jesus Christ. To him be the glory both now and to the day of eternity. Amen. (2 Peter 3:14-18)

Psalm
Psalm 146:5-10
God lifts up those bowed down

Additional Reading
Ruth 4:13-17
God's fidelity toward Ruth and her posterity

Hymn: In Deepest Night, ELW 699

God of wisdom, you grant understanding to those who seek you and reveal hidden things to those who love you. By your Spirit, enlighten our bodies, minds, and hearts, that we may know you and serve you.

Saturday, December 13, 2025
Week of Advent 2

Lucy, martyr, died 304

1 Samuel 2:1-8
Hannah sings in praise of God's fidelity

Hannah prayed and said,
"My heart exults in the Lord;
    my strength is exalted in my God.
My mouth derides my enemies,
    because I rejoice in my victory.

"There is no Holy One like the Lord,
    no one besides you;
    there is no Rock like our God.

"He raises up the poor from the dust;
    he lifts the needy from the ash heap,
to make them sit with princes
    and inherit a seat of honor.
For the pillars of the earth are the Lord's,
    and on them he has set the world." (1 Sam. 2:1-2, 8)

Psalm
Psalm 146:5-10
God lifts up those bowed down

Additional Reading
Luke 3:1-18
The proclamation of John the Baptist

Hymn: Filled with Hope and Gratitude, ACS 907

Holy God, our hearts exult in your great mercy and mighty love. Lead us by your Spirit to prepare the way and clear the path for all people to experience your salvation and rejoice in your redemption.

Lighting the Advent Wreath

Use this blessing when lighting the first three candles.

Blessed are you, God of might and majesty, for you promise to make the desert rejoice and blossom, to watch over strangers, and to set prisoners free.

As we light these candles, satisfy our hunger with your good gifts, open our eyes to the great things you have done for us, and fill us with patience until the coming of the Lord Jesus.

O ransomed people of the Lord, come,
let us travel on God's holy way
and enter into Zion with singing. Amen.

Sunday, December 14, 2025
Third Sunday of Advent

John of the Cross, renewer of the church, died 1591

Matthew 11:2-11
The forerunner of Christ

Jesus began to speak to the crowds about John: "What did you go out into the wilderness to look at? A reed shaken by the wind? What then did you go out to see? Someone dressed in soft robes? Look, those who wear soft robes are in royal palaces. What then did you go out to see? A prophet? Yes, I tell you, and more than a prophet. This is the one about whom it is written,

    'See, I am sending my messenger ahead of you,

        who will prepare your way before you.'

Truly I tell you, among those born of women no one has arisen greater than John the Baptist; yet the least in the kingdom of heaven is greater than he." (Matt. 11:7b-11)

Psalm
Psalm 146:5-10
God lifts up those bowed down

Additional Readings
Isaiah 35:1-10
The desert blooms

James 5:7-10
Patience until the Lord's coming

Hymn: Prepare the Royal Highway, ELW 264

Stir up the wills of all who look to you, Lord God, and strengthen our faith in your coming, that, transformed by grace, we may walk in your way; through Jesus Christ, our Savior and Lord, who lives and reigns with you and the Holy Spirit, one God, now and forever.

Monday, December 15, 2025
Week of Advent 3

Psalm 42
Hope in God

I say to God, my rock,
    "Why have you forgotten me?
Why must I walk about mournfully
    because the enemy oppresses me?"
As with a deadly wound in my body,
    my adversaries taunt me,
while they say to me continually,
    "Where is your God?"

Why are you cast down, O my soul,
    and why are you disquieted within me?
Hope in God; for I shall again praise him,
    my help and my God. (Ps. 42:9-11)

Additional Readings

Isaiah 29:17-24
The infirm will be healed

Acts 5:12-16
Many people healed by the apostles

Hymn: Comfort, Comfort Now My People, ELW 256

Consoling God, you are always here and always near, closer to us than we are to ourselves. Reveal your presence in our midst, especially when we are fearful, despondent, or grieving, that we may find healing and comfort in you.

Jude 17-25

Prepare for the Lord's coming

Now to him who is able to keep you from falling, and to make you stand without blemish in the presence of his glory with rejoicing, to the only God our Saviour, through Jesus Christ our Lord, be glory, majesty, power, and authority, before all time and now and for ever. Amen. (Jude 24-25)

Psalm

Psalm 42
Hope in God

Additional Reading

Ezekiel 47:1-12
The wilderness will flower

Hymn: All Earth Is Hopeful, ELW 266, TFF 47

God of mercy, fill us with your Holy Spirit, that rooted in faith and grounded in love, we may till and water the soil of your kin-dom until it blooms and flowers amid the wilderness of the world.

Wednesday, December 17, 2025
Week of Advent 3

Zechariah 8:1-17
God's promise to Zion

For thus says the LORD of hosts: Just as I purposed to bring disaster upon you, when your ancestors provoked me to wrath, and I did not relent, says the LORD of hosts, so again I have purposed in these days to do good to Jerusalem and to the house of Judah; do not be afraid. These are the things that you shall do: Speak the truth to one another, render in your gates judgments that are true and make for peace, do not devise evil in your hearts against one another, and love no false oath; for all these are things that I hate, says the LORD. (Zech. 8:14-17)

Psalm
Psalm 42
Hope in God

Additional Reading
Matthew 8:14-17, 28-34
Jesus heals

Hymn: Goodness Is Stronger Than Evil, ELW 721

Faithful God, you renew us each day with your abundant goodness. Remove every evil from our hearts. Let your Holy Spirit bear the fruits of healing, peace, and justice in our lives, for the sake of this world you love.

Thursday, December 18, 2025
Week of Advent 3

Psalm 80:1-7, 17-19
Show the light of your countenance

O Lᴏʀᴅ God of hosts,
> how long will you be angry with your people's prayers?

You have fed them with the bread of tears,
> and given them tears to drink in full measure.

You make us the scorn of our neighbors;
> our enemies laugh among themselves.

Restore us, O God of hosts;
> let your face shine, that we may be saved. (Ps. 80:4-7)

Additional Readings

2 Samuel 7:1-17
God will build you a house

Galatians 3:23-29
Children of God by Christ's coming

Hymn: All Are Welcome, ELW 641

Mothering God, we praise you for birthing us anew with the gift of faith in baptism. Call us back when our hearts go astray, and let the light of your face guide us in every step of the way.

Friday, December 19, 2025
Week of Advent 3

2 Samuel 7:18-22

David prays for God's faithfulness toward Israel

Then King David went in and sat before the LORD, and said, "Who am I, O Lord GOD, and what is my house, that you have brought me thus far? And yet this was a small thing in your eyes, O Lord GOD; you have spoken also of your servant's house for a great while to come. May this be instruction for the people, O Lord GOD! And what more can David say to you? For you know your servant, O Lord GOD! Because of your promise, and according to your own heart, you have wrought all this greatness, so that your servant may know it. Therefore you are great, O LORD God; for there is no one like you, and there is no God besides you, according to all that we have heard with our ears." (2 Sam. 7:18-22)

Psalm

Psalm 80:1-7, 17-19
Show the light of your countenance

Additional Reading

Galatians 4:1-7
God's Son, sent in the fullness of time

Hymn: Blessed Be the God of Israel, ELW 250

Liberating God, you sent your Son to release the captives and liberate the oppressed. Set us free from all idolatry, that surrendering our lives to your grace, we may serve you for the life and liberation of the world.

Saturday, December 20, 2025
Week of Advent 3

Katharina von Bora Luther, renewer of the church, died 1552

John 3:31-36
The one who comes from above

The one who comes from above is above all; the one who is of the earth belongs to the earth and speaks about earthly things. The one who comes from heaven is above all. He testifies to what he has seen and heard, yet no one accepts his testimony. Whoever has accepted his testimony has certified this, that God is true. He whom God has sent speaks the words of God, for he gives the Spirit without measure. The Father loves the Son and has placed all things in his hands. Whoever believes in the Son has eternal life; whoever disobeys the Son will not see life, but must endure God's wrath. (John 3:31-36)

Psalm
Psalm 80:1-7, 17-19
Show the light of your countenance

Additional Reading
2 Samuel 7:23-29
David reminds God of God's promise

Hymn: O God, Whose Word Well-Planted, ACS 975

Living God, you send witnesses to reveal your promises and testify to your faithfulness. Speak to us through your Spirit, let your word take root in our hearts, and raise prophets to proclaim your truth in our midst.

Lighting the Advent Wreath

Use this blessing when lighting all four candles.

Blessed are you, God of hosts, for you promised to send a son, Emmanuel, who brought your presence among us; and you promise through your Son Jesus to save us from our sin.

As we light these candles, turn again to us in mercy; strengthen our faith in the word spoken by your prophets; restore us and give us life that we may be saved.

O house of David, come,
**let us rejoice, for the Son of God, Emmanuel,
comes to be with us. Amen.**

Sunday, December 21, 2025
Fourth Sunday of Advent

Matthew 1:18-25
Our God near at hand

An angel of the Lord appeared to [Joseph] in a dream and said, "Joseph, son of David, do not be afraid to take Mary as your wife, for the child conceived in her is from the Holy Spirit. She will bear a son, and you are to name him Jesus, for he will save his people from their sins." All this took place to fulfill what had been spoken by the Lord through the prophet:

"Look, the virgin shall conceive and bear a son,
and they shall name him Emmanuel,"
which means, "God is with us." (Matt. 1:20b-23)

Psalm
Psalm 80:1-7, 17-19
Show the light of your countenance

Additional Readings
Isaiah 7:10-16
The sign of Immanuel

Romans 1:1-7
Paul's greeting to the church at Rome

Hymn: Come Now, O God, ACS 902

Stir up your power, Lord Christ, and come. With your abundant grace and might, free us from the sin that hinders our faith, that eagerly we may receive your promises, for you live and reign with the Father and the Holy Spirit, one God, now and forever.

Monday, December 22, 2025
Week of Advent 4

1 Samuel 2:1-10
Hannah's song

Hannah prayed and said,

> "My heart exults in the LORD;
> my strength is exalted in my God.
> My mouth derides my enemies,
> because I rejoice in my victory.

> "There is no Holy One like the LORD,
> no one besides you;
> there is no Rock like our God.
> Talk no more so very proudly,
> let not arrogance come from your mouth;
> for the LORD is a God of knowledge,
> and by him actions are weighed.
> The bows of the mighty are broken,
> but the feeble gird on strength." (1 Sam. 2:1-4)

Additional Readings

Genesis 17:15-22
God promises Sarah a son

Galatians 4:8-20
Paul's labor for the Galatian church

Hymn: O Day of Peace, ELW 587/711

Almighty God, strengthen our hearts through your Holy Spirit, that in our dying and rising each day, we may reveal your joyful victory over injustice, sin, and death, laboring for your kin-dom in all the world.

Tuesday, December 23, 2025
Week of Advent 4

Genesis 21:1-21

God saves Hagar and Ishmael

Sarah saw the son of Hagar the Egyptian, whom she had borne to Abraham, playing with her son Isaac. So she said to Abraham, "Cast out this slave woman with her son; for the son of this slave woman shall not inherit along with my son Isaac." The matter was very distressing to Abraham on account of his son. But God said to Abraham, "Do not be distressed because of the boy and because of your slave woman; whatever Sarah says to you, do as she tells you, for it is through Isaac that offspring shall be named for you. As for the son of the slave woman, I will make a nation of him also, because he is your offspring." (Gen. 21:9-13)

Psalm
1 Samuel 2:1-10
Hannah's song

Additional Reading
Galatians 4:21—5:1
Two women, two covenants, one freedom

Hymn: There's a Wideness in God's Mercy, ELW 587/588

Loving God, you raise up the poor from the dust and lift the needy from the ash heap. Comfort the outcast and widen the welcome of your church, that all people may find home in Christ's arms.

Christmas

During the Christmas season we celebrate Christ's coming in the flesh to sojourn among us. Each family and community marks this event in ways steeped in tradition. We adorn our homes, give one another gifts, and sing familiar carols. We meditate on the mystery of the incarnation as we look into the eyes of babies who have been born among us.

We do this at a time of year in the northern hemisphere when the days are shortest and the nights are longest. The darkness of this time is like that of a womb delivering us into new life. In the silence of these long nights, flames of hope come to light.

In the Christian church we celebrate the birth of Christ not only on Christmas Day, but for a season of twelve days. Christmas culminates with the Day of Epiphany on January 6. Through the Christmas season we remember the One born among us who has come to draw the whole world to God.

Table Prayer for the Twelve Days of Christmas

O God, with joy we celebrate the birth of your Son.
Born of Mary, he came to live among us
and is with us now at this table.
May Christ also be born in us,
that we might bear his love to all the world
and offer each other grace upon grace.
In Jesus' name we pray.
Amen.

Lighting the Christmas Tree

Use this prayer when you first illumine the tree or when you gather at the tree.

Holy God,
we praise you as we light this tree.
It casts beauty and warmth in this place
just as you illuminate our lives through Jesus,
the light of the world.

God of all,
we thank you for your love,
the love that has come to us in Jesus.
Be with us now as we remember that gift of love,
and help us to share that love with a yearning world.

Creator God,
you made the stars in the heavens.
Thank you for the hope that shines on us in Jesus,
the bright morning star.
Amen.

Blessing of the Nativity Scene

This blessing may be used when figures are added to the nativity scene and throughout the days of Christmas.

Bless us, O God, as we remember Jesus' birth. With each angel and shepherd we place here before you, show us the wonder found in a stable. In song and prayer, silence and awe, we adore your gift of love, Christ Jesus our Savior.
Amen.

Wednesday, December 24, 2025
Nativity of Our Lord
Christmas Eve

Luke 2:1-14 [15-20]
God with us

But the angel said to [the shepherds], "Do not be afraid; for see—I am bringing you good news of great joy for all the people: to you is born this day in the city of David a Savior, who is the Messiah, the Lord. This will be a sign for you: you will find a child wrapped in bands of cloth and lying in a manger." And suddenly there was with the angel a multitude of the heavenly host, praising God and saying,

"Glory to God in the highest heaven,
and on earth peace among those whom he favors!"
(Luke 2:10-14)

Psalm

Psalm 96
Let the earth be glad

Additional Readings

Isaiah 9:2-7
A child is born for us

Titus 2:11-14
The grace of God has appeared

Hymn: O Come, All Ye Faithful, ELW 283

Almighty God, you made this holy night shine with the brightness of the true Light. Grant that here on earth we may walk in the light of Jesus' presence and in the last day wake to the brightness of his glory; through your Son, Jesus Christ our Lord, who lives and reigns with you and the Holy Spirit, one God, now and forever.

Thursday, December 25, 2025
Nativity of Our Lord
Christmas Day

John 1:1-14
The Word became flesh

In the beginning was the Word, and the Word was with God, and the Word was God. He was in the beginning with God. All things came into being through him, and without him not one thing came into being. What has come into being in him was life, and the life was the light of all people. The light shines in the darkness, and the darkness did not overcome it. . . .

And the Word became flesh and lived among us, and we have seen his glory, the glory as of a father's only son, full of grace and truth. (John 1:1-5, 14)

Psalm
Psalm 98
The victory of our God

Additional Readings
Isaiah 52:7-10
Heralds announce God's salvation

Hebrews 1:1-4 [5-12]
God has spoken by a son

Hymn: The Word Who Sang the Light into Creation, ACS 973

Almighty God, you gave us your only Son to take on our human nature and to illumine the world with your light. By your grace adopt us as your children and enlighten us with your Spirit, through Jesus Christ, our Redeemer and Lord, who lives and reigns with you and the Holy Spirit, one God, now and forever.

Friday, December 26, 2025
Stephen, Deacon and Martyr

Matthew 23:34-39
Jesus laments that Jerusalem kills her prophets

[Jesus said,] "Therefore I send you prophets, sages, and scribes, some of whom you will kill and crucify, and some you will flog in your synagogues and pursue from town to town, so that upon you may come all the righteous blood shed on earth, from the blood of righteous Abel to the blood of Zechariah son of Barachiah, whom you murdered between the sanctuary and the altar. Truly I tell you, all this will come upon this generation.

"Jerusalem, Jerusalem, the city that kills the prophets and stones those who are sent to it! How often have I desired to gather your children together as a hen gathers her brood under her wings, and you were not willing! See, your house is left to you, desolate. For I tell you, you will not see me again until you say, 'Blessed is the one who comes in the name of the Lord.'" (Matt. 23:34-39)

Psalm
Psalm 17:1-9, 15
I call upon you, O God

Additional Readings
2 Chronicles 24:17-22
Zechariah is stoned to death

Acts 6:8—7:2a, 51-60
Stephen is stoned to death

Hymn: Give Thanks for Saints, ELW 428

We give you thanks, O Lord of glory, for the example of Stephen, the first martyr, who looked to heaven and prayed for his persecutors. Grant that we also may pray for our enemies and seek forgiveness for those who hurt us, through Jesus Christ, our Savior and Lord, who lives and reigns with you and the Holy Spirit, one God, now and forever.

Saturday, December 27, 2025
John, Apostle and Evangelist

John 21:20-25
The beloved disciple remains with Jesus

Peter turned and saw the disciple whom Jesus loved following them; he was the one who had reclined next to Jesus at the supper and had said, "Lord, who is it that is going to betray you?" When Peter saw him, he said to Jesus, "Lord, what about him?" Jesus said to him, "If it is my will that he remain until I come, what is that to you? Follow me!" So the rumor spread in the community that this disciple would not die. Yet Jesus did not say to him that he would not die, but, "If it is my will that he remain until I come, what is that to you?"

This is the disciple who is testifying to these things and has written them, and we know that his testimony is true. But there are also many other things that Jesus did; if every one of them were written down, I suppose that the world itself could not contain the books that would be written. (John 21:20-25)

Psalm

Psalm 116:12-19
The death of faithful servants

Additional Readings

Genesis 1:1-5, 26-31
Humankind is created by God

1 John 1:1—2:2
Jesus, the word of life

Hymn: By All Your Saints, ELW 420, st. 1, 5, and Last

Merciful God, through John the apostle and evangelist you have revealed the mysteries of your Word made flesh. Let the brightness of your light shine on your church, so that all your people, instructed in the holy gospel, may walk in the light of your truth and attain eternal life, through Jesus Christ, our Savior and Lord, who lives and reigns with you and the Holy Spirit, one God, now and forever.

Sunday, December 28, 2025
First Sunday of Christmas

The Holy Innocents, Martyrs (Transferred to December 29)

Isaiah 63:7-9

Israel saved by God's own presence

I will recount the gracious deeds of the LORD,
    the praiseworthy acts of the LORD,
because of all that the LORD has done for us,
    and the great favor to the house of Israel
that he has shown them according to his mercy,
    according to the abundance of his steadfast love.
For he said, "Surely they are my people,
    children who will not deal falsely";
and he became their savior
    in all their distress.
It was no messenger or angel
    but his presence that saved them;
in his love and in his pity he redeemed them;
    he lifted them up and carried them all the days of old. (Isa. 63:7-9)

Psalm

Psalm 148
God's splendor is over earth and heaven

Additional Readings

Hebrews 2:10-18
Christ frees humankind

Matthew 2:13-23
Herod kills innocent children

Hymn: A Stable Lamp Is Lighted, ACS 910

O Lord God, you know that we cannot place our trust in our own powers. As you protected the infant Jesus, so defend us and all the needy from harm and adversity, through Jesus Christ, our Savior and Lord, who lives and reigns with you and the Holy Spirit, one God, now and forever.

Monday, December 29, 2025
The Holy Innocents, Martyrs (Transferred)

1 Peter 4:12-19
Continue to do good while suffering

Beloved, do not be surprised at the fiery ordeal that is taking place among you to test you, as though something strange were happening to you. But rejoice insofar as you are sharing Christ's sufferings, so that you may also be glad and shout for joy when his glory is revealed. If you are reviled for the name of Christ, you are blessed, because the spirit of glory, which is the Spirit of God, is resting on you. (1 Peter 4:12-14)

Psalm
Psalm 124
We have escaped like a bird

Additional Readings
Jeremiah 31:15-17
Rachel weeps for her children

Matthew 2:13-18
Herod kills innocent children

Hymn: How Long, O God, ELW 698

We remember today, O God, the slaughter of the innocent children of Bethlehem by order of King Herod. Receive into the arms of your mercy all innocent victims. By your great might frustrate the designs of evil tyrants and establish your rule of justice, love, and peace, through Jesus Christ, our Savior and Lord, who lives and reigns with you and the Holy Spirit, one God, now and forever.

Tuesday, December 30, 2025
Sixth Day of Christmas

2 Corinthians 4:16-18
The temporary and the eternal

So we do not lose heart. Even though our outer nature is wasting away, our inner nature is being renewed day by day. For this slight momentary affliction is preparing us for an eternal weight of glory beyond all measure, because we look not at what can be seen but at what cannot be seen; for what can be seen is temporary, but what cannot be seen is eternal. (2 Cor. 4:16-18)

Psalm
Psalm 20
Answer us when we call

Additional Reading
Isaiah 26:1-9
Trust in God forever

Hymn: Lead On, O King Eternal! ELW 805

Eternal God, renew our hearts each day with your grace, that we may persevere in faith and, at the end of this earthly pilgrimage, receive the promise of your immeasurable glory in Jesus Christ, our Savior.

Wednesday, December 31, 2025
Seventh Day of Christmas

1 Kings 3:5-14
God grants a discerning mind

At Gibeon the LORD appeared to Solomon in a dream by night; and God said, "Ask what I should give you." And Solomon said, "You have shown great and steadfast love to your servant my father David, because he walked before you in faithfulness, in righteousness, and in uprightness of heart toward you; and you have kept for him this great and steadfast love, and have given him a son to sit on his throne today. And now, O LORD my God, you have made your servant king in place of my father David, although I am only a little child; I do not know how to go out or come in. And your servant is in the midst of the people whom you have chosen, a great people, so numerous they cannot be numbered or counted. Give your servant therefore an understanding mind to govern your people, able to discern between good and evil; for who can govern this your great people?" (1 Kings 3:5-9)

Psalm
Psalm 20
Answer us when we call

Additional Reading
John 8:12-19
I am the light

Hymn: Peace Came to Earth, ELW 285

Gracious God, we thank you for your steadfast love throughout this year, in blessings small and great. Grant us to walk into the coming year with faith, righteousness, and uprightness of heart, following the way of the Light of the world.

Lesser Festivals and Commemorations

For more see Gail Ramshaw's *More Days for Praise: Festivals and Commemorations in Evangelical Lutheran Worship* (Augsburg Fortress, 2016).

January 1—Name of Jesus Every Jewish boy was circumcised and formally named on the eighth day of his life. Already in his infancy, Jesus bore the mark of a covenant that he made new through the shedding of his blood on the cross.

January 2—Johann Konrad Wilhelm Loehe Wilhelm Loehe was a pastor in nineteenth-century Germany. From the small town of Neuendettelsau he sent pastors to North America, Australia, New Guinea, Brazil, and Ukraine.

January 15—Martin Luther King Jr. Martin Luther King Jr. is remembered as an American prophet of justice among races and nations. Many churches hold commemorations near Dr. King's birth date of January 15, in conjunction with the American civil holiday honoring him.

January 17—Antony of Egypt Antony was one of the earliest Egyptian desert fathers. He became the head of a group of monks who lived in a cluster of huts and devoted themselves to communal prayer, worship, and manual labor.

January 17—Pachomius Another of the desert fathers, Pachomius was born in Egypt about 290. He organized hermits into a religious community in which the members prayed together and held their goods in common.

January 18—Confession of Peter; *Week of Prayer for Christian Unity begins* The Week of Prayer for Christian Unity is framed by two commemorations, the Confession of Peter and the Conversion of Paul. On this day the church remembers that Peter was led by God's grace to acknowledge Jesus as "the Christ, the Son of the living God" (Matt. 16:16).

January 19—Henry When Erik, king of Sweden, determined to invade Finland for the purpose of converting the people there to Christianity, Henry went with him. Henry is recognized as the patron saint of Finland.

January 21—Agnes Agnes was a girl of about thirteen living in Rome, who had chosen a life of service to Christ as a virgin, despite the Roman emperor Diocletian's ruling that had outlawed all Christian activity. She gave witness to her faith and was put to death as a result.

January 25—Conversion of Paul; *Week of Prayer for Christian Unity ends* As the Week of Prayer for Christian Unity comes to an end, the church remembers how a man of Tarsus named Saul, a former persecutor of the early Christian church, was led to become one of its chief preachers.

January 26—Timothy, Titus, Silas On the two days following the celebration of the Conversion of Paul, his companions are remembered. Timothy, Titus, and Silas were missionary coworkers with Paul.

January 27—Lydia, Dorcas, Phoebe On this day the church remembers three women who were companions in Paul's ministry.

January 28—Thomas Aquinas Thomas Aquinas was a brilliant and creative theologian who immersed himself in the thought of Aristotle and worked to explain Christian beliefs amid the philosophical culture of the day.

February 2—Presentation of Our Lord Forty days after the birth of Christ, the church marks the day Mary and Joseph presented him in the temple in accordance with Jewish law. Simeon greeted Mary and Joseph, responding with a canticle that begins "Now, Lord, you let your servant go in peace" (see ELW S113).

February 3—Ansgar Ansgar was a monk who led a mission to Denmark and later to Sweden. His work ran into difficulties with the rulers of the day, and he was forced to withdraw into Germany, where he served as a bishop in Hamburg.

February 5—The Martyrs of Japan In the sixteenth century, Jesuit missionaries, followed by Franciscans, introduced the Christian faith in Japan. By 1630, Christianity was driven underground. This day commemorates the first martyrs of Japan, twenty-six missionaries and converts, who were killed by crucifixion.

February 14—Cyril, Methodius These brothers from a noble family in Thessalonika in northeastern Greece were priests who are regarded as the founders of Slavic literature. Their work in preaching and worshiping in the language of the people is honored by Christians in both East and West.

February 18—Martin Luther On this day Luther died at the age of sixty-two. For a time, he was an Augustinian monk, but it is primarily for his work as a biblical scholar, translator of the Bible, reformer of the liturgy, theologian, educator, and father of German vernacular literature that he is remembered.

February 23—Polycarp Polycarp was bishop of Smyrna and a link between the apostolic age and the church at the end of the second century. At the age of eighty-six he was martyred for his faith.

February 25—Elizabeth Fedde Fedde was born in Norway and trained as a deaconess. Among her notable achievements is the establishment of the Deaconess House in Brooklyn and the Deaconess House and Hospital of the Lutheran Free Church in Minneapolis.

March 1—George Herbert Herbert was ordained a priest in 1630 and served the little parish of St. Andrew Bremerton until his death. He is best remembered, however, as a writer of poems and hymns, such as "Come, My Way, My Truth, My Life" and "The King of Love My Shepherd Is."

March 2—John Wesley, Charles Wesley The Wesleys were leaders of a revival in the Church of England. Their spiritual methods of frequent communion, fasting, and advocacy for the poor earned them the name "Methodists."

March 7—Perpetua, Felicity In the year 202 the emperor Septimius Severus forbade conversions to Christianity. Perpetua, a noblewoman; Felicity, an enslaved woman; and other companions were all catechumens at Carthage in North Africa, where they were imprisoned and sentenced to death.

March 10—Harriet Tubman, Sojourner Truth Harriet Tubman helped about three hundred enslaved people escape via the Underground Railroad until slavery was abolished in the United States. After slavery was abolished in New York in 1827, Sojourner Truth became deeply involved in Christianity, and in later life she was a popular speaker against slavery and for women's rights.

March 12—Gregory the Great Gregory held political office and at another time lived as a monk, all before he was elected to the papacy. He also established a school to train church musicians; thus Gregorian chant is named in his honor.

March 17—Patrick Patrick went to Ireland from Britain to serve as a bishop and missionary. He made his base in the north of Ireland and from there made many missionary journeys, with much success.

March 19—Joseph The Gospel of Luke shows Joseph acting in accordance with both civil and religious law by returning to Bethlehem for the census and by presenting the child Jesus in the temple on the fortieth day after his birth.

March 21—Thomas Cranmer Cranmer's lasting achievement is contributing to and overseeing the creation of the *Book of Common Prayer*, which remains (in revised form) the worship book of the Anglican Communion. He was burned at the stake under Queen Mary for his support of the Protestant Reformation.

March 22—Jonathan Edwards Edwards was a minister in Connecticut and has been described as the greatest of the New England Puritan preachers. Edwards carried out mission work among the Housatonic Indians of Massachusetts and became president of the College of New Jersey, later to be known as Princeton University.

March 24—Oscar Arnulfo Romero Romero is remembered for his advocacy on behalf of the poor in El Salvador, though it was not a characteristic of his early priesthood. After several years of threats to his life, Romero was assassinated while presiding at the eucharist.

March 25—Annunciation of Our Lord Nine months before Christmas, the church celebrates the annunciation. In Luke the angel Gabriel announces to Mary that she will give birth to the Son of God, and she responds, "Here am I, the servant of the Lord" (Luke 1:38).

March 29—Hans Nielsen Hauge Hans Nielsen Hauge was a layperson who began preaching in Norway and Denmark after a mystical experience that he believed called him to share the assurance of salvation with others. At the time, itinerant preaching and religious gatherings held without the supervision of a pastor were illegal, and Hauge was arrested several times.

March 31—John Donne This priest of the Church of England is commemorated for his poetry and spiritual writing. Most of his poetry was written before his ordination and is sacred and secular, intellectual and sensuous.

April 4—Benedict the African Benedict's fame as a confessor brought many visitors to him, and he was eventually named superior of a Franciscan community.

April 6—Albrecht Dürer, Matthias Grünewald, Lucas Cranach These great artists revealed through their work the mystery of salvation and the wonder of creation. Though Dürer remained a Roman Catholic, at his death Martin Luther wrote to a friend, "Affection bids us mourn for one who was the best." Several religious works are included in Grünewald's small surviving corpus, the most famous being the Isenheim Altarpiece. Cranach was widely known for his woodcuts, some of which illustrated the first German printing of the New Testament.

April 9—Dietrich Bonhoeffer In 1933, and with Hitler's rise to power, Bonhoeffer became a leading spokesman for the Confessing Church, a resistance movement against the Nazis. After leading a worship service on April 8, 1945, at Schönberg prison, he was taken away to be hanged the next day.

April 10—Mikael Agricola Agricola began a reform of the Finnish church along Lutheran lines. He translated the New Testament, the prayer book, hymns, and the mass into Finnish and through this work set the rules of orthography that are the basis of modern Finnish spelling.

April 19—Olavus Petri, Laurentius Petri These two brothers are commemorated for their introduction of the Lutheran movement to the Church of Sweden after studying at the University of Wittenberg. Together the brothers published a complete Bible in Swedish and a revised liturgy in 1541.

April 21—Anselm This eleventh-century Benedictine monk stands out as one of the greatest theologians between Augustine and Thomas Aquinas. He is perhaps best known for his "satisfaction" theory of atonement, in which God takes on human nature in Jesus Christ in order to make the perfect payment for sin.

April 23—Toyohiko Kagawa Toyohiko Kagawa's vocation to help the poor led him to live among them. He was arrested for his efforts to reconcile Japan and China after the Japanese attack of 1940.

April 25—Mark Though Mark himself was not an apostle, it is likely that he was a member of one of the early Christian communities. The gospel attributed to him is brief and direct and is considered by many to be the earliest gospel.

April 29—Catherine of Siena Catherine was a member of the Order of Preachers (Dominicans), and among Roman Catholics she was the first woman to receive the title Doctor of the Church. She also advised popes and any uncertain persons who told her their problems.

May 1—Philip, James Philip and James are commemorated together because the remains of these two saints were placed in the Church of the Apostles in Rome on this day in 561.

May 2—Athanasius At the Council of Nicea in 325 and when he himself served as bishop of Alexandria, Athanasius defended the full divinity of Christ against the Arian position held by emperors, magistrates, and theologians.

May 4—Monica Almost everything known about Monica comes from Augustine's *Confessions*, his autobiography. Her dying wish was that her son remember her at the altar of the Lord, wherever he was.

May 8—Julian of Norwich Julian was most likely a Benedictine nun living in an isolated cell attached to the Carrow Priory in Norwich, England. When she was about thirty years old, she reported visions that she later compiled into a book, *Sixteen Revelations of Divine Love*, which is a classic of medieval mysticism.

May 9—Nicolaus Ludwig von Zinzendorf Drawn from an overly intellectual Lutheran faith to Pietism, at the age of twenty-two Count Zinzendorf permitted a group of Moravians to live on his lands. Zinzendorf participated in worldwide missions emanating from this community and is also remembered for writing hymns characteristic of his Pietistic faith.

May 14—Matthias After Christ's ascension, the apostles met in Jerusalem to choose a replacement for Judas. Though little is known about him, Matthias had traveled among the disciples from the time of Jesus' baptism until his ascension.

May 18—Erik Erik, long considered the patron saint of Sweden, ruled there from 1150 to 1160. He is honored for efforts to bring peace to the nearby pagan kingdoms and for his crusades to spread the Christian faith in Scandinavia.

May 21—Helena Helena was the mother of Constantine, a man who later became the Roman emperor. Helena is remembered for traveling through Palestine and building churches on the sites she believed to be where Jesus was born, where he was buried, and from which he ascended.

May 24—Nicolaus Copernicus, Leonhard Euler Copernicus formally studied astronomy, mathematics, Greek, Plato, law, medicine, and canon law and is chiefly remembered for his work as an astronomer and his idea that the sun, not the earth, is the center of the solar system. Euler is regarded as one of the founders of the science of pure mathematics and made important contributions to mechanics, hydrodynamics, astronomy, optics, and acoustics.

May 27—John Calvin Having embraced the views of the Reformation by his mid-twenties, John Calvin was a preacher in Geneva, was banished once, and later returned to reform the city with a rigid, theocratic discipline. Calvin is considered the father of the Reformed churches.

May 29—Jiří Tranovský Jiří Tranovský is considered the "Luther of the Slavs" and the father of Slovak hymnody. He produced a translation of the Augsburg Confession and published his hymn collection *Cithara Sanctorum (Lyre of the Saints)*, also known as the Tranoscius, which is the foundation of Slovak Lutheran hymnody.

May 31—Visit of Mary to Elizabeth Sometime after the annunciation, Mary visited her cousin Elizabeth, who greeted Mary with the words "Blessed are you among women" (Luke 1:42), and Mary responded with her famous song, the Magnificat.

June 1—Justin Justin was a teacher of philosophy and engaged in debates about the truth of the Christian faith. Having been arrested and jailed for practicing an unauthorized religion, he refused to renounce his faith, and he and six of his students were beheaded.

June 3—The Martyrs of Uganda King Mwanga of Uganda was angered by Christian members of the court whose first allegiance was not to him but to Christ. On this date in 1886, thirty-two young men were burned to death for refusing to renounce Christianity. Their persecution led to a much stronger Christian presence in the country.

June 3—John XXIII Despite the expectation upon his election that the seventy-seven-year-old John XXIII would be a transitional pope, he had great energy and spirit. He convened the Second Vatican Council in order to "open the windows" of the church. The council brought about great changes in Roman Catholic worship and ecumenical relationships.

June 5—Boniface Boniface led large numbers of Benedictine monks and nuns in establishing churches, schools, and seminaries. Boniface was preparing a group for confirmation on the eve of Pentecost when he and others were killed by a band of pagans.

June 7—Seattle The city of Seattle was named after Noah Seattle against his wishes. After Chief Seattle became a Roman Catholic, he began the practice of morning and evening prayer in the tribe, a practice that continued after his death.

June 9—Columba, Aidan, Bede These three monks from the British Isles were pillars among those who kept alive the light of learning and devotion during the Middle Ages. Columba founded three monasteries, including one on the island of Iona, off the coast of Scotland. Aidan, who helped bring Christianity to the Northumbria area of England, was known for his pastoral style and ability to stir people to charity and good works. Bede was a Bible translator and scripture scholar who wrote a history of the English church and was the first historian to date events "anno Domini" (AD), the "year of our Lord."

June 11—Barnabas Though Barnabas was not among the Twelve mentioned in the gospels, the book of Acts gives him the title of apostle. When Paul came to Jerusalem after his conversion, Barnabas took him in over the fears of the other apostles who doubted Paul's discipleship.

June 14—Basil the Great, Gregory of Nyssa, Gregory of Nazianzus, Macrina The three men in this group are known as the Cappadocian fathers; all three explored the mystery of the Holy Trinity. Basil's Longer Rule and Shorter Rule for monastic life are the basis for Eastern monasticism to this day, and express a preference for communal monastic life over that of hermits. Gregory of Nazianzus defended Orthodox trinitarian and christological doctrines, and his preaching won over the city of Constantinople. Gregory of Nyssa is remembered as a writer on spiritual life and the contemplation of God in worship and sacraments. Macrina was the older sister of Basil and Gregory of Nyssa, and her teaching was influential within the early church.

June 17—Emanuel Nine On June 17, 2015, Clementa C. Pinckney, Cynthia Marie Graham Hurd, Susie Jackson, Ethel Lee Lance, DePayne Middleton-Doctor, Tywanza Sanders, Daniel Lee Simmons, Sharonda Coleman-Singleton, and Myra Thompson were murdered by a self-professed white supremacist while they were gathered for Bible study and prayer at the Emanuel African Methodist Episcopal Church (often referred to as Mother Emanuel) in Charleston, South Carolina. A resolution to commemorate June 17 as a day of repentance for the martyrdom of the Emanuel Nine was adopted by the Churchwide Assembly of the Evangelical Lutheran Church in America on August 8, 2019.

June 21—Onesimos Nesib Nesib, an Ethiopian, was captured by slave traders and taken from his homeland to Eritrea, where he was bought, freed, and educated by Swedish missionaries. He translated the Bible into Oromo and returned to his homeland to preach the gospel there.

June 24—John the Baptist The birth of John the Baptist is celebrated exactly six months before Christmas Eve. For Christians in the northern hemisphere, these two dates are deeply symbolic, since John said that he must decrease as Jesus increased. John was born as the days are longest and then steadily decrease, while Jesus was born as the days are shortest and then steadily increase.

June 25—Presentation of the Augsburg Confession On this day in 1530 the German and Latin editions of the Augsburg Confession were presented to Emperor Charles of the Holy Roman Empire. The Augsburg Confession was written by Philipp Melanchthon and endorsed by Martin Luther and consists of a brief summary of points in which the reformers saw their teaching as either agreeing with or differing from that of the Roman Catholic Church of the time.

June 25—Philipp Melanchthon Though he died on April 19, Philipp Melanchthon is commemorated today because of his connection with the Augsburg Confession. Colleague and co-reformer with Martin Luther, Melanchthon was a brilliant scholar, known as "the teacher of Germany."

June 27—Cyril Remembered as an outstanding theologian, Cyril defended the Orthodox teachings about the person of Christ against Nestorius, who was at that time bishop of Constantinople. Eventually it was decided that Cyril's interpretation that Christ's person included both divine and human natures was correct.

June 28—Irenaeus Irenaeus believed that only Matthew, Mark, Luke, and John were trustworthy gospels. As a result of his battles with the Gnostics, he was one of the first to speak of the church as "catholic," meaning that congregations did not exist by themselves but were linked to one another throughout the whole church.

June 29—Peter, Paul One of the things that unites Peter and Paul is the tradition that says they were martyred together on this date in 67 or 68 CE. What unites them even more closely is their common confession of Jesus Christ.

July 1—Catherine Winkworth, John Mason Neale Many of the most beloved hymns in the English language are the work of these gifted poets. Catherine Winkworth devoted herself to the translation of German hymns into English, while John Mason Neale specialized in translating many ancient Latin and Greek hymns.

July 3—Thomas Alongside the doubt for which Thomas is famous, the Gospel according to John shows Thomas moving from doubt to deep faith. Thomas makes one of the strongest confessions of faith in the New Testament, "My Lord and my God!" (John 20:28).

July 6—Jan Hus Jan Hus was a Bohemian priest who spoke against abuses in the church of his day in many of the same ways Luther would a century later. The followers of Hus became known as the Czech Brethren and later became the Moravian Church.

July 11—Benedict of Nursia Benedict is known as the father of Western monasticism. Benedict encouraged a generous spirit of hospitality. Visitors to Benedictine communities are to be welcomed as Christ himself.

July 12—Nathan Söderblom In 1930 this Swedish theologian, ecumenist, and social activist received the Nobel Peace Prize. Söderblom organized the Universal Christian Council on Life and Work, which was one of the organizations that in 1948 came together to form the World Council of Churches.

July 17—Bartolomé de Las Casas Bartolomé de Las Casas was a Spanish priest and a missionary in the Western Hemisphere. Throughout the Caribbean and Central America, he worked to stop the enslavement of Indigenous peoples, to halt the brutal treatment of women by military forces, and to promote laws that humanized the process of colonization.

July 22—Mary Magdalene The gospels report that Mary Magdalene was one of the women of Galilee who followed Jesus. As the first person to whom the risen Lord appeared, she returned to the disciples with the news and has been called "the apostle to the apostles" for her proclamation of the resurrection.

July 23—Birgitta of Sweden Birgitta's devotional commitments led her to give to the poor and needy all that she owned while she began to live a more ascetic life. She founded an order of monks and nuns, the Order of the Holy Savior (Birgittines), whose superior was a woman.

July 25—James James was one of the sons of Zebedee and is counted as one of the twelve disciples. James was the first of the Twelve to suffer martyrdom and is the only apostle whose martyrdom is recorded in scripture.

July 28—Johann Sebastian Bach, Heinrich Schütz, George Frederick Handel These three composers did much to enrich the worship life of the church. Johann Sebastian Bach drew on the Lutheran tradition of hymnody and wrote about two hundred cantatas, including at least two for each Sunday and festival day in the Lutheran calendar of his day. George Frederick Handel was not primarily a church musician, but his great work *Messiah* is a musical proclamation of the scriptures. Heinrich Schütz wrote choral settings of biblical texts and paid special attention to ways his composition would underscore the meaning of the words.

July 29—Mary, Martha, Lazarus of Bethany Mary and Martha are remembered for the hospitality and refreshment they offered Jesus in their home. Following the characterization drawn by Luke, Martha represents the active life, and Mary, the contemplative.

July 29—Olaf Olaf is considered the patron saint of Norway. While at war in the Baltic and in Normandy, he became a Christian; then he returned to Norway and declared himself king, and from then on Christianity was the dominant religion of the realm.

August 8—Dominic Dominic believed that a stumbling block to restoring heretics to the church was the wealth of clergy, so he formed an itinerant religious order, the Order of Preachers (Dominicans), who lived in poverty, studied philosophy and theology, and preached against heresy.

August 10—Lawrence Lawrence was one of seven deacons of the congregation at Rome and, like the deacons appointed in Acts, was responsible for financial matters in the church and for the care of the poor.

August 11—Clare At age eighteen, Clare of Assisi heard Francis preach a sermon. With Francis's help she and a growing number of companions established a women's Franciscan community called the Order of Poor Ladies, or Poor Clares.

August 13—Florence Nightingale, Clara Maass Nightingale led a group of thirty-eight nurses to serve in the Crimean War, where they worked in appalling conditions. She returned to London as a hero and there resumed her work for hospital reform. Clara Maass was born in New Jersey and served as a nurse in the Spanish-American War, where she encountered the horrors of yellow fever. Later responding to a call for subjects in research on yellow fever, Maass contracted the disease and died.

August 14—Maximilian Kolbe, Kaj Munk Confined in Auschwitz, Father Kolbe was a Franciscan priest who gave generously of his meager resources and finally volunteered to be starved to death in place of another man who was a husband and father. Kaj Munk, a Danish Lutheran pastor and playwright, was an outspoken critic of the Nazis. His plays frequently highlighted the eventual victory of the Christian faith despite the church's weak and ineffective witness.

August 15—Mary, Mother of Our Lord The honor paid to Mary as mother of our Lord goes back to biblical times, when Mary herself sang, "From now on all generations will call me blessed" (Luke 1:48). Mary's song speaks of reversals in the reign of God: the mighty are cast down, the lowly are lifted up, the hungry are fed, and the rich are sent away empty-handed.

August 20—Bernard of Clairvaux Bernard was a Cistercian monk who became an abbot of great spiritual depth. Through translation his several devotional writings and hymns are still read and sung today.

August 24—Bartholomew Bartholomew is mentioned as one of Jesus' disciples in Matthew, Mark, and Luke. Except for his name on these lists of the Twelve, little is known about him.

August 28—Augustine As an adult, Augustine came to see Christianity as a religion appropriate for a philosopher. Augustine was baptized by Ambrose at the Easter Vigil in 387, was made bishop of Hippo in 396, and was one of the greatest theologians of the Western church.

August 28—Moses the Black A man of great strength and rough character, Moses the Black was converted to Christian faith toward the close of the fourth century. The change in his heart and life had a profound impact on his native Ethiopia.

September 2—Nikolai Frederik Severin Grundtvig Grundtvig was a prominent Danish theologian of the nineteenth century. From his university days, he was convinced that poetry spoke to the human spirit better than prose, and he wrote more than a thousand hymns.

September 9—Peter Claver Peter Claver was born into Spanish nobility and was persuaded to become a Jesuit missionary. He served in Cartagena (in what is now Colombia) by teaching and caring for enslaved people.

September 13—John Chrysostom John was a priest in Antioch and an outstanding preacher. His eloquence earned him the nickname Chrysostom ("golden mouth"), but he also preached against corruption among the royal court, whereupon the empress sent him into exile.

September 14—Holy Cross Day The celebration of Holy Cross Day commemorates the dedication of the Church of the Resurrection in 335 CE on the location believed to be where Christ was buried.

September 16—Cyprian During Cyprian's time as bishop, many people had denied the faith under duress. In contrast to some who held the belief that the church should not receive these people back, Cyprian believed they ought to be welcomed into full communion after a period of penance.

September 17—Hildegard, Abbess of Bingen Hildegard lived virtually her entire life in convents yet was widely influential. She advised and reproved kings and popes, wrote poems and hymns, and produced treatises in medicine, theology, and natural history.

September 18—Dag Hammarskjöld Dag Hammarskjöld was a Swedish diplomat and humanitarian who served as secretary general of the United Nations. The depth of Hammarskjöld's Christian faith was unknown until his private journal, *Markings*, was published following his death.

September 21—Matthew Matthew was a tax collector, an occupation that was distrusted, because tax collectors were frequently dishonest and worked as agents for the occupying Roman government; yet it was these outcasts to whom Jesus showed his love. Since the second century, tradition has attributed the first gospel to him.

September 29—Michael and All Angels The scriptures speak of angels who worship God in heaven, and in both testaments angels are God's messengers on earth. Michael is an angel whose name appears in Daniel as the heavenly being who leads the faithful dead to God's throne on the day of resurrection, while in the book of Revelation, Michael fights in a cosmic battle against Satan.

September 30—Jerome Jerome translated the scriptures into the Latin that was spoken and written by the majority of people in his day. His translation is known as the Vulgate, which comes from the Latin word for "common."

October 4—Francis of Assisi Francis renounced wealth and future inheritance and devoted himself to serving the poor. Since Francis had a spirit of gratitude for all of God's creation, this commemoration has been a traditional time to bless pets and animals, creatures Francis called his brothers and sisters.

October 4—Theodor Fliedner Fliedner's work was instrumental in the revival of the ministry of deaconesses among Lutherans. Fliedner's deaconess motherhouse in Kaiserswerth, Germany, inspired Lutherans all over the world to commission deaconesses to serve in parishes, schools, prisons, and hospitals.

October 6—William Tyndale Tyndale's plan to translate the scriptures into English met opposition from Henry VIII. Though Tyndale completed work on the New Testament in 1525 and worked on a portion of the Old Testament, he was tried for heresy and burned at the stake.

October 7—Henry Melchior Muhlenberg Muhlenberg was prominent in setting the course for Lutheranism in the United States by helping Lutheran churches make the transition from the state churches of Europe to independent churches of America. Among other things, he established the first Lutheran synod in America and developed an American Lutheran liturgy.

October 15—Teresa of Avila Teresa of Avila (also known as Teresa de Jesús) chose the life of a Carmelite nun after reading the letters of Jerome. Teresa's writings on devotional life are widely read by members of various denominations.

October 17—Ignatius Ignatius was the second bishop of Antioch in Syria. When his own martyrdom approached, he wrote in one of his letters, "I prefer death in Christ Jesus to power over the farthest limits of the earth.... Do not stand in the way of my birth to real life."

October 18—Luke Luke, as author of both Luke and Acts, was careful to place the events of Jesus' life in both their social and religious contexts. Some of the most loved parables and canticles are found only in this gospel.

October 23—James of Jerusalem James is described in the New Testament as the brother of Jesus, and the secular historian Josephus called him "the brother of Jesus, the so-called Christ." Little is known about James, but Josephus reported that the Pharisees respected him for his piety and observance of the law.

October 26—Philipp Nicolai, Johann Heermann, Paul Gerhardt These three outstanding hymnwriters all worked in Germany in the seventeenth century during times of war and plague. Philipp Nicolai's hymns "Wake, Awake, for Night Is Flying" and "O Morning Star, How Fair and Bright!" were included in a series of meditations he wrote to comfort his parishioners during the plague. The style of Johann Heermann's hymns (including "Ah, Holy Jesus") moved away from the more objective style of Reformation hymnody toward expressing the emotions of faith. Paul Gerhardt, whom some have called the greatest of Lutheran hymnwriters, lost a preaching position at St. Nicholas's Church in Berlin because he refused to sign a document stating he would not make theological arguments in his sermons.

October 28—Simon, Jude Little is known about Simon and Jude. In New Testament lists of the apostles, Simon the Zealot is mentioned, but he is never mentioned apart from these lists. Jude, sometimes called Thaddaeus, is also mentioned in lists of the Twelve.

October 31—Reformation Day By the end of the seventeenth century, many Lutheran churches celebrated a festival commemorating Martin Luther's posting of the 95 Theses, a summary of abuses in the church of his time. At the heart of the reform movement was the gospel, the good news that it is by grace through faith that we are justified and set free.

November 1—All Saints Day The custom of commemorating all of the saints of the church on a single day goes back at least to the third century. All Saints Day celebrates the baptized people of God, living and dead, who make up the body of Christ.

November 3—Martín de Porres Martín was a lay brother in the Order of Preachers (Dominicans) and engaged in many charitable works. He is recognized as an advocate for Christian charity and interracial justice.

November 7—John Christian Frederick Heyer, Bartholomaeus Ziegenbalg, Ludwig Nommensen Heyer was the first missionary sent out by American Lutherans, and he became a missionary in the Andhra region of India. Ziegenbalg was a missionary to the Tamils of Tranquebar on the southeast coast of India. Nommensen worked among the Batak people, who had previously not seen Christian missionaries.

November 11—Martin of Tours In 371 Martin was elected bishop of Tours. As bishop he developed a reputation for intervening on behalf of prisoners and heretics who had been sentenced to death.

November 11—Søren Aabye Kierkegaard Kierkegaard, a nineteenth-century Danish theologian whose writings reflect his Lutheran heritage, was the founder of modern existentialism. Kierkegaard's work attacked the established church of his day—its complacency, its tendency to intellectualize faith, and its desire to be accepted by polite society.

November 17—Elizabeth of Hungary This Hungarian princess gave away large sums of money, including her dowry, for relief of the poor and sick. She founded hospitals, cared for 392 orphans, and used the royal food supplies to feed the hungry.

November 23—Clement Clement is best remembered for a letter he wrote to the Corinthian congregation still having difficulty with divisions in spite of Paul's canonical letters. Clement's letter is also a witness to early understandings of church government and the way each office in the church works for the good of the whole.

November 23—Miguel Agustín Pro Miguel Agustín Pro grew up amid oppression in Mexico and worked on behalf of the poor and homeless. Miguel and his two brothers were arrested, falsely accused of throwing a bomb at the car of a government official, and executed by a firing squad.

November 24—Justus Falckner, Jehu Jones, William Passavant Not only was Falckner the first Lutheran pastor to be ordained in North America, but he published a catechism that was the first Lutheran book published on the continent. Jones was the Lutheran Church's first African American pastor and carried out missionary work in Philadelphia, which led to the formation there of the first African American Lutheran congregation (St. Paul's). William Passavant helped to establish hospitals and orphanages in a number of cities and was the first to introduce deaconesses to the work of hospitals in the United States.

November 25—Isaac Watts Watts wrote about six hundred hymns, many of them in a two-year period beginning when he was twenty years old. When criticized for writing hymns not taken from scripture, he responded that if we can pray prayers that are not from scripture but written by us, then surely we can sing hymns that we have made up ourselves.

November 30—Andrew Andrew was the first of the Twelve. As a part of his calling, he brought other people, including Simon Peter, to meet Jesus.

December 3—Francis Xavier Francis Xavier became a missionary to India, Southeast Asia, Japan, and the Philippines. Together with Ignatius Loyola and five others, Francis formed the Society of Jesus (Jesuits).

December 4—John of Damascus John left a career in finance and government to become a monk in an abbey near Jerusalem. He wrote many hymns as well as theological works, including *The Fount of Wisdom*, a work that touches on philosophy, heresy, and the orthodox faith.

December 6—Nicholas Nicholas was a bishop in what is now Turkey. Legends that surround Nicholas tell of his love for God and neighbor, especially the poor.

December 7—Ambrose Ambrose was baptized, ordained, and consecrated a bishop all on the same day. While bishop, he gave away his wealth and lived in simplicity.

December 13—Lucy Lucy was a young Christian of Sicily who was martyred during the persecutions under Emperor Diocletian. Her celebration became particularly important in Sweden and Norway, perhaps because the feast of Lucia (whose name means "light") originally fell on the shortest day of the year.

December 14—John of the Cross John was a monk of the Carmelite religious order who met Teresa of Avila when she was working to reform the Carmelite Order and return it to a stricter observance of its rules. His writings, like Teresa's, reflect a deep interest in mystical thought and meditation.

December 20—Katharina von Bora Luther Katharina took vows as a nun, but around age twenty-four she and several other nuns who were influenced by the writings of Martin Luther left the convent. When she later became Luther's wife, she proved herself a gifted household manager and became a trusted partner.

December 26—Stephen Stephen, a deacon and the first martyr of the church, was one of those seven upon whom the apostles laid hands after they had been chosen to serve widows and others in need. Later, Stephen's preaching angered the temple authorities, and they ordered him to be put to death by stoning.

December 27—John John, a son of Zebedee, was a fisherman and one of the Twelve. Tradition has attributed authorship of the gospel and the three epistles bearing his name to the apostle John.

December 28—The Holy Innocents The infant martyrs commemorated on this day were the children of Bethlehem, two years old and younger, who were killed by Herod, who worried that his reign was threatened by the birth of a new king named Jesus.

Anniversary of Baptism (abbreviated)

This order is intended for use in the home. It may be adapted for use in another context, such as a Christian education setting. When used in the home, a parent or sponsor may be the leader. A more expanded version of this order appears in *Evangelical Lutheran Worship Pastoral Care* (pp. 128–135).

A bowl of water may be placed in the midst of those who are present.

Gathering

A baptismal hymn or acclamation (see Evangelical Lutheran Worship #209–217, 442–459) may be sung.

The sign of the cross may be made by all in remembrance of their baptism as the leader begins.

In the name of the Father, and of the + Son, and of the Holy Spirit.
Amen.

The candle received at baptism or another candle may be used. As it is lighted, the leader may say:

Jesus said, I am the light of the world.
Whoever follows me will have the light of life.

Reading

One or more scripture readings follow. Those present may share in reading.

A reading from Mark: People were bringing little children to Jesus in order that he might touch them; and the disciples spoke sternly to them. But when Jesus saw this, he was indignant and said, "Let the little children come to me; do not stop them; for it is to such as these that the kingdom of God belongs.". . . And he took them up in his arms, laid his hands on them, and blessed them. *(Mark 10:13-14, 16)*

A reading from Second Corinthians: If anyone is in Christ, there is a new creation: everything old has passed away; see, everything has become new! (*2 Corinthians 5:17*)

A reading from First John: Beloved, let us love one another, because love is from God; everyone who loves is born of God and knows God. (*1 John 4:7*)

Those present may share experiences related to baptism and their lives as baptized children of God. A portion of the Small Catechism (Evangelical Lutheran Worship, pp. 1160–1167) may be read as part of this conversation.

A baptismal hymn or acclamation may be sung.

Baptismal Remembrance

A parent or sponsor may trace a cross on the forehead of the person celebrating a baptismal anniversary. Water from a bowl placed in the midst of those present may be used. These or similar words may be said.

Name, when you were baptized, you were marked with the cross of Christ forever.
Remember your baptism with thanksgiving and joy.

Prayers

Prayers may include the following or other appropriate prayers. Others who are present may place a hand on the head or shoulder of the one who is celebrating the anniversary.

Let us pray.
Gracious God, we thank you for the new life you give us through holy baptism. Especially, we ask you to bless *name* on the anniversary of *her/his* baptism. Continue to strengthen *name* with the Holy Spirit, and increase in *her/him* your gifts of grace: the spirit of wisdom and understanding, the spirit of counsel and might, the spirit of knowledge and the fear of the Lord, the spirit of joy in your presence; through Jesus Christ, our Savior and Lord.
Amen.
Other prayers may be added. Those present may offer petitions and thanksgivings.

The prayers may conclude with the Lord's Prayer.

Our Father in heaven,
>   **hallowed be your name, your kingdom come,**
>   **your will be done, on earth as in heaven.**

Give us today our daily bread.

Forgive us our sins
>   **as we forgive those who sin against us.**

Save us from the time of trial and deliver us from evil.

For the kingdom, the power, and the glory are yours,
>   **now and forever. Amen.**

Blessing

The order may conclude with this or another suitable blessing.

Almighty God, who gives us a new birth by water and the Holy Spirit and forgives us all our sins, strengthen us in all goodness and by the power of the Holy Spirit keep us in eternal life through Jesus Christ our Lord.

Amen.

The greeting of peace may be shared by all.

Other suggested readings for this service:

John 3:1-8: *Born again from above*

Romans 6:3-11: *Raised with Christ in baptism*

Galatians 3:26-28: *All are one in Christ*

Ephesians 4:1-6: *There is one body and one Spirit*

Colossians 1:11-13: *Claimed by Christ, heirs of light*

1 Peter 2:2-3: *Long for spiritual food*

1 Peter 2:9: *Chosen in baptism to tell about God*

Revelation 22:1-2: *The river of the water of life*

Prayers for Various Situations

A prayer to begin the work day

May the graciousness of the Lord our God be upon us;
prosper the work of our hands. (Ps. 90:17, *ELW*)
Generous God, you call us to lives of service.
In my words and actions this day, move me to serve in Christ's name.
When I lack energy, inspire me. When I lack courage, strengthen me.
When I lack compassion, be merciful to me.

You may make the sign of the cross.

In all things, O God, you are our way, our truth, and our life. Reveal through
me your life-giving work, that I love my neighbors as myself. I ask this in Jesus'
name. Amen.

A prayer to begin the school day

Show me your ways, O Lord, and teach me your paths. (Ps. 25:4, *ELW*)
Christ be with me: in you I am never alone.
Christ within me: your Spirit is at work in me.
Christ behind me: reassure me when I struggle.
Christ before me: lead me when I am uncertain.
Christ beneath me: support me when I am weak.
Christ above me: encourage me to do my best.
Christ in quiet: I listen for the sound of your voice.
Christ in danger: I will not fear, for you are with me.

You may make the sign of the cross.

In all things, O God, you are our way, our truth, and our life.
Teach me to love you and my neighbors as myself.
I ask this in Jesus' name. Amen.
(Based on the Prayer of St. Patrick)

Meal time

Every good and perfect gift comes from you, O God. Bless this food, and help us to receive it with thankful hearts. By your Spirit nourish our love for one another and for our neighbor in need; through Jesus Christ, our Savior and Lord. Amen.

Living alone

Gracious God, none who trust in your Son can be separated from your love. Give to all who live alone peace and contentment in their solitude, hope and fulfillment in their love of you, and joy and companionship in their relations with others; through Jesus Christ our Lord. Amen.

Blessing for pets and animals

Use this prayer on St. Francis Day, October 4, or whenever it is appropriate.

Gracious God,
in your love you created us in your image
and made us stewards of the animals
that live in the skies, the earth, and the sea.
Bless us in our care for our *pet/s* (*animal/s*) (*names may be added here*).
Help us recognize your power and wisdom
in the variety of creatures that live in our world,
and hear our prayer for all that suffer overwork, hunger, and ill-treatment.
Protect your creatures and guard them from all evil, now and forever. Amen.

Time of conflict, crisis, disaster

O God, where hearts are fearful and constricted, grant courage and hope. Where anxiety is infectious and widening, grant peace and reassurance. Where impossibilities close every door and window, grant imagination and resistance. Where distrust twists our thinking, grant healing and illumination. Where spirits are daunted and weakened, grant soaring wings and strengthened dreams. All these things we ask in the name of Jesus Christ, our Savior and Lord. Amen.

Health of body and soul

By your power, great God, our Lord Jesus healed the sick and gave new hope to the hopeless. Though we cannot command or possess your power, we pray for those who want to be healed. Mend their wounds, soothe fevered brows, and make broken people whole again. Help us to welcome every healing as a sign that, though death is against us, you are for us, and have promised renewed and risen life in Jesus Christ the Lord. Amen.

Time of grief

Merciful Creator, your Holy Spirit intercedes for us even when we do not know how to pray. Send your Spirit now to comfort us in these days of need and loss, and help us to commend (*name*) to your merciful care; through Jesus Christ, our Savior and Lord. Amen.

Those suffering from addiction

O blessed Jesus, you ministered to all who came to you. Look with compassion upon all who through addiction have lost their health and freedom. Restore to them the assurance of your unfailing mercy; remove the fears that attack them; strengthen those who are engaged in the work of recovery; and to those who care for them, give honesty, understanding, and persevering love; for your mercy's sake. Amen.

The chronically ill and those who support them

Loving God, your heart overflows with compassion for your whole creation. Pour out your Spirit on all people living with illness for which there is no cure, as well as their families and loved ones. Help them to know that you claim them as your own and deliver them from fear and pain; for the sake of Jesus Christ, our healer and Lord. Amen.

Living with mental illness

Mighty God, in Jesus Christ you know the spirits that cloud our minds and set us against ourselves. Comfort those who are torn by conflict, cast down, or lost in worlds of illusion. By your power, drive from us the powers that shake confidence and shatter love. Tame unruly forces within us, and bring us to your truth, so that we may know peace and accept ourselves as your beloved children in Jesus Christ. Amen.

A prayer attributed to Francis of Assisi

Lord, make us instruments of your peace. Where there is hatred, let us sow love; where there is injury, pardon; where there is discord, union; where there is doubt, faith; where there is despair, hope; where there is darkness, light; where there is sadness, joy. Grant that we may not so much seek to be consoled as to console; to be understood as to understand; to be loved as to love. For it is in giving that we receive; it is in pardoning that we are pardoned; and it is in dying that we are born to eternal life. Amen.

A prayer of Catherine of Siena

Power of the eternal Father, help me. Wisdom of the Son, enlighten the eye of my understanding. Tender mercy of the Holy Spirit, unite my heart to yourself. Eternal God, restore health to the sick and life to the dead. Give us a voice, your own voice, to cry out to you for mercy for the world. You, light, give us light. You, wisdom, give us wisdom. You, supreme strength, strengthen us. Amen.

A prayer of Julian of Norwich

In you, Father all-mighty, we have our preservation and our bliss. In you, Christ, we have our restoring and our saving. You are our mother, brother, and savior. In you, our Lord the Holy Spirit, is marvelous and plenteous grace. You are our clothing; for love you wrap us and embrace us. You are our maker, our lover, our keeper. Teach us to believe that by your grace all shall be well, and all shall be well, and all manner of things shall be well. Amen.

A prayer of Martin Luther

Behold, Lord, an empty vessel that needs to be filled. My Lord, fill it. I am weak in the faith; strengthen me. I am cold in love; warm me and make me fervent, that my love may go out to my neighbor. I do not have a strong and firm faith; at times I doubt and am unable to trust you altogether. O Lord, help me. Strengthen my faith and trust in you. In you I have sealed the treasure of all I have. I am poor; you are rich and came to be merciful to the poor. I am a sinner; you are upright. With me, there is an abundance of sin; in you is the fullness of righteousness. Therefore I will remain with you, of whom I can receive, but to whom I may not give. Amen.

Prayers on pages 419–422 from *Evangelical Lutheran Worship, All Creation Sings,* and *Pastoral Care.*

Morning Blessing

You may make the sign of the cross.

I am a beloved child of God, marked with the cross of Christ forever.

Your mercies are new every morning. *(Based on Lam. 3:23)*

Thank you, gracious God, for the gift of this new day.
Awaken me to your abiding presence;
open my eyes to your creation;
open my ears to your promises;
open my heart to the needs of others.
Fill me with your Spirit and guide me this day
in works of kindness, justice, and mercy.
I ask this in the name of Jesus, the light and life of the world.
Amen.

A Simplified Form for Morning Prayer

Opening

O Lord, open my lips,
and my mouth shall proclaim your praise.
Glory to the Father, and to the Son,
and to the Holy Spirit:
as it was in the beginning, is now,
and will be forever. Amen.
The alleluia is omitted during Lent.

Alleluia.

Psalmody

The psalmody may begin with Psalm 63, Psalm 67, Psalm 95, Psalm 100, or another
psalm appropriate for morning. Psalms provided in this book for each day may be used
instead of or in addition to the psalms mentioned.

A time of silence follows.

A hymn may follow (see the suggested hymn for each day).

Readings

One or more readings for each day may be selected from those provided in this book.
The reading of scripture may be followed by silence for reflection.

The reflection may conclude with these or similar words.

Long ago God spoke to our ancestors
in many and various ways by the prophets,
but in these last days God has spoken to us by the Son.

Gospel Canticle

The song of Zechariah may be sung or said.

Blessed are you, Lord, the God of Israel,
you have come to your people and set them free.
You have raised up for us a mighty Savior,
born of the house of your servant David.
Through your holy prophets, you promised of old
to save us from our enemies,
from the hands of all who hate us,
to show mercy to our forebears,
and to remember your holy covenant.
This was the oath you swore to our father Abraham:
to set us free from the hands of our enemies,
free to worship you without fear,
holy and righteous before you, all the days of our life.
And you, child, shall be called the prophet of the Most High,
for you will go before the Lord to prepare the way,
to give God's people knowledge of salvation
by the forgiveness of their sins.
In the tender compassion of our God
the dawn from on high shall break upon us,
to shine on those who dwell in darkness and the shadow of death,
and to guide our feet into the way of peace.

Prayers

*Various intercessions may be spoken at this time. The prayer provided in this book for
each day may also be used.*

The following prayer is especially appropriate for morning.

Almighty and everlasting God,
you have brought us in safety to this new day.
Preserve us with your mighty power,
that we may not fall into sin

nor be overcome in adversity.
In all we do, direct us to the fulfilling of your purpose;
through Jesus Christ our Lord.
Amen.

The Lord's Prayer

Our Father in heaven,
    hallowed be your name,
    your kingdom come,
    your will be done, on earth as in heaven.
Give us today our daily bread.
Forgive us our sins
    as we forgive those who sin against us.
Save us from the time of trial
    and deliver us from evil.
For the kingdom, the power, and the glory are yours,
    now and forever. Amen.

Blessing

Let us bless the Lord.
Thanks be to God.

Almighty God,
the Father, + the Son, and the Holy Spirit,
bless and preserve us.
Amen.

Additional materials for daily prayer are available in Evangelical Lutheran Worship
(pp. 295–331) and may supplement this simple order.

A Simplified Form for Evening Prayer

Opening
Jesus Christ is the light of the world,
the light no darkness can overcome.
Stay with us, Lord, for it is evening,
and the day is almost over.
Let your light scatter the darkness
and illumine your church.

Psalmody
The psalmody may begin with Psalm 141, Psalm 121, or another psalm appropriate for evening. Psalms provided in this book for each day may be used instead of or in addition to the psalms mentioned.

A time of silence follows.

A hymn may follow (see the suggested hymn for each day).

Readings
One or more readings for each day may be selected from those provided in this book. The reading of scripture may be followed by silence for reflection.

The reflection may conclude with these or similar words.

Jesus said, I am the light of the world.
Whoever follows me will never walk in darkness.

Gospel Canticle

The song of Mary may be sung or said.

My soul proclaims the greatness of the Lord,
my spirit rejoices in God my Savior,
for you, Lord, have looked with favor on your lowly servant.
From this day all generations will call me blessed:
you, the Almighty, have done great things for me,
and holy is your name.
You have mercy on those who fear you,
from generation to generation.
You have shown strength with your arm
and scattered the proud in their conceit,
casting down the mighty from their thrones
and lifting up the lowly.
You have filled the hungry with good things
and sent the rich away empty.
You have come to the aid of your servant Israel,
to remember the promise of mercy,
the promise made to our forebears,
to Abraham and his children forever.

Prayers

*Various intercessions may be spoken at this time. The prayer provided in this book for
each day may also be used.*

The following prayer is especially appropriate for evening.

We give thanks to you, heavenly Father,
through Jesus Christ your dear Son,
that you have graciously protected us today.
We ask you to forgive us all our sins, where we have done wrong,
and graciously to protect us tonight.
For into your hands we commend ourselves:
our bodies, our souls, and all that is ours.

Let your holy angels be with us,
so that the wicked foe may have no power over us.
Amen.

The Lord's Prayer

Our Father in heaven,
hallowed be your name,
your kingdom come,
your will be done, on earth as in heaven.
Give us today our daily bread.
Forgive us our sins
as we forgive those who sin against us.
Save us from the time of trial
and deliver us from evil.
For the kingdom, the power, and the glory are yours,
now and forever. Amen.

Blessing

Let us bless the Lord.
Thanks be to God.

The peace of God,
which surpasses all understanding,
keep our hearts and our minds in Christ Jesus.
Amen.

Additional materials for daily prayer are available in Evangelical Lutheran Worship
(pp. 295–331) and may supplement this simple order.

Evening Blessing

You may make the sign of the cross.

I am a beloved child of God, marked with the cross of Christ forever.
Come to me, all you that are weary . . . and I will give you rest.
(Matt. 11:28)

Thank you, gracious God, for the gift of this coming night.
Restore me with your right spirit. Calm my mind. Quiet my heart.
Enfold me with your bountiful mercy.
Protect me from all harm,
that I sleep assured of the peace found in you alone.
I ask this in the name of Jesus, who gives us rest. Amen.

Night Prayers with Children

Dear Jesus, as a hen covers her chicks with her wings to keep them safe,
protect us this night under your golden wings; for your mercy's sake.
Amen.

We bless you, God, for the day just spent,
for laughter, tears, and all you've sent.
Grant us, Good Shepherd, through this night,
a peaceful sleep till morning light.

*A parent or caregiver may trace the cross on the child's forehead or heart and say one of
these blessings:*

God the Father, Son, and Holy Spirit watch over you.
May God protect you through the night.
May the Lord Jesus keep you in his love.

Suggestions for Daily Reflection

God's word for me this day is:

God's word will shape my day by:

I will share God's word with others through:

My prayers today will include:

- Jesus' church throughout the whole earth and all the ways it serves the gospel

- The safeguarding and restoration of God's creation

- Peace and justice in our community, our nation, and our world

- All who suffer from poverty, oppression, sickness, grief, or loneliness

- All who suffer in body, mind, or spirit

- Specific concerns today